Advance praise for
Educational Leadership Policies and Practices: Voices from the Developing Countries

In an area where so little has been written on school and system leaders, *Educational Leadership Policies and Practices: Voices from the Developing Countries* is a very welcome contribution to the field. The various authors do a great job of portraying how radically different the contexts are for making education progress as leaders. We see the familiar concepts: transformational, moral, pedagogical, capacity building, contingent, mobilizing community, and so on, but the contexts are so different that the findings and lessons generate new ideas about leadership. The six main leadership lessons for less developed countries examined in the final chapter are especially powerful.

— MICHAEL FULLAN, Professor Emeritus, OISE/University of Toronto, Canada

Education Leadership is an emerging area in education, research, and practice. This becomes even more challenging when we deal with developing countries. This book takes a holistic view of this challenge. The authors, with their diverse and rich research background, have presented their experiences in a very inspirational way. This provides real life examples for the teachers, academic leaders, researchers, policymakers, principals, and interested readers who can learn from these examples to improve their leadership skills and behaviours. The work of the authors is highly commendable, and it will serve as a guide and handbook for the education practitioners from diverse backgrounds for their personal and professional development.

— ENGR. PROF. DR ATTAULLAH SHAH, Vice Chancellor Karakoram International University, GB, Pakistan

The educational leadership models adopted in developing countries seem to be highly influenced by the leadership theories developed in the context of the most developed countries which are normally constrained by contextual realities and challenges of the less developed countries. The contributors of the book have rightly reminded as well as advocated an indigenous perspective of educational leadership in the institutions and have also offered several thought-provoking practices and insightful learnings for developing contextually-responsive educational leadership underpinned by the wisdom 'think globally, act locally' in order to improve institutional performance which appears to be quite appealing, convincing, and fascinating. Great Work!

— PROFESSOR DR MUHAMMAD MEMON, Chairman, Board of Intermediate & Secondary Education, Hyderabad Sindh and Chairman, National Accreditation Council for Teacher Education, Pakistan.

This book is an important contribution to the international educational leadership literature. Drawing on the knowledge and wisdom of researchers in Pakistan, Afghanistan, and Kyrgyzstan, the chapters integrate theory and practice to provide a deeply grounded, contextualised portrayal of educational leadership in these countries, and to offer pathways for future research and action.
– LYNNE PARMENTER, Professor, Nazarbayev University, Graduate School of Education, Kazakhstan

The work of leadership is inherently stakeholder driven. Yet, a multitude of education reform initiatives in developing countries are either pushed down through the use of authority or informed by theories of influence formulated in foreign contexts. This book is a significant contribution to our understanding of educational leadership in developing countries because it gives centre stage to local perspectives. The contributors of the book underscore the importance of trust and embeddedness in the system which is essential for any change to be successfully envisioned, realised, and sustained. Great work!
– MARIAM CHUGHTAI, EdD. (Harvard University); Director, National Curriculum Council; Assistant Professor and Associate Dean, Lahore University of Management Sciences (LUMS)

This timely book provides empirical policy and practice studies of educational leadership from less developed countries. Based on the scholarly evidence of the review of leadership studies both from the less and more developed countries, the book reflects the global educational trends of the 21st century. Each chapter of this book amply reflects why leadership matters, and what the required core skills are to develop educational leaders best suited to the less developed countries.
– ALMAS KAYANI, PhD., Associate Professor of Education, Arid Agriculture University, Pakistan

This book explores educational leadership: how it is situated, developed, its impact, and how different contexts conceptualise it. The authors acknowledge the challenges educational leaders in developing countries experience and help imagine how leadership could be transformed to deal with these challenges. This book further chronicles transformations that must occur both in the culture and practice of leadership and in leadership preparation programmes to fully embrace the imperative for transformational leadership.
– WACHIRA NICHOLAS, Assistant Professor, Aga Khan University, Institute for Educational Development- East Africa

Educational Leadership Policies and Practices
Voices from the Developing Countries

Educational Leadership Policies and Practices
Voices from the Developing Countries

Editors
JAN-E-ALAM KHAKI
GULAB KHAN
MOLA DAD SHAFA
SADRUDDIN BAHADUR QUTOSHI

OXFORD
UNIVERSITY PRESS

Oxford University Press is a department of the University of Oxford.
It furthers the University's objective of excellence in research, scholarship, and education by publishing worldwide. Oxford is a registered trade mark of Oxford University Press in the UK and in certain other countries

Published in Pakistan by
Oxford University Press
No. 38, Sector 15, Korangi Industrial Area,
PO Box 8214, Karachi-74900, Pakistan

© Oxford University Press 2023

The moral rights of the author have been asserted

First Edition published in 2023

All rights reserved. No part of this publication may be reproduced, stored in a retrieval system, or transmitted, in any form or by any means, without the prior permission in writing of Oxford University Press, or as expressly permitted by law, by licence, or under terms agreed with the appropriate reprographics rights organization. Enquiries concerning reproduction outside the scope of the above should be sent to the Rights Department, Oxford University Press, at the address above

You must not circulate this work in any other form
and you must impose this same condition on any acquirer

ISBN 978-0-19-070644-9

Typeset in Times New Roman
Printed on 80gsm Offset Paper

Printed by Delta Dot Technologies (Pvt.) Ltd., Karachi

To

All those Educational Leaders who have dared to innovate leadership policies and practices in many Less Developed Countries

Contents

List of Abbreviations — xi
Foreword — xiii
Acknowledgements — xvii

Introduction — 1

1. High Aspirations, Unmet Expectations: Leadership Policy Conceptions in Public Universities — 11
   GULAB KHAN, TAJ-UD-DIN SHARAR, ASIF KHAN, AND SAJJAD HUSSAIN

2. Toothless Tigers or Selfless Servants? Role Perceptions of DEOs in Pakistan — 31
   JAN-E-ALAM KHAKI, ZUBEDA BANA, QAMAR SAFDAR, AND MIR AFZAL TAJIK

3. School Supervision: A Tool for Effective Governance or an Institutional Burden? — 49
   TAKBIR ALI

4. Pedagogies for Developing Pedagogical Leaders — 74
   MIR AFZAL TAJIK

5. A Leadership Development Programme: Challenges, Opportunities, and Lessons Learnt — 92
   DHANI BUX SHAH

6. The Nature of School Administrators' Support of Beginning Teachers in Kyrgyzstan — 110
   DUISHON ALIEVICH SHAMATOV

7. Supporting Students Affected by War and Terrorism: School Leadership Challenges — 126
   NEELOFAR AHMED

8. School Improvement Leadership: Lessons Learnt in the Mountainous Region of Gilgit-Baltistan — 148
MOLA DAD SHAFA AND SHARIFULLAH BAIG

9. Transformative Leadership as/for Emancipation: A Journey Towards Exploring Self and Beyond in the Field of Educational Leadership — 173
SADRUDDIN BAHADUR QUTOSHI AND BAL CHANDRA LUITEL

10. Culture and Organisational Knowledge Creation Processes: A Case Study in Afghanistan — 192
OMIDULLAH KHAWARY

11. Educational Leadership Policies and Practices: Key Lessons and Way Forward — 209
GULAB KHAN AND JAN-E-ALAM KHAKI

References — 226
About Editors and Contributors — 247
Index — 253

List of Abbreviations

ADISM	Advanced Diploma In School Management
ADO	Assistant District Official/er
ADOE	Assistant District Officer of Education
AKDN	Aga Khan Development Network
AKPBS	Aga Khan Planning and Building Services
AKU-IED	Aga Khan University, Institute for Educational Development
CE: ELM	Certificate in Education: Educational Leadership and Management
CEO	Chief Executive Officer
CPs	Course Participants
CPEC	China-Pakistan Economic Corridor
CSRC	Civil Society Resource Center
DA/TA	Daily Allowance/Travel Allowance
DDO	Drawing and Disbursing Officer
DEO	District Education Officer/official
DoE	Director of Education
EDIP	Education Development and Improvement Programme
ED-LINKS	Links to Education
EDO	Executive District Officer
EFA	Education for All
ELM	Educational Leadership and Management
FATA	Federally Administered Tribal Area
GB	Gilgit-Baltistan
GoP	Government of Pakistan
HE	Higher Education
HEC	Higher Education Commission
HEIs	Higher Education Institutions
ICT	Islamabad Capital Territory
ICTy	Information and Communications Technology
IDPs	Internally Displaced Persons
K–12	Grades K–12
KIU	Karakoram International University
LDCs	Less Developed Countries

LIST OF ABBREVIATIONS

LftM	Leadership from Middle
LUMS	Lahore University of Management Sciences
MA	Master of Arts
M&E	Monitoring and Evaluation
MDCs	More Developed Countries
MERLU	Monitoring, Evaluation, Research and Learning Unit
MDGs	Millennium Development Goals
MoE	Ministry of Education
MRD	Multi-paradigmatic Research Design
MSGs	Mothers' Support Groups
NEP	National Education Policy
NOWPDP	Network of Organisations Working with People with Disability in Pakistan
OISE/UT	Ontario Institute of Studies in Education, University of Toronto, Canada
PDCN	Professional Development Centre, North
PDT	Professional Development Teacher
PhD	Doctor of Philosophy
SMC	School Management Committee
SoE	School of Education
STEP	Strengthening Teacher Education Programme
SDP	School Development Plan
TA/DA	Transport Allowance/Daily Allowance
TEO	Taluqa Education Officer
UC	Union Council
UGC	University Grants Commission
UNESCO	United Nations, Educational, Scientific and Cultural Organisation
USAID	United States Agency for International Development

Foreword

We have entered an age of both great promise and great concern: A complex and daunting age, in need of inspiring and visionary leadership in all fields of endeavour, especially the field of education.

The 21st century digital era has ushered in the *fourth industrial revolution*. New technologies are enabling us to communicate instantly almost anywhere in the world. Robots are increasing our industrial productivity. Genetic engineering is offering pest resistant, high yield crops. Transport systems are becoming more energy efficient. We are exploring the solar system and preparing to land on Mars. Our national markets are an inextricable part of a global economic system. We are living increasingly in an interconnected and interdependent global village.

At the same time, however, all is not right with the world of modern progress. Our technological advances have ushered in the *Anthropocene*, an unprecedented era in which the metaphorical human footprint is altering in disastrous ways our planet's ability to sustain life. Atmospheric warming from fossil fuel emissions is precipitating climate change: sea-level rise, catastrophic wildfires and hurricanes, and prolonged droughts are threatening our survival. We are drastically polluting our marine ecosystems with microplastics deadly to wildlife, and we are overharvesting fish stocks, the lifeblood of millions of coastal villagers. We are deploying sophisticated weaponised technology to (fruitlessly) resolve cultural differences. And we are losing indigenous wisdom traditions about how to live sustainably in natural ecosystems.

To help us resolve the ethical dilemma of how to benefit from the fourth industrial revolution while, at the same time, resolving the dire challenges of the Anthropocene, we need transformative leadership. Transformative leadership is based on a broad ethical vision of *the public good*. Transformative leaders strive to inspire and empower others to become visionary and inspiring leaders (not simply obedient followers) in their many and varied spheres of influence and walks of life, from politics, business and government, to family and community.

Transformative leaders have a unique set of capabilities that separates them from managers who understand progress in narrow technical terms as ensuring the uncritical reproduction of established social systems. Transformative leaders are alive to the importance of serving the competing interests of both the economy and sustainability, which contribute equally to a 21st century vision of the public good. In the field of education, transformative leaders (district officers, headteachers, teachers) understand their ultimate goal as preparing young people not only with knowledge and skills for employment in the digital economy, but also with the moral values and agency of responsible citizens committed to ensuring the viability of the ecosystems that support life on Earth.

Educational research plays an important role in addressing the need to create inspiring and visionary leadership for transforming the world. To fully harness the power of educational research it is important to understand the multi-paradigmatic nature of contemporary approaches which offer a rich array of epistemologies (or ways of knowing), enabling us to generate different forms of knowledge—objective, subjective, critical, integral—depending on the purpose of our research (Taylor & Luitel, 2019).

Classical educational research, which adopts a *quasi-scientific* approach framed by an objectivist epistemology, focuses the researcher on exploring the social world 'out there' (beyond him/herself), drawing on theoretical models of leadership to measure the impact (or lack thereof) of leadership practices; seeking to answer the question: What is the impact of existing leadership practices, how well are they achieving their primary goal? This approach serves well the purpose of evaluating the implementation by educational leaders of policies framed by the system's official values.

By contrast, *interpretive research* approaches, based on a constructivist epistemology, focus primarily on the world 'in here', delving into the subjective perspectives of educational leaders (and those being led), endeavouring to understand their vision and situational agency, exploring how local contextual factors enable and constrain, inspire and frustrate, their practices. They seek to answer the question: Given local cultural sensitivities, how are leadership practices being experienced by all stakeholders? The main purpose served by this research approach is to investigate the extent to which the framing assumptions and values of the education system serve all cultural contexts equally well.

Contemporary multi-paradigm research approaches, which combine *interpretive* and *critical* epistemologies, seek not only to understand but also to transform the framing assumptions and values of both our outer and inner worlds. This approach generates an empowering *integral* form of enhanced self-knowing in relation to significant others and the world at large. In *critical auto-ethnographic studies*, an established leader adopts the role of *critical reflective practitioner* and collaborates with a mentor (e.g. postgraduate supervisor) who empowers him/her to explore critically the cultural assumptions and values that frame (often invisibly) his/her professional practice, and to develop a culture-sensitive, visionary, and inspiring philosophy of transformative leadership. He/she seeks to pursue an answer to the question: How can I transform my leadership practice to empower my colleagues as visionary and inspiring professional educators committed to developing their students' capabilities to resolve the ethical dilemma of living and working in a world that is being shaped by both the fourth industrial revolution and the Anthropocene?

This timely, multinational book demonstrates a range of educational research approaches employed to investigate and develop innovative and aspirational approaches to educational leadership. As you read each chapter, in turn, I encourage you to ask yourself the following questions.

- What types of knowledge about educational leadership practice are being evidenced by this particular research study?
- How well is the particular model/s of leadership likely to prepare young people to live and work both digitally and sustainably in a rapidly changing world?

Peter Charles Taylor
Chair, International Transformative Education Research Network
Adjunct Professor, Murdoch University, Australia

Acknowledgements

From the beginning, we called this book project a 'labour of love'. We envisioned it as a voluntary adventure, embarked on out of our own deep interest, not out of any compulsion. This labour of love, thanks to the efforts of all involved, has now reached its maturation stage.

Right from the beginning there were a few friends who worked as 'triggers' and motivators to start this book. Increasingly, I, as the Chief Editor, was receiving messages from students, faculty, and readers in different organisations as to how they benefitted from the previous book *Educational Leadership in Pakistan: Ideals and Realities* (Oxford University Press, 2010), edited with Qamar Safdar, one of my colleagues at the Aga Khan University, Institute for the Educational Development (AKU-IED). When that book was being conceived, we had been hoping that a sequel would soon follow, but the pressure of engagements did not allow us enough time to fulfil this dream. However, colleagues within and outside AKU continued motivating us to consider writing the second book, particularly when even the second impression of the book went out of print soon after its publication.

Among those who particularly pushed and motivated me to start this volume are the other three editors of this book—Gulab Khan, Mola Dad Shafa, and Sadruddin Bahadur Qutoshi. Respecting their wish and following my own dream, I prepared the book proposal and, having got feedback from them, we embarked on it. True to their word, the colleagues fully honoured their commitment right from the beginning to the end, despite their heavy commitments to their universities.

Another faculty member, Dr Almas Kayani, the then Director, Women Development Studies Centre, University of Arid Agriculture, Rawalpindi, also played an inspirational role in initiating this project. After having worked with us at the conceptualisation stage, she had to move overseas owing to family commitments and, sadly, had to leave the project. Nevertheless, I thank her for her inspiration to push us to start this project. Showing her support to the work, she has kindly provided a blurb.

To these, and many others who became our source of inspiration to embark on this project, I offer my profound gratitude for their commitment to scholarship and promotion of literature on educational leadership in the less developed countries (LDCs). The steady encouragement coming from many scholars has successfully guided us through the thick and thin of writing this book.

In addition, my gratitude goes to all those who contributed chapters to this volume and did their best to maintain the highest possible academic rigour and quality needed for this book. Despite their ongoing professional engagements, they spared their invaluable time. Thank you all!

Many others have made valuable contributions to this volume, including Dr Peter Charles Taylor, Adjunct Professor of Transformative STEAM Education, Murdoch University, Australia, and Director, International Transformative Educational Research Network (ITERN), who has kindly written the Foreword to this volume. Also, all those imminent scholars who have written blurbs for this volume deserve our wholehearted gratitude.

Last but not the least, Oxford University Press and its staff deserve our gratitude for obliging us by publishing this volume. To you all, I say a big 'Thank you'.

Jan-e-Alam Khaki

Introduction

Leadership matters! This is what can safely be concluded from the educational leadership literature of the last five decades, both from the more developed countries (MDCs) as well as from the less developed countries (LDCs).[1] Leadership has become a truly interesting and potent subject in many disciplines, including business—where it originated—and now education, because of its appeal as an increasingly important factor to improve quality. With the advancement of behavioural sciences, the notion of leadership has grown further, and been borrowed by other disciplines such as educational administration. With this trend, a difference is made between a 'manager' and a 'leader,' the former being a gatekeeper and the latter being a vision builder, inspirer, and mentor.

Today, the academia, including universities, colleges, schools, and other professional development centres (PDCs), has been permeated by the newly found 'love' of leadership with accompanying claim of success and effectiveness. As a result, an increasing number of competing leadership theories has inundated the book industry, management and leadership journals, and the courses and programmes offered from undergraduate to graduate levels. The latest trends have helped leadership theories filter down even to early childhood education, termed as 'leadership in early years'.

The scholarship on leadership in both the MDCs and LDCs has led to a race on generating models and theories of leadership with the aim of showing the relative efficacy of each model. While this has created so many possibilities to choose from different theories, equally, the emergence of numerous leadership development models has made selection and prioritisation of theories a daunting task.

This phenomenon has been especially prevalent in the MDCs over half a century; in contrast, in the LDCs, it is a relatively younger field, spanning over four to five decades. A body of research, including theoretical frameworks, normative studies, and even training manuals, has sprung up. The interest of scholars, researchers, practitioners, and trainers in the field has continued to surge.

Amidst the increasingly complex maze of the body of knowledge, an interesting question has been raised about the scope of leadership knowledge: Can the knowledge of leadership or research conclusions drawn from one context (say the MDCs) be reflective of and applicable to the realities of another context (i.e. LDCs) with no consideration to the compelling contextual ground realities or limitations? The situational approach of leadership theory amply demonstrates otherwise, arguing that the situation is critical to the success or failure of leadership. Omni-application of leadership knowledge regardless of the context is bound to face enormous challenges as socio-cultural demands in one context may be very different from another even within the same country or city, let alone across continents that are so diverse in every sense of the term.

Application of the findings of leadership studies from one context or culture to another, say, in Toronto, Tokyo, New York, or Timbuktu, may be highly questionable due largely to the contextual differences. However, this does not mean that lessons learnt from research in one context cannot be helpful in understanding educational complexities elsewhere. The key point here is that research findings and the lessons learnt may not be automatically applicable in another, largely different, context. The literature produced from research in the MDCs cannot be taken for granted as equally applicable in the LDCs. Even within LDCs, knowledge generated in one country, such as Kenya, may not be applicable, say, in Bangladesh.

This goes to show that contextual knowledge and vernacular wisdom is directly relevant to, and helpful in understanding, a particular context where we want to apply a particular type of knowledge. If this argument is accepted, it means that research done and knowledge generated from within the LDCs may have a more direct relevance and value to policymakers, practitioners, and researchers.

In addition, this realisation has necessitated doing local research to generate vernacular knowledge, reflecting practical experiences, including training and professional development programmes carried out in the educational institutions, particularly at the universities. So, this volume reflects this dual role, the role of a researcher and of a practitioner.

We, the editors, having been researchers and practitioners, working in such LDCs as Afghanistan, Kyrgyzstan, Nepal, and Pakistan, have faced this acute need both as doctoral scholars ourselves as well as faculty members and practitioners. This volume, therefore, is an attempt towards meeting this felt need. It draws on the wisdom coming from both MDCs and LDCs integrating it in a way that provides a reservoir of knowledge for policymakers, researchers, and practitioners to draw from and make use of, according to the contextual needs.

These stories, which we poetically call the 'Voices' for sharpening the messages, are shared with the readers hoping that they (the stories) will be heard and appreciated. Some of these voices may be melodious, others loud, or still others soft. But each 'singer' or contributor 'sings' a song of their own, unique to their context and culture, yet sharing many essential features of the policy and practice of leadership. These 'songs' will be intelligible when they are heard in *their* 'language' and context; any attempt to decontextualise them may yield less tangible lessons that we hope others can learn. We are trying to find the undercurrents below these apparently individual chapters. This will be clearer in Chapter 11, where the key lessons are highlighted.

Almost all the contributors to this volume are both researchers as well as practitioners in higher education institutions or organisations dealing with education. Sharing the fruits of our labour in these two roles, we believe, may be worthwhile for other researchers and practitioners particularly in the LDCs. Having situated the rationale of writing this volume, we would like to quickly give a brief history of leadership studies in Pakistan and how this book is situated within that context.

The history of leadership as a field of study, particularly in the area of school and higher education, is two or three decades old in Pakistan. For example, when the Aga Khan University's Institute for Educational Development (AKU-IED) started a programme for the principals (both public and private schools) during 1998–99, it (AKU) was among the leading universities starting professional enhancement programmes for headteachers[2] in Karachi. A few of the teacher training institutions did sporadically offer managerial programmes for public sector institutions for the management cadres, but not specifically for the headteachers. In the private sector, this practice was still uncommon up until the second half of the 1990s. It may be noted that the heads were/are appointed to their positions on the basis of their seniority and there were no criteria or training programme necessary to be a school head. Even after promotion, no formal training is required nor given to any headteacher.

As a result of the introduction of leadership programmes as well as the stakeholders' fascination with leadership notions in developing countries, many doctoral and masters level students studying abroad started contributing to leadership studies. A pioneering book *Educational Leadership in Pakistan: Ideals and Realities* (Oxford University Press, 2010) was edited by the first editor of this volume and another faculty, Qamar Safdar—both at the time working with the AKU-IED as full-time faculty dealing with a number of educational leadership programmes as part of the regular courses offered at AKU-IED. The book, first of its kind in Pakistan, generated an enormous positive response from readers, professors, researchers, and students. They reported that they found the book very useful as an indigenous and primary resource on leadership practices in Pakistan and elsewhere.

In the last two decades, the AKU-IED has mainstreamed the leadership programmes offered up to graduate levels. As a result, many of the faculty members and graduate students have undertaken research projects and contributed to the studies on educational leadership. Meanwhile, other universities and professional development institutions and centres have sprung up, including the most recent addition in Pakistan in the form of the Syed Ahsan Ali and Syed Maratib Ali School of Education (abbreviated as SoE in this volume) at the Lahore University of Management Sciences (LUMS). The schools are now offering courses and workshops, shorter and longer, which are attracting a sizeable clientele, reflecting an increased interest in the area.

Based on these and similar developments, the editors of this volume embarked on this project to further enhance the leadership knowledge greatly needed by the local researchers, faculty members, students, practitioners, and general readers. The difference between the earlier book (*Educational Leadership in Pakistan*) and this one is that, while the former volume was exclusively limited to contributors from Pakistan, this volume is relatively international as chapters have been contributed by scholars from Afghanistan, Kyrgyzstan, and Nepal, as well.

The chapters in this volume contribute to the scope of the educational leadership domain, including policy studies, leadership models, supervision, monitoring and evaluation, leadership of school heads for supporting war and terror affected students, and organisational learning, aiming to develop a broader knowledge of the area of educational leadership in LDCs. Having outlined the context in which this volume has been conceptualised, we now move on to sharing brief contours of the chapters included in this volume to help readers follow the structure of the book.

Chapter 1 by Gulab Khan, Taj-Ud-Din Sharar, Asif Khan, and Sajjad Hussain examines the policy with regard to educational leadership in higher education in Pakistan. The chapter analyses the educational policies in Pakistan through the leadership lens and how, for the last many decades, the policy-makers have or have not focused on leadership in higher education. The writers argue that the higher education leadership has been largely overlooked or not brought into the educational policy radar largely because empirical studies of leadership have emerged mostly in K–12 (school grades K–12) contexts over the last couple of decades—more specifically, since the 1990s. However, the writers emphasise that 'educational leadership' in higher education needs to be focused as has been demonstrated elsewhere in the world to make a difference in the quality of education in Higher Education Institutions (HEIs).

Chapter 2, by Jan-e-Alam Khaki, Zubeda Bana, Qamar Safdar, and Mir Afzal Tajik, focuses on the office that is responsible for the implementation of policies in the K-12 setting in Pakistan. The chapter outlines the district education officers' (DEOs) self-perceived images and roles. They report that often they see themselves as helpless officers, having big titles but little power to actually make a difference on the ground, due to a number of hampering factors. These include, but are not limited to, corruption, nepotism, tribalism, frequent changes of education secretaries and ministers, and, most of all, political interference. The authors describe the role of the DEOs as being mere *toothless tigers*—big titles versus little power to effect change. Of course, there are notable exceptions to this situation, where the officers *do* make a difference, to the extent possible, yet, the overall position remains unchanged with little to no signs of improvement in schools and classrooms. The discussion leads to the fact that there is no easy solution to these problems unless there is a systemic change.

Chapter 3, authored by Takbir Ali, highlights the place of school supervision in the context of Pakistani schools, focusing on Sindh, a province of Pakistan. Ali argues that school supervision, which is meant for the improvement of teaching, learning, and leadership in schools, ends up as a futile exercise in Sindh, chiefly due to corruption in the education department. He argues that school supervision proves to be a waste of time and resources, due largely to the ineffective processes characterizing the whole system. His analysis concludes that, despite good intentions and policies, the practical realities render school supervision a fruitless and wasteful exercise. At the end, Ali suggests ways and means of improving the supervision process.

The following three chapters (4, 5, and 6) relate to the headteacher capacity building models as well as their mentoring roles for staff and students in schools.

Chapter 4 by Mir Afzal Tajik looks at the various headteacher development models. More specifically, his chapter presents analyses of a variety of school leadership models, options, and strategies, including both the continuous professional development of the experienced headteachers and the induction programmes for those beginning in those roles. Anchoring his study in a private university in Pakistan, Tajik talks about the pedagogical model used for the professional development of headteachers and assistant headteachers. Reporting about the nature of the programme, its aims and objectives and how it evolved, Tajik shares the lessons learnt from the programme and how it influenced the heads in their professional development processes. The chapter highlights the challenges of developing and implementing such pedagogies in the context of Pakistan and more generally, in the developing countries. The chapter concludes with a discussion on the implications of these pedagogies and recommendations for policy and practice.

Dhani Bux Shah (Chapter 5) shares his experiences and learnings from a leadership programme involving a group of headteachers from the provinces of Sindh and Balochistan at a private university in Pakistan. He worked with the programme as a professional development teacher (PDT) and was involved in it from conceptualisation to implementation, including teaching and follow up. Shah's study reflects how a meticulously conceived and carefully delivered professional enhancement programme can help even the senior personnel re-conceptualise their roles and revisit their long-held notions. The chapter tells how the leadership programme helped address school leadership challenges and provided learning opportunities. Those who run the headteachers' professional development programmes such as these can learn many lessons from the chapter in terms of both the model, its implementation, and follow up.

Shamatov in Chapter 6 shares his study on the role of school headteachers in the induction of beginning teachers in the context of Kyrgyzstan, which reflects yet another dimension of the role of school heads. The writer shares his study on how the school heads support the beginning teachers during their early induction period. His study demonstrates how perceptions, more than realities, play a role in developing beginning teachers' conceptions about the school leadership. The study shows that the beginning teachers need significant support, not only in their teaching work or disciplinary matters but also in working with colleagues, pupils, parents, and education officials. He recommends that the beginning teachers should have more positive perceptions of their administrators in order to build more exciting relations with school leadership.

Among the drawbacks of the 21st century are the scourges of war and of terrorism. These two sources of plight and fear have caused so much devastation to humanity in general and children in particular.

Millions of children have been brutally affected by war and terrorist violence. Education is one sure key for societies to secure themselves from debilitating damage by putting in place appropriate psychological, social, and physical safeguards for children affected by war and terrorist violence. Neelofar Ahmad takes these up in Chapter 7 and unpacks how the education policies and school leadership can help address education leadership challenges generated as a result of war and terror. She discusses cross-cultural cooperation in this area to benefit from the lessons learnt in one context and make use of it in another context with concomitant strengths and limitations. All those who have an interest in how education and war and terrorism intertwine will find valuable insights in this chapter.

The locus of studies in the chapters introduced so far is largely in urban mega cities. Mola Dad Shafa and Sharifullah Baig in Chapter 8 take the reader to the mountainous rural region of Gilgit-Baltistan (GB) of Pakistan. The authors report on the development and progress of teacher leadership through what they call a comprehensive, integrated, and consortium-based school improvement project known as the Educational Development and Improvement Programme (EDIP). It specifically highlights the role of teachers as the leaders to navigate the dynamics of the EDIP model in the targeted public sector schools of GB. The insights emanating from this study highlight EDIP's significant contributions in changing teacher perceptions and perspectives in improving their role as teacher leaders. The contributors identify many aspects of the programme as key to sustainability of the work, such as a well-thought-out sustainability plan and a carefully engineered gradual phase-out strategy as part of the future education projects. This, they warn, could be a challenging task for the government education department, the donor community, and the implementing partners as all of them have their own priorities and limitations.

Raising the discourse from the practical application of policy studies and leadership theories and models to a more theoretical level, Sadruddin Bahadur Qutoshi and Bal Chandra Luitel (Chapter 9) problematise leadership conceptions, particularly the transformational model, by arguing that transforma*tive* rather than transforma*tional* leadership is what should be aimed at as a leadership theory. They argue that emancipatory interest of education that is embedded within such a transformative leadership theory is both revealing and rewarding, in that both leaders and followers come closer to each other in order to create an environment of trust, cooperation, and collaboration to build what they call 'an organisational citizenship behaviour'. In so doing, the authors argue, the leader and follower can collectively raise the performance of themselves and others in the institution and beyond, developing the concept of co-leading, co-becoming, and co-evolving. To this end, the task of leader is to develop institution/s as learning organisations. This, they claim, is a journey of exploration and discovery through the practice of dialogic engagement of two individuals—mentee and mentor—as a template for the transformative experience of true learning and transformation from one stage of learning to another without any final limit (i.e. an engagement with the philosophy of lifelong learning through critical reflective practices).

Situating his study in the backdrop of an organisation in Afghanistan, Omidullah Khawary in Chapter 10 explores the dynamics of how organisations learn in an intra-institutional context. He studies the intricate stages of learning among and between individuals and unpacks the dynamics of its relation in an organisational framework. Khawary concludes that the leadership should have a clear knowledge vision that has the ability to determine the type of knowledge to be created, including its appropriate means and domains. As the organisation studied reportedly has a wide scope of mandate, Khawary argues that it should articulate a knowledge vision that can transcend the boundaries of knowledge creation, its long-term direction, and how it should evolve in the years and decades ahead. He argues that the knowledge vision should highlight the value system of the organisations defining what is considered to be the truth, goodness, and beauty for the organisation.

The volume concludes with Chapter 11 wherein the key learnings of all the chapters are summarised, discussed, and concluded with recommendations. Gulab Khan and Jan-e-Alam Khaki synthesise five themes from all the chapters to help the reader grasp the key messages and recommendations. A sixth meta-theme in the chapter concludes an exercise of exploration of educational leadership with a special focus on policy, school and district leadership situated in the context of the developing countries with a particular focus on Pakistan, Afghanistan, and Kyrgyzstan.

It may be noted that this volume is not meant to be a training module. It intends to first help *understand* the theoretical underpinnings, drawn from the study of literature related to leadership both from the MDCs and LDCs. Second, the book aims to show some *pathways* to practice leadership in different contexts. Leadership trainers, of course, may gain insights from the book as to how training institutions use leadership models, such as pedagogical leadership and/or transform*ative* leadership, to offer deeper insights in nurturing leaders using well-thought-out conceptions and strategies.

The editors hope that this volume will make a meaningful contribution to the existing knowledge-base on educational leadership and management studies, bringing an additional layer of new and much-needed knowledge to the rapidly expanding global scholarship on this subject. We do hope that the readers, including researchers, policymakers, district education officials, headteachers or principals, practitioners, professional development teams, students, and general readers will find the volume insightful and useful to their pursuit of improving the quality of education through a contextual understanding and enhancement of educational leadership skills. This we emphasise, because, LEADERS DO MATTER!

Jan-e-Alam Khaki
Gulab Khan
Mola Dad Shafa
Sadruddin Bahadur Qutoshi
13 December 2019

Notes

1. The LDCs are referred largely to less developed countries, such as Pakistan, and MDCs are more developed (i.e. technologically advanced) countries, such as, the United States of America.
2. Generally, in Pakistan the public schools use the terms 'head/teacher/master/mistress' more commonly for schools from K–10; while the private schools often use the term 'principal' for all stages and years of schooling.

1

High Aspirations, Unmet Expectations: Leadership Policy Conceptions in Public Universities

GULAB KHAN, TAJ-UD-DIN SHARAR, ASIF KHAN, AND SAJJAD HUSSAIN

Successive governments have always focused on education policies right from the birth of Pakistan. This attention has been largely driven by the utility of education as an ideological tool to cement firmly the ideology of Pakistan among the masses and give a homogenous texture to the federation. While there have been extensive analyses of how policy development has been anchored in an ideological framework, policy on educational leadership, especially higher education, has received much less attention in scholarship. With the objective of filling this gap, this chapter explores education policy proposals specific to leadership in public sector universities in Pakistan. The chapter is based on textual analysis of the major conferences, policy documents, and relevant scholarship on education policy development in Pakistan. The various policy and conference documents retrieved from government sources were openly coded followed by categorisation of themes on leadership in higher education.

The chapter first discusses how policy discourse in the last seven decades has treated conceptions of leadership in public universities in the country. The second section assesses the tensions arising from internal versus external controls and an attendant objective of creating synergy among public universities in Pakistan. The third section discusses the competing demands for quality and access, and how university leadership is engaged to forge a balance between the two. The fourth section ties back to where it began by discussing concepts of the knowledge-based economy and associated leadership dynamics in universities.

Starting with the first educational conference in 1947, major education policies have come through the various governments over the last seven and a half decades of Pakistan's existence. The chapter ventures to reveal in the policy discourse the stark absence of leadership in universities, where the predominant focus is on 'administration' and 'management' within a framework of 'positional leadership'. While, in some contexts, 'leadership', 'management', and 'administration' are taken as synonymous, this chapter considers the three terms as being different, as discussed in the section below.

POLICY DISCOURSE: ABSENCE OF *LEADERSHIP* AND A PREDOMINANT FOCUS ON *ADMINISTRATION* AND *MANAGEMENT*

Educational leadership discourse and scholarship in Pakistan has largely been conducted around conceptions and practices of educational leadership in the K-12 educational settings. For example, Simkins, Sisum, and Memon (2003) explored the headteachers' role in public schools in Pakistan. Another significant scholarly piece that gives insights on educational leadership mainly in the K-12 settings in Pakistan is a most comprehensive work compiled by Khaki and Safdar (2010). Similarly, Ali and Babur (2010) trace the history of the making of the leadership structure in schools in the subcontinent going as far back as the time of the British Empire. Furthermore, a relatively comprehensive account of education policies by Siddiqui (2016) lays down the political and ideological backdrops against which educational policy has evolued in Pakistan.

In these studies, however, there is little theoretical and empirical focus on how leadership is conceived and practiced in higher education, particularly at the university level. Part of the reason has been the complex leadership structure in universities, which assumes many layers of decision-making juggernauts, including faculty unions. The reason for such an absence in policy discourse on university leadership can also be traced back to the beginnings of university education in the sub-continent and subsequently in Pakistan.

At the time of independence, Pakistan was faced with a dearth of resources for running its affairs. Moreover, security became the topmost concern, while the social sector, including higher education, took a backseat in policy arenas. Partition also resulted in very few universities falling within its geographic domains. The first policies, conferences, and commissions reflect this serious handicap. As a corollary, 'efficiency' in running the affairs of universities remained at the centre of leadership conceptions and practices. At the same time, universities were tasked with the heavy responsibility of accelerating the pace of progress in the fields of commerce and industry as well as having to provide intellectual impetus to aid 'academic freedom' for the overall development of the country. Along the years, it seems that the objective of 'administration', translated as 'efficiency' and 'accountability' in a knowledge-based environment (in itself a worthy goal when running a system with limited resources), has won the race.

A predominant focus on administrative and managerial conceptions and practices of leadership in universities can be traced back to the first educational conference held in November 1947, henceforth termed as the 'Conference'. The proceedings of the Conference only mention 'administrative machinery' under Appendix A and 'educational administration' in passing in an annexure to Appendix E (Government of Pakistan (GoP), 1947). Even there, 'educational administration' fell under a category of 'overseas scholarship' schemes for training of 'other educational personnel' who would be '...specialised in various aspects e.g. recreative and Social Activities, Juvenile Employment, Infants' training, Education of the Handicapped....' (GoP, 1947: 70). Save the latest policy rounds, a perilous absence of treatment of university leadership runs as a striking common in all phases of education policy development in Pakistan.

As a result, 'administering' higher education emerges as the predominant framework within which leadership has been conceived and practiced in universities. Especially towards the mid-1970s, the University Grants Commission Act, promulgated in 1974, laid out an extensive administrative and management structure for universities—a structure that has largely retained its original texture to this day. Analysis of university ordinances and successive policies shows that almost invariably, 'administration' has been conceived as controlling and managing the higher education system. This suggests that higher education policy has treated leadership in narrow terms, often equating it with the managerial functions of the university. This, as one can see is at variance with the conceptions and practices of leadership which, unlike 'managing' and 'administering', are about motivating individuals and teams to rally for a deep and strategic vision through cultural transformation of the social unit where reform is needed

(Bertocci, 2009; Bryan & Wilson, 2015; Schein, 2010). It is, however, only very lately, and especially after 2002, that the concepts of vision and mission for universities and constituent units have come to the fore, but that too as a part of the accountability and quality assurance mechanisms in universities.

Thus, from the beginning of policy development in the country, universities have invested greater intellectual, financial, and human resources to achieve administrative efficiency. This investment can be looked at primarily in three dimensions of policy development and analysis and associated demands on university leadership. The first dimension can be seen as creating coordination among universities and the tension between the competing demands of establishing control of the university, the second as maintaining a balance between access and quality in higher education, and the third as tuning higher education to the demands of industry and the needs and dynamics of national development.

The following section deals with the genesis of the administrative structure and governance of the university in Pakistan with associated efforts to establish the balance of internal versus external control and creating synergy among universities.

INTERNAL VERSUS EXTERNAL CONTROL AND CREATING SYNERGY AMONG UNIVERSITIES

At the time of independence, Pakistani universities inherited an administrative structure along the lines of colonial models, such as the London University with the primary function of arranging examinations for the affiliated colleges (GoP, 1947). However, over the decades running into the post-Partition era, universities increasingly assumed teaching and research activities as well.

The genesis of a governance and administrative structure for the university in Pakistan begins with the noteworthy absence of any discussions on the leadership structure and vision for universities in the Conference in 1947, held under the chairmanship of Mr Fazlur Rahman, Minister for Interior, Information and Broadcasting and Education, Government of Pakistan. The Conference is noteworthy in that the term 'leadership' does not appear in the deliberations of the Committee on university education, henceforth termed as the 'Committee', that was tasked primarily with thrashing out the possibility of setting up a self-governing, Inter-universities Board for Pakistan, a precursor to the University Grants Commission formed in 1974. This board was envisioned as creating synergies and coordination among the universities of the new republic. It is important to note that the proposed board for Pakistan was not a new entity. A similar board had been in existence in pre-Partition India since 1925 (GoP, 1947). 'The Committee proposed, and the Conference resolved, that the Board be continued in Pakistan by elevating its status to a more robust and authority-intensive entity.' Thus, the Committee's primary responsibility of creating an external board and the associated absence of deliberations on how universities should 'lead' themselves, suggests an effort to establish an external locus of control to ensure efficient use of limited resources in an environment when higher education was not in high demand.

The powers of the board, with vice chancellors or their nominees as members, were significant including, inter alia, exchange of information and opinion among the universities, equivalence of degrees and diplomas, initiation of fresh developments, and maintenance of standards of teaching and examinations, to name a few. Thus, with respect to leadership, the Conference appeared hooked to three administrative goals for universities: (a) administrative efficiency, (b) standardisation of practices across universities, and (c) coordination among universities.

A predominant focus on 'administering' the university suggests that the university leadership at the time and in the years and decades to come would be invested more with the administrative aspects and not with setting vision and promoting a culture of genuine scholarship. Furthermore, lesser attention of the Conference to deliberating on and recommending improvements in the quality of scholarship and teaching in the university can also be assessed from the instance when Dr C.H. Rice, a member of the Committee, proposed granting greater freedom and initiative to universities. The Committee did not consider his proposal and left it to the proposed board for deliberation and further action. Thus, an opportune moment in the history of higher education to set the tone of 'academic freedom' in universities in Pakistan and, accordingly, an opportunity to tune the university leadership and governance towards genuine efforts to raise quality of teaching and research, appears to have been lost. Had the committee deliberated on Dr Rice's proposal, the possibility of developing a truly 'free' university, a pre-requisite for a strong and robust academic and research culture in any country, could have come to fruition sooner than later. Interestingly enough, the need to sustain academic freedom reverberates in future policies as well, such as the National Education Policy 1998–2010, wherein the guiding principles for the policy included, among others, 'academic freedom' and 'institutional autonomy' (GoP, 1998: 59). This suggests that the goal of 'academic freedom' remained only on the wish-list of policy with an absence of concrete leadership action to enable the university to truly acquire an independent status so that a genuine and indigenous scholarship of high quality could be developed in the country.

The years between 1947 and the 1960s are also characterised by a tussle between autonomy to and control of universities. For example, the Proposals for a New Education Policy 1969, henceforth referred to as the Proposal, reiterated the deteriorating standards in universities. To address this problem, three ways forward were suggested in the Proposal: (a) Financial autonomy, (b) Administrative autonomy, and (c) Streamlining of internal administration of the university. To give effect to these, the Proposals drafted a bill for a University Act 1969, which proposed to annul the earlier ordinance of 1961 (itself amended by West Pakistan Ordinances Nos. XXIV of 1962, XXX of 1962, I of 1966, V of 1966, and III of 1967) (GoP, 1969: 66). It can be inferred from such ordinances, propositions of which are discussed in more detail below, that the Proposals, which were reviewed significantly in the New Education Policy of 1970, produced many ripples that would ultimately shape the administrative and governance structure that the universities would be governed by. These bills and proposals or components therein largely remained ineffective until 1974 when the Act No. XXIII (Josh & Mak International, 1974) on the University Grants Commission (UGC), henceforth named as the Commission, was enacted on 22 April 1974 (National Assembly Secretariat, 1974).

The Proposal and the ordinances and legislative amendments aimed to grant vast autonomy to universities with a division of power among Chancellor, Vice Chancellor, Senate, Syndicate, Academic Council, and other bodies. Within the university, the Vice Chancellor was given huge powers to run the administrative and academic matters of the university. Under these ordinances, the Senate was proposed as a large body, with a membership of 'not more than 100', including the Vice Chancellor, nominees of the government, 50 elected teachers, 15 elected students including presidents and secretaries of the student unions (GoP, 1969).

The proposed structures are significant in that the notion of leadership in higher education assumed a formal and hierarchical setup on the lines of 'positional leadership' (Lovett, 2018; Sourthworth, 2004) in the university. Even though universities in Pakistan have maintained administrative and leadership structure and texture originally proposed in the draft bill for a University Act 1969, a lot has also changed especially with regard to how lower tiers such as students and teachers can have a say in university matters. The supreme authority in the proposed University Act 1969 lays with the Senate, which had powers of (a) making and ratifying or amending statutes and of amending, repealing, or adding to the university ordinances, and (b) of ratifying and cancelling university ordinances and of amending, modifying, or repealing any regulations, among others (GoP, 1969: 74). The next in line of authority, the Syndicate, was to be the executive body of the university with the Vice Chancellor as the Chairperson. The composition of the Syndicate consisted, in addition to Chairperson, of the Deans of Faculties of Arts and Sciences, two Principals from affiliated colleges, eight university teachers, and two government representatives. The Syndicate would be a supervisory body for overall management and administration in consonance with the proposed Act, Statutes, and university Ordinances (GoP, 1969: 74–5).

Parallel to granting internal autonomy to the university through the proposed University Act 1969, UGC Ordinance 1969 proposed having two UGCs, one each for East and West Pakistan, with representatives from universities. The UGC of West Pakistan, enacted in 1974 and repealed in 2002 under the HEC Ordinance, was awarded significant powers to the extent that they had the jurisdiction to assess and evaluate programmes and needs, to advise the Syndicate to take necessary actions, and to provide grants and funding to universities (GoP, 1969: 70). This meant that autonomy was conceived as the channelling of government funds to universities, not through the education departments, as was the practice at the time, but through the UGC with powers to determine, allocate, and disburse funds, and '…advise the Central or Provincial Government on the allocation of any grants for any general or specified purpose' (GoP, 1969: 50). In addition, the UGC had the mandate also to advise on establishing new universities and to '…collect information on all such matters relating to university education…as it thinks fit and make the same available to any university of Central or Provincial Government…' (GoP, 1969: 50).

These and other functions gave wide leeway to the Commission to steer and influence the decision-making and administration of the universities in the direction that it desired. Thus, the Proposal, which set out with the objective of giving more autonomy to universities in financial, administrative, and academic matters, laid down a foundation for another body that would assume greater powers than individual universities in the future, leaving a significant control of decision-making and influence outside the university. As can be seen, the Commission morphed into a heavy body, with an extensive governance structure of its own, having a secretariat with a full body of professional and support structures. With the Commission in place for greater external control, universities found themselves tackling a host of issues, chiefly the balancing of access and quality, efficiency, accountability, and the heavy mandate of contributing in the national development of the country.

In the long line of administrative structuring and restructuring, the draft National Education Policy of 2017 made an exception as it explicitly deliberated on the administration and governance of higher education. It stated:

> Administrative structure of public sector modern universities shall be reformed, to streamline the role and contribution of Vice Chancellor, Controller and Registrar to effectively manage the Academic Affairs and Student Services, Graduate Studies and Research, Budget planning/Finance and Institutional Development. (GoP, 2017: 85)

However, even here, it is still the original discourse of 'administrative' restructuring suggesting that the future direction of such reforms would aim at the administrative functions of the university leadership. Having said this, it can be expected that with these policy provisions, the policy discourse may finally shift towards reimagining university administration as 'university leadership'. With the VCs and Rectors given 'additional responsibility' to raise funds (GoP, 2017: 85), the primary locus of decision-making may finally shift to the universities themselves, with greater and truer self-control and autonomy that could lead to positive and sustainable innovations in universities. However, in the post 18th Constitution Amendment scenario, with education at all levels devolved to provinces, it appears murky as to how the provincial higher education commissions/departments will emulate the propositions of the NEP 2017 or a later policy, because these bodies either need to be in place, as in Balochistan and Sindh, or are in evolutionary phase, as in Punjab and Khyber Pakhtunkhwa.

The section below describes policy evolution on how access and quality have made headway into policy development and analysis. Accordingly, it can be inferred how leadership in the university may have engaged to maintain a balance between the two.

Providing Leadership on Access and Quality: Two Forces in the Imbalance

In 1947, Pakistan inherited three universities from among 21 at the time in united India. These universities were: Dacca (renamed Dhaka) University in East Pakistan, University of the Punjab, and University of Sindh in West Pakistan, with the latter newly founded and the former undergoing transition due to Partition. Between 1947 and 1969, a steady increase in the number of universities in Pakistan can be observed with 12 universities combined in East and West Pakistan and a student enrolment of 22,000 (GoP, 1969). Parallel to this increase and coupled with the dynamics of structural reformations in the competing aims of internal versus external control, quality has become a perennial struggle for leadership at the university.

The New Education Policy 1970, while lamenting the seriously declining standards in education, pinned its greater hope on expansion of university education. Moving on, the expansionist agenda made it to the Education Policy 1972–1980 through a comparative analysis of access to higher education with some of the developed counterparts at the time. The policy noted that, compared with countries like the USA, Japan, and Canada, Pakistan at the time had relatively lower ratio of university students per 100,000 of the population (GoP, 1972)—a fact that appears to have changed very little to this day. To increase access, this policy set a target of creating an additional 100,000 university places by 1980 to cover 3 per cent of the university age group of the population. However, the National Education Policy 2009 acknowledged equitable access as a 'formidable challenge' amid low per capita expenditure and the increased demand for resources, particularly in the science subjects. According to the HEC (n.d.), as of the year 2015, there were 1,295,178 students enroled combined in over 160 public and private universities in the country, whereas the National Education Policy 2017 reports an enrolment of a mere 8 per cent (against a target of 7 per cent by 2010 in the education policy of 1998–2010) of the university age group (17–23) (GoP, 2017: 79). With access as the primary agenda for higher education, the draft Education Policy 2017 aimed to increase the number of public universities to 195 by the year 2025 and private universities to 300 from the existing 76.

However, at the same time that universities expanded their reach and access, quality came into the spotlight. Along with quality issues, as universities kept growing in size and numbers, administrative and structural issues also emerged more prominently. Each successive policy almost invariably lamented the deteriorating standards of teaching and research at universities. For example, the 1970 policy asked Provincial Governments to restore university Senates and to develop '…universities as centres of learning and nurseries of values and ideals in an atmosphere of academic freedom' (GoP, 1970: 10). This could be achieved, according to the provisions of this policy by, among other steps, improving the pay-scales and service structures of teaching staff such that these incentives are tied to improved qualification and research output. These policy aims appear to be the first indication of the current incentives-based service structure for faculty in an effort to improve quality at the universities. Thus, the policy not only brought in dynamism related to teacher accountability, but it also added external accountability frameworks to deal with after the Commission was formed. This meant that the new policy laid clear demands on university leadership to put in place internal regulatory checks as well as to deal with regulations from central government in addition to addressing the issues of quality, academic freedom, and administrative efficiency.

Similarly, with an increasing student population on campuses, the tensions between students and university administration started cropping up around the time of the Education Policy 1972–80. For example, student riots on campuses suggested that student voices were absent in decision-making on issues that affected student lives in universities. According to Siddiqui (2016), these riots resulted from one-sided decision making by the universities, a facet of *positional leadership*, to have three-year degree programmes as against two years. The wide gap at the time, that largely still exists, between students and leadership and administrative structures is not only a university phenomenon but also a feature of lower tiers in schooling where, with fewer exceptions, school and college heads are often at the farthest distance in relation to students (Khan, 2010). According to Hofstede (1997), the 'power distance' in social organisations, including schools and universities, is often wide with those in power often situated out of sight, especially for students, thereby triggering dynamics of social importance such as accessibility, trust, and openness. The increase in the gap between students and university administrations thus appeared a function of increasing student populations on campuses, a fact that has become a permanent feature of universities in Pakistan. Some of the latest outbreaks of violence or agitation on campuses in some of the well-established universities in the country went to the extent that universities had to shut down for many days in a row (Abbasi, 2017;

Ahmed, 2018). The gravity of the issue can also be realised from the policy action that a need for campus security forces, with magisterial powers, was felt necessary for teachers to address untoward incidents on campus (GoP, 1998: 81). The most recent student protests to revive their unions led to a crackdown on them (Masood, 2019). Reacting to this, Amnesty International (2019) called on the government to end the crackdown. This shows that the tensions between students and university leadership in Pakistan still exists and may have aggravated further.

These and other administrative issues affecting quality of education can be attributed to other factors, such as a push for increasing access to higher education without a deeper vision for doing so and without enabling the university leadership to deal with associated dynamics. Quality has also come under the spotlight, as the later trends in policy development suggest, to gear higher education towards a knowledge-based economy. The Draft National Education Policy 2017 deplores the matter, noting that quality has often lagged behind international standards, given that no Pakistani university has made it to the list of the top 500 in the world (GoP, 2017: 80). Situations like these suggest that the university authorities need to focus on providing leadership, more than merely administering the university, to be able to successfully juggle the imbalance between access and quality.

With an emphasis on increasing access and maintaining quality, higher education policy has also repeatedly called on university leadership to align standards of quality with the new developments in services and industry and the emerging needs of national development. The consistent push to link outputs with industry demands has led universities in directions that have presented challenges of greater complexity.

The next section deals with the policy of pushing university leadership to develop a close parity of educational objectives with the needs of industry and of national development.

KNOWLEDGE-BASED ECONOMY: NEW DEMANDS, OLD STRUCTURES

A key formulation of the various policies on higher education, especially since the 1970s, asks universities to respond to the emerging national needs in the wake of globalisation and rapid technological and economic changes around the world. This demand on university administration and leadership has lately been presented within the framework of the 'knowledge-based economy', with the first such thoughts appearing in the National Education Policy and Implementation Programme 1979. The policy emphasised the need to consolidate higher education such that national development required universities to take upon themselves the new calling of providing leadership (GoP, 1979: 78). This was also a time when there were about 15 universities in the country. The way forward for these universities, as laid out in this policy, was to bring them under the federal ambit instead of provincial so as to ensure proper inputs in resources because the provinces had failed to appropriately fund the universities. The impetus came from the National Education Conference held in October 1977 wherein different stakeholders felt the need to federalise the universities. Resultantly, the Commission assumed greater authority and reach in coordinating and regulating affairs of the universities nationwide. Further, 'market demand' was considered important as against churning out graduates with '...unnecessary duplication of efforts and wastage of resources' (GoP, 1979: 80). A strong emphasis on the economic pay-offs of higher education brought in dynamics that the university leadership appeared caught off guard in dealing with in the coming years and decades.

The National Education Policy (NEP, 1992) took the 'knowledge-economy' concept a step further by asking university leaderships to engage in high-tech pursuits so as to make the future workforce tech-literate because the technological developments levied on universities the duty to impart skills on '...acquisition and use of high technologies....' (GoP, 1992: 34). Furthermore, the policy argued that broad based and high end research in science and technology had not been established in the country. Therefore, an increasing focus on technology and science was visible in the policy lines, which suggests that university leadership in this era would have primarily focused on increasing curricular provision in science and technology in the country. It also highlights, for the first time in a policy document the relative failure of the Commission in bringing the desired impact in higher education by stating, 'The University Grants Commission has yet to play a more definite role in raising standards of teaching, examination and research, and in orientating university programs to national needs' (GoP, 1992: 43).

The concept of a 'knowledge-based' economy and its relations with the university leadership functions can be looked at in three dimensions: financial sustainability, higher education in service of industry, and accountability.

Financial Sustainability

The decades after the 1970s, and especially after the 1990s, brought in new dynamics that would hit universities hard in their financial coffers. Echoes of financial self-sustainability can be traced back to the 1970s but policy becomes very explicit towards the 1990s, when the National Education Policy of 1992 'encouraged' universities to look for 'various means' to generate funds (GoP, 1992: 35). The policy push to achieve financial sustainability also gave directions to university leadership on how to increase the budget of universities. The 1998 policy was very vocal on this, stating that 'the recovery of the cost of higher education was minimal' (GoP, 1998: 67) and hence stressing the necessity for universities to share the burden of the cost in the form of students' fee and donations from alumni and philanthropists.

In order to address the challenging demand of financial viability, universities started rolling out four-year BS degrees with a greater focus on high-selling programs in science and technology and by introducing self-finance streams. In addition to dealing with a younger student body, which the university leadership was not previously used to, unseen administrative and leadership dynamics started to emerge for universities. These included, among others, accreditation of BS programs and dynamics associated with free-market approaches such as the self-finance schemes. The implementation of such policy actions enabled universities to generate internal funds through contract research, internships, and consultancy services. This policy, however, pushed universities to reimagine their status as financially viable and self-sustaining entities which in many ways would also lead to a decline in overall rigour and quality of teaching and research on campuses. For example, in a bid to attract large numbers of students, the universities reviewed their admissions criteria and procedures, teaching and learning standards, and examination system in ways that led to the dilution of the rigour of higher education.

The financial viability model also led universities to grant more college affiliations. This move can be looked at in multiple perspectives. First, through the college affiliation process, the outreach of universities had to be widened and through it management of higher education. The universities increased student intake through these affiliations and hence more revenue and greater reach. However, a step that required deeper vision and acumen backfired as the 1998 policy acknowledged the deteriorating standards in higher education. Thus, management of the affiliated colleges came forth as a subsidiary dynamic to the policy's objective of financial viability, which the leaderships in many universities found themselves less able to deal with, given the involvement of provincial governments in the process. This difficult relationship of universities and affiliated colleges remains a challenge to this day to the extent that the NEP 2009 made specific references to it by stating, 'On the governance side, the academic and administrative management of colleges remains an unresolved issue since the degrees are awarded by the universities while the administrative control of colleges themselves lies with the provincial governments' (GoP, 2009: 56). Therefore, the policy asked universities to develop standards for college affiliation and to disaffiliate any college that did not perform well. However, it has been the general observation that there have been no or very fewer disaffiliations although the quality of many affiliated colleges remains seriously questionable. This highlights the complex and difficult situation that university-college relationships have grown into in many universities where such relationships exist.

Higher Education Subservient to Industry

A second important dimension of the 'knowledge-based economy' conception of higher education was that universities were to establish, sustain, and deepen links with the industry. As a corollary, a resultant leadership function was to make university programmes relevant to economic realities and challenges. To this effect, the 1998 Education Policy looked forward to a new beginning in higher education by stating, 'Accordingly higher education institutions must be responsive to the challenges of a rapidly changing and challenging new world; expectations of society and growing demands of the rising student population' (GoP, 1998: 59).

The above was a vision of a new model of university education which was responsive to the needs of industry. While the concept of a knowledge-based economy is modern, the need for maintaining close links with industry runs deep in educational policy development in the country. Modern concepts of the close linkages between the university and industry are in essence the first policy actions incarnate as suggested in the Conference when the Scientific Research and Technical Education Committee proposed setting up a Council of Scientific and Industrial Research (GoP, 1947). The policy proposed to launch committee with membership from both industry and education to improve industry-university linkages. More recently, however, this push to strengthen industry-university linkages became more tangible in action by setting up of the Offices of Research, Innovation and Commercialisation (ORICs) that are functional and accredited by the HEC in many universities in the country. This suggests that the university leadership has to now ensure that the university programmes are geared towards a 'knowledge economy', a concept that gained full momentum in the NEP 2009 and the draft proposals of NEP 2017. A key policy objective of the NEP 2009 for universities was to produce 'marketable graduates' with a balanced worldview who are able to perform at a higher level in industry and the job market. In this regard, the policy stated, 'In the modern global knowledge-economy, employers increasingly look to universities and colleges to deliver the *well-educated workforce* they require in the form of *articulate, flexible,* and *readily employable graduates* to remain competitive' (GoP, 2009: 57).

The draft proposals NEP 2017 takes this task of university leadership a step further and includes the contemporary geostrategic dynamics including the most recent and much-touted economic game changer, the China-Pakistan Economic Corridor (CPEC) in the equation of industry-university linkage by laying out that 'HEIs shall be prepared and reinforced to contribute significantly…' (GoP, 2017: 85). These are the new dynamics that the university leadership needs to be engaged with in the context of the fourth industrial revolution and to respond to the whiplash of accountability.

Accountability for Quality

With the economic viability and the requirement to address the needs of industry and the service sector taking front seats in policy development, university leadership has to now also deal with elaborate evaluation and accountability mechanisms for teachers and programmes. Especially since 2002, with the HEC branding the bandwagon of the knowledge economy, high-stakes accountability of teachers and programmes is the new order that university leadership must deal with so as to shift the balance towards quality higher education.

Since the inception of the NEP 2009, quality assurance and accreditation mechanisms on a massive scale have been a hallmark of policy development. At the programmatic level, and as a step towards demand-driven reforms, university leadership now has to 'accredit' and 'validate' their degree programmes, with failure to do so leading to serious consequences for the affected programmes. Thus, in the policy developments since 2002, university leadership can be seen under increasing pressure from the HEC to hold their programmes accountable to various statutory bodies, such as the Pakistan Engineering Council, National Computing Education Accreditation Council, National Business Education Accreditation Council, and the National Council for Accreditation of Teacher Education, to name a few. According to the NEP 2009, the accreditations are supposed to be at par with international standards of quality and transparency. However, with few exceptions, international branding that was aspired as flowing out from the high accountability mechanisms is yet to be seen in the universities.

The stress on a knowledge-based economy has also led to consequences with regard to the evaluation and accountability of teachers. Holding teachers accountable has been an aim from the earliest decades of policy making in the country. However, this aim assumes explicit status in later policies. For example, the Education Policy 1992 stated that 'teachers shall be subjected to a strict regimen of accountability through performance evaluation, on the basis of which rewards and punishments will be awarded by review boards established for the purpose' (GoP, 1992: 37). Identifying 'commitment' and 'implementation' gaps as primary reasons for slow development in education, the 2009 Policy set as its target 'good quality, merit-oriented, equitable and efficient higher education...' and considered it a pivotal tool to transform the '...dream of a knowledge-based economy into reality' (GoP, 2009: 55). The high-stakes also involved promotions becoming conditional on research publications in reputed journals. The most recent Tenure Track System, formally institutionalised in the aftermath of NEP 2009, is part of the same effort to bump up quality in universities. However, the yardstick to measure quality, particularly the quality of research for faculty promotion, has largely remained illusory at best. Making things worse, the consequences have included some serious malpractices occurring, thereby seriously maligning the culture and ethos of genuine scholarship in the country.

In addition, administrative and governance dynamics in the NEP 2009 also led university leadership in the direction of increased accountability through shared decision making by engaging key stakeholders such that university programs are aligned to 'economic imperatives.' This further highlights the very high importance that the NEP 2009 has placed on increased and strong industry and academia linkages. Thus, universities are steered to roll out programmes in Engineering and other subjects that may yield swift economic pay offs. Research, according to the NEP 2009, needed to be aligned so as to ensure economic competitiveness, to the extent that any PhDs awarded should reflect the rigours of strong scholarship. Thus, the aims of the NEP 2009 are as much global as they are local, so that the country should move forward in an increasingly sophisticated technological world, with a structure in place that taps into the potential of technology, and the natural and human resources that the country is immensely bestowed with.

Conclusions: Perennial Demands, Unmet Aspirations

From the beginning, higher education policy has placed demands on universities and their leaderships to pursue goals that were heavenly in stature but earthly in practice. The challenges of these demands have been multipronged. At the same time as universities were asked to contribute significantly to national development, they were also engaged in balancing the dynamics of internal and external controls, while marching forward to meet the demands of the changing times. Along the way, the well-intentioned policy aims have led to situations that are not desired at places of higher learning called universities. With 'leadership' on the sidelines and 'administrative efficiency' as the primary unit of action in policy discourses, the challenges for university leadership multiply as the university is steered into a highly uncertain future.

First, a push for accountability to achieve 'excellence', a worthy goal in itself, has led to unimagined results in the reach and quality of higher education. At the time that this policy of accountability was being rolled out with its peculiar criteria, its potential outcomes were not clearly appreciated. Universities and their leaderships might have overlooked the disastrous potential of such policy aims that Campbell's Law sums up as:

> The more any quantitative social indicator is used for social decision-making, the more subject it will be to corruption pressures and the more apt it will be to distort and corrupt the social processes it is intended to monitor. (Campbell, 1976, quoted in Sidorkin, 2015: 321).

Strong evidence favouring Campbell's Law can be seen in the K-12 settings where serious unintended consequences have come forth as a result of high stakes accountability approaches (Khan, 2017; Khan, Khan, Hussain & Shaheen, 2017; Koretz, 1998; Nichols & Berliner, 2007; Suen, & Yu, 2006). In the eyes of some, the outcomes of high-stakes approaches to performance evaluation have not been different in universities where yard sticks of numbers of MPhil and PhD graduates produced and numbers of publications have led to the creation of a 'professor mafia' (e.g. Hoodbhoy, 2017). The focus on quantity of publication has locked teachers into a rat-race wherein a culture of genuine scholarship has been seriously undermined with many gross violations of ethical nature and the gaming of the system. Quality of teaching in classrooms has also become a victim because an emphasis on producing greater numbers of MPhil and PhD graduates and the race for publications has led faculty to invest a greater amount of their time and energy into these quantitative indicators, rather than teaching. Campbell's Law appears to hold sway in Pakistan's academe with serious consequences for the public's trust in universities as places of learning and research.

This suggests that the metrics to measure teacher quality, though relevant in themselves, need to be made more meaningful yet less prone to corruption and gaming. This can be achieved when the university leadership is deeply engaged with the cultural undertones of these accountability mechanisms because reforming culture is one of the primary functions of leadership in any social organisation (Bryan & Wilson, 2015; Hendrickson, Lane, Harris, & Dorman, 2013; Schein, 2010). The criteria of MPhils and PhDs produced and papers published should be based more on an inherent culture of genuine scholarship. To achieve this, university leaderships will need to provide appropriate support structures and inputs so that novices and the young are able to setup viable and authentic research and publication agendas for themselves. Additionally, the Quality Enhancement Cells setup at universities and the ORICs should reposition themselves to play a proactive role by providing constructive feedback with support mechanisms as their hallmark of action. As much as possible, high-stakes approaches to accountability should be curtailed and a culture of collegiality promoted such that faculty collaborate rather than compete to achieve their desired objectives in research, teaching, and career. This is easier said than done but the university leadership has a significant role to play in setting these dynamics right and in their appropriate direction.

In a knowledge-based economic concept of higher education, an inevitable corollary for universities in the new global milieu, the new directions in the draft Education Policy of 2017 were important on their own, in that the Policy required researchers to publish only in those journals that are well reputed. The university based leadership will need to engage with such new policy directions and promote genuine scholarship on their campuses. Because, essentially, the idea is still the use of quantifiable metrics to make teachers accountable. With such high-stake approaches, the threat of Campbell's Law looms large in the research laboratories and desks. Thus, ensuring fidelity to this policy will be a challenge to university leaderships, given the many dubious practices that have made inroads to the publishing efforts of university faculty. Increased pressure on university leadership to forge closer links with business and industry will also likely increase the demands on universities to balance 'academic freedom' and 'industry needs' in an environment of squeezed funding opportunities.

In pursuits of financial viability, university leaderships will need to reconsider the rolling out of new programmes, both at the undergraduate and graduate levels. Instead, they should be looking at consolidating and realigning their existing programmes, a policy ambition from the Education Policies of the 1970s and the NEP 2009. Churning out graduates with minimum to no employability will tarnish the value of higher education, ultimately affecting the long term survival of the universities. At the same time, the Walmart approach to higher education will need to be curtailed and more strategic depth given to the expansionist agenda in the universities (Pratt, 2013). Commercialisation of higher education will most likely lead to a decline in public's trust in university (Bok, 2003). University leadership, instead of vying for '...ephemeral gains in the continuing struggle for progress and prestige,...', which will cost universities the essential values of higher education, should look at market places as sectors in transition and hence, accordingly, should aim for programmes that will have relevance in the deep future. Similarly, dynamics associated with such processes as the university rankings and college affiliations will also need to be revisited. To this end, the Draft Education Policy of 2017 gives a classification of tiers in higher education. If implemented, the policy will bring in new and challenging dynamics that the university leadership will need to deal with in the coming years and decades.

HEC will need to play a critical role in leading the universities to greater autonomy but with necessary capacity building of university leadership. In order for its intended reforms to take roots in universities, HEC will need to develop a critical mass of university leaders who would be in a position to balance the challenging demands of access and quality in the contemporary world, where competing geostrategic, economic, technological, and political dynamics, make higher education a very fluid social sector. The phenomenon of MOOCs (Massive Open Online Courses) appears to be the new and emerging face of higher education. With advances in Artificial Intelligence (AI), higher education may increasingly shift to online platforms. With Machine Learning (ML) and

AI marching on fast to take on many professions in the coming decades, the rush to produce 'marketable graduates' needs serious and close inspection. The need for university leadership to assess the 'marketability' of graduates has never been as complex and challenging as today. The fast-emerging realities in ML and AI make it necessary that the universities are engaged in deeper, critical, and careful analysis of what their programmes mean with regard to the current and future job market (Mahroum, 2018). All this coupled with climate change as a reality and a serious threat to humanity, universities would need visionary leadership that is capable of aligning the strategic direction of universities with the needs of a modern economic system as well as ensuring true academic freedom…a tall but achievable order indeed!

2

Toothless Tigers or Selfless Servants? Role Perceptions of DEOs in Pakistan

JAN-E-ALAM KHAKI, ZUBEDA BANA, QAMAR SAFDAR, AND MIR AFZAL TAJIK

The District Education Officers (DEOs) in Pakistan have a critical middle position between the high officials under the Secretary Education and/or the Director Education, at the top, and the headteachers and teachers at the bottom. They are the critical channel through which the government authority flows downwards and reporting processes from the grassroots go upwards. This chapter presents the findings and their analysis of a small-scale exploratory case study undertaken to investigate the role perceptions of these middle level education officials, seen as a critical link for the effectiveness of the implementation of government policies, and sharing of the grassroots problems of governance. The sample of the study was drawn from the eleven districts of Balochistan, eleven districts of Sindh, and ten officials from Islamabad Capital Territory (ICT), who were selected for their professional development to be held at the Aga Khan University, Institute for Educational Development (AKU-IED) under a donor-funded project. The study investigated these DEOs' self-perceived roles and responsibilities and the ways in which the selected headteachers perceived the efficacy of these roles through interviews and documents analysis, largely based on newspaper reports. The findings of the study reveal that most of the DEOs perceive their roles as more administrative, at best managerial, than academic or instructional. Reportedly, they do this work very often in complex circumstances, pressurised by political influences, local traditions, tribal dynamics, and uncertain law and order situations. They feel almost besieged with debilitating rather than enabling circumstances. Despite these limitations, they try their best to do at least the minimum they are required to; but find it difficult to go beyond. Self-efficacy in this case is in short supply; though some do claim that they are able to accomplish what they can in the given circumstances. Though good intentions are in abundance but materializing them is seen as a herculean task. On paper, they appear to be 'powerful senior government officials', at the district level. But, in practice, they are the proverbial 'toothless tigers', because their actual influence on their juniors appears too little; in most cases they cannot even hold their humblest employees accountable. The reasons for this are discussed in this chapter. The perception of their juniors, such as the headteachers, is not very different. They consider the DEOs more a burden than a support. This study suggests that the entire system needs to be revisited to make it more aware of and responsive to 21st century governance demands of a huge and complex system in the words of the writers, a 'difficult' country.

RATIONALE AND BACKGROUND

The study of educational leadership and management in Pakistan is a relatively new territory—a road less travelled (GoP, 2009). This is truer when it comes to the study of DEOs' ways of managing education. These officials actually bridge the government's higher functionaries and policies with grassroots policy implementation, monitoring, and supervision of the schools in their respective districts. These officials, theoretically, should exercise significant control over the functioning of schools in their jurisdiction. Although on paper they have heavy responsibilities, but they actually have limited scope to exercise due largely to a complex web of power centres in a weak democracy and a poorly disciplined bureaucracy in their respective provinces.

Having inherited a pre-colonial culture of public administration in education, in the post-colonial era the push for 'modernisation' and 'decentralisation' or 'devolution' has not always worked (Ali & Babur, 2010; Chapman, 2000; Shah, 2003; UNESCO, 1983). For example, administrators were held accountable to elected councils and ultimately to the electorate in the Musharraf led government in 2000s. The new local government system was designed to take decision-making closer to the people's representatives. It meant, theoretically, planning and development would be carried out in accordance with local needs (UNESCO, 2006). However, the ground realities have largely remained unchanged due to many reasons, including corruption.

The UNESCO Report (1983) laments that governance of education (in Pakistan) is 'in several ways seriously deficient owing partly to lack of qualified administrative staff but mainly to out-dated, inadequate or irrelevant civil service rules and regulations' (pp. 3, 4). The report concludes by arguing that these structural impediments 'obstruct ready and appropriate administrative and management changes and the creation of structures and procedures to meet educational needs'. A UNESCO Report (2017) adds, 'Pakistan's education sector faces several stark challenges. A mix of issues related to poor leadership and governance, institutional imbalances and a lack of political consensus building have resulted in a milieu of (numerous) issues'. The report further adds, 'An extremely inefficient managerial capacity and an evident lack of dedication/motivation of low salaried teachers, likely reduce the quality of offered services' (p. 3). One cannot fail to notice in these reports the highlighting of leadership and governance as the two key issues, among, of course, many others that affect the smooth functioning of the educational administration.

In order to meet some of these limitations, there was a huge push by the Pervez Musharraf government during the 2000s for 'decentralisation' of governance of many departments, including education. At the policy level, it might have been seen as a panacea for educational improvement. However, how faulty this politically motivated decentralisation was can be gauged by a comment made by one of the DEOs who once told the first writer of this chapter in a meeting, 'Whatever decision-making freedom we had, in the name of devolution even that was taken away'. The problem was that the power of decision-making was given to the political leaders and the actual professionals, dealing with educational administration, were made mere rubber stamps. Thus, making the ground realities further complicated due to complex dynamics of power clashes.

After late 2000s, these officers were provided with many in-service skills development opportunities at various fora and universities, including the AKU-IED, for continuing professional development, with the funding provided by donor agencies such as USAID/ED-LINKS. The AKU-IED conducted a series of programmes aiming at the enhancement of the knowledge and skills as in-service projects. It is during this time that a small scale exploratory qualitative study was undertaken to investigate the perceptions and practices of the DEOs. With interviews as the main data collection tool, the study investigated the DEOs' self-perceived roles and responsibilities in their respective districts. Additionally, some headteachers were interviewed to see how they viewed the roles and responsibilities of these officials, with whom they interact frequently for the implementation of government policies and procedures. This chapter is the first attempt at putting together their self-reported and perceived roles and responsibilities. Those respondents were drawn from the course participants who had come from Balochistan, Sindh, and Islamabad Capital Territory. The total number of research participants, the nature of the interviews, and other methodological questions are discussed in the respective sections below.

The chapter reports here the findings and analysis of the study, hoping that more systematic and longitudinal studies would be undertaken to build a strong base of evidence-based knowledge for better understanding of the complex roles and responsibilities of the officials who are seen often as toothless tigers but, equally important, many of whom try their best in less than a perfect world to do what they can. It is easier to pass judgment on what they *do not do*, but difficult to say what they do; in a country like Pakistan, regarded by Lieven (2011) as a 'hard country'.

The context and background of the study indicate that school success largely depends on its leadership (Khaki & Qamar, 2010; Leithwood & Duke, 1999; Leithwood & Riehl, 2003; Leithwood, Begley & Cousins, 1992; Memon, 2000; Sergiovanni, 1998). However, the majority of schools in the public sector lack leadership, effective management skills, a vision for school development and improvement, or knowledge of new trends in curricula, instruction, assessment, and professional development (Memon, 2010). In order to address these dire needs, ED-LINKS,[1] through a consortium, had entered into an agreement with AKU-IED to take a number of systemic and systematic initiatives, such as, the recruitment of qualified and professionally developed headteachers, orientation and induction programmes, and continuing professional education of headteachers. Lastly, providing professional development opportunities to district officials during 2008–2010 was part of the ED-LINKS programme for the DEOs (AKU-IED, 2008).

The National Education Policy Review Team's White Paper (Aly, 2007) also emphasised the need for professional development of school heads and others (like DEOs) to make them effective educational leaders in order to improve school management. The initial meeting at the leadership level among the stakeholders (Government, USAID-ED-LINKS, and AKU-IED) reflected that district officials needed greater exposure to the research on educational leadership and management, leading to better governance of educational institutions. This required a sort of 'paradigm shift' in these officials' thinking and practices. They needed to be exposed to new ideas and trends in educational leadership and management, change management, educational standards, curriculum, instruction, student assessment, continuing professional education for teachers, school development planning, monitoring school performance, and managing human and non-human resources. Based on the felt needs, the AKU-IED planned to offer a three-phased programme to the serving DEOs to help them further improve their capacity for better education governance. The project was funded by USAID through ED-LINKS. The key stakeholders of this project included the governments of Sindh (11 districts), Government of Balochistan (11 districts), ICT (10 officials), Provincial Institutes of Teacher Education (PITEs) and, Bureaus of Curriculum (BoCs) of both provinces. The framework encouraged engagement and participation of key stakeholders in enhancing quality of education and focus on academic learning, professional learning, social learning, improving infrastructure, community mobilisation, and promoting effective school leadership and management at all levels.

The AKU-IED was approached to offer a certificate level course to DEOs, headteachers, and first assistants (FAs). The programme was spread over a 3-phase framework. The first phase included a four-week residential programme of face-to-face sessions at AKU-IED, followed by fieldwork according to a pre-specified plan for school improvement. After the fieldwork, the participants came back to critically reflect on and share their field experiences with their colleagues. The participants were expected to support the headteachers during their work. The project was required to provide a two-week interim immersion programme to the various cadres of DEOs. As a result of the programme, it was hoped that the DEOs would revisit their notions of educational management, and provide better leadership to their organisations.

THEORETICAL AND CONTEXTUAL PERSPECTIVES

Since Pakistan's independence in 1947, attempts have been made to reform educational administration in many ways (Bergman & Mohammad, 1998; GoP, 2009; Siddiqui, 2016). More often than not, these attempts have focused on teacher education, curricula, and other dimensions. Sadly, educational administration has been given less attention than it deserved (UNESCO, 2017; Tajik, 2008, 2004; Aly, 2007). Even the latest attempt by the Musharraf regime at devolution had failed to produce any noticeable change for a number of reasons, including lack of acceptance of these changes at various levels of the administration, as well as in the political spheres (Saqib, 2008). Now, even the whole notion of devolution is being reversed because, allegedly, it has not worked. Like the famous Urdu verse, *marz badhta gaya joon joon dawa kee* (meaning, as more medicines were administered to the patient, the disease continued to grow), educational administration and management continue to remain moribund. The reasons are many but the most compelling one is that educational administration, management, and leadership have been taken for granted, believing that 'anybody could do this job'. It was not seen as a professional job, but a job of any and all, as senior teachers are promoted to the position of headship and then promoted to the positions of DEOs without any further training whatsoever for the job accomplishment. The fact is that there are no additional qualifications required for appointing a headteacher or an EDO (Khaki, 2005; Khaki & Safdar, 2010; Memon, 2010; UNESCO, 1983). The overriding culture in educational institutions was geared more towards following than leading, proving Hofstede (1997, 1991) true yet again, in his fourth category of compliant cultures. Education managers, generally, are seen as government 'servants' (not leaders).

This attitude was predicated on maintaining the status quo rather than creating a new culture of 'leadership', characterised by innovation, change, and experimentation to improve the efficiency and effectiveness of the system (Memon & Bana, 2005), many calling this the 'colonial mould' that has remained intact to this day (Ali & Babur, 2010). The psychosocial model has been so ingrained in the psyche of the people that 'obedience' and 'discipline', rather than commitment to a cause, have been the hallmarks of a 'good' officer. A UNESCO Report (1983) presented the same conclusion when it portrayed the educational management culture in Pakistan by confirming that 'the line of command is rigid. Each officer is expected to take orders only from his immediate superior and may take no decisions, no matter how minor, without the latter's approval…' (p. 3).

How strongly this compliant culture is ingrained in the minds of the officers could be demonstrated by a small dictum of a DEO. During a particular professional development session for DEOs at AKU-IED in late 1990s, one senior DEO proudly stated, 'My standing order for my subordinates is: Do or die but don't say why'. This has been the general attitude of the administration in many government offices of education for a long time, attesting to the compliant culture and to a high-power distance' (Hofstede, 1980; 1984; 1991; 1997) in Pakistan's public education system. These attitudes have led to a sort of inertia in running of education in Pakistan, the breaking of which has been very difficult, if not impossible. Due to many authoritarian regimes, such attitudes have been further reinforced, making change a herculean task (Ali & Babur, 2010; Ali & Saqib, 2008; Hoodbhoy, 1998; Khaki & Safdar, 2010; Memon, 2010).

Hambrick and Mason (1984) in their relatively old but still valid study argue that 'organisational outcomes are based in part on managerial values' and, very generally, 'organisation is a reflection of its top management-their values, cognitive biases, cognitive styles, and various aptitudes' (p. 4). Managers would view the situation differently and identify different solutions for the same problem. Hambrick and Mason in the same study rightly assert, 'No two managers or management teams will necessarily opt for—or even identify—the same solutions' (p. 4). In order to understand this phenomenon, Hambrick and Mason further suggest, 'We need to understand the managers themselves' (p. 4). Early studies (e.g. Hambrick & Brandon, 1988) argue that complex decisions are largely the result of behavioural factors rather than techno-economic optimizing attempts. In their view, bounded rationality, multiple and conflicting goals, ill-defined options, and varying aspiration levels all derive from what they call 'givens', that each decision-maker bring to the administrative issues.

Explaining human behaviour, Mintzberg (1973) contends, 'Managers must react to pressures and introduce short-term adjustments or long-term structural changes balancing stability and change so as to achieve 'a dynamic type of stability' (p. 20). In the case of Pakistan, this equilibrium, we argue, is tilted towards stagnation, not really even stability, leading to Milne's (1970) old typology of organic and inorganic organisations. Tending towards a less organic organisational ethos, age-old wisdom prevails which has no relation to the realities of 21st century. Cultural barriers, local pressures, organisational inertia, an obsolete system of governance, lack of exposure to better practices, and lack of on-the-job learning opportunities in the most modern management and leadership practices characterised by dynamism, are all missing elements of the government's senior management bureaucracy (LaRocque, 2001). Added to this apathy are the social problems, such as downright dishonesty in the workforce, brazen political interference, nepotism, and harassment of the district officials, as well as corruption in selection and promotion (Takbir, chapter in this volume; Fergoson & Earley, 1999). The system cannot be corrected at only one level; it needs an overall systemic overhaul (Hofstede, 1993, 1997; Senge, 1990) to breathe life into it. We wonder if even a messiah could fix this system unless governments review the structures of governance and their dynamic relations to other sectors and factors that can help improve the quality of governance and lead to better outcomes in educational management.

In many cases, issues of administration and management have crippled the DEOs' work due to conflicts between the education administrators and the politicians. The showcase below of the case of one EDO is symptomatic of the systemic issues facing the educational administration in Pakistan. The news was reported by *Dawn*, a highly reliable newspaper in Pakistan (*Dawn*, 26 September 2009). This is not just an isolated story; such stories abound among DEOs. This is one of the many thorny issues that hamper the smooth functioning of the education department. There are many reasons why these education departments/personnel do not function well. Some of the key problems frequently identified for poor performance of the governance of education in the literature are: (a) fragmentation and lack of clarity in inter-tier relationships; (b) poor monitoring; (c) lack of resources and corruption; (d) political interference; (e) rowdiness and transfers; (f) lack of appropriate, relevant and continued professional development opportunities (Memon, 2010; Takbir Ali, Chapter 3 in this volume).

Many developing countries, including Pakistan, suffer from disjointed and fragmented coordination. Often, within the same province, district officials are located at far distances, making coordination with one another and with schools very difficult due to communication and transportation problems. Similarly, different layers of officials do not always coordinate in a coherent manner for policy implementation, leading thus to a lack of clarity in inter-tier relationships. Additionally, poor monitoring is reported as one of the major impediments to the smooth running of schools and other educational institutions. Due to lack of resources (for example, not many education officials have enough vehicles in the first place and, even if they do, there is no budget for fuel to visit schools). In cases where these officials do manage to visit schools, they are unable to effect change or monitor properly because actions are inhibited by political, tribal, social, and other pressures. Their image, therefore, is that of toothless tigers. Whatever the stated magnitude of their official role, they are unable to take any strong action against erring or undisciplined teachers or headteachers because of the latter's political and/or tribal clout. In this very programme, during a discussion, one of the DEOs related solemnly that he had issued transfer letters to one school teacher *seven times* in a single day but had to cancel them each time due to a conflict between two political leaders in his jurisdiction.

Similarly, corruption in many forms has been reported as plaguing the department (Aly, 2007). Another DEO in a session reported that there was a rumour that a particular district official paid more than one lac rupees to get his transfer from one (disliked) place to another (preferred place). He opined that, obviously, he would recover this amount from headteachers and teachers wherever he had been posted. In order to gauge the extent of the problem of transfers in quick succession based on political expediencies and exigencies, a report from the *Dawn* is discussed below in order to highlight the kind of inefficiencies caused by quick transfers. This problem is not just related to middle managers but goes even higher, up to the Secretary of Education.

Lack of Continuity in Leadership

According to a *Dawn* report (13 December 2009), describing the transfers and postings of Departmental Secretaries in such rapid succession as 'uncalled for', the senior officials of the Department said that it not only caused disruption in the delivery of services and uncertainty among the subordinate staff, but it also affected the routine working of the department. 'It has often been observed that almost all important and complex issues remain unresolved until a new secretary is fully apprised of the status of the department's business. Normally, the process of such briefings takes around six months', one official added.

Two of the Education Secretaries had been transferred to some other department even before they were able to start their work after getting their initial briefings. One official said that decisions on a number of important matters had been pending for many months and with the posting of a new Secretary, they would remain pending for another six months or so (*Dawn*, 14 December 2010). This report shows how even the otherwise very stable posts of Departmental Secretaries are changed in the provinces in such quick succession due to the political interests, thus leading to inefficiency. They obviously cause instability and delays in decision-making. In an interview (Daily *Jang*, 14 December 2010) the new Secretary considered 'governance' as the prime issue in the Department of Education. The above cited newspaper report regarded the department as a 'heap of problems', which the new Secretary had to address. Yet, another problem that dogs the system is reportedly rowdiness of aggrieved teachers or pressurizing unions. Again, this rowdiness is not just related to only the lower-level officials, but even Education Secretaries have not been spared.

In such an event, one Education Secretary was roughed up on a certain occasion by the employees in the department (*Dawn*, 8 May 2009).

Last, but by no means least, a key problem plaguing the administrative machinery in the Education department has to do with lack of access to sound, up to date, and quality PD opportunities. Although off and on workshops are organised for various purposes for teachers but, according to Memon (2010), 'not a single institution exists in the public sector' (p. 284) that offers continued PD programmes to the educational leaders. Their promotions are often based on the years of service, not so much on their performances with consequence that gerontocracy, and not meritocracy, is upheld.

Thus, this is the larger context in which DEOs function (or malfunction!) in their respective districts. The provincial governments and the donor agencies are trying their best to remedy the situation and help to somehow improve a little at a time, to meet at least the basic minimum standards of performance. Programmes are being conducted to expose these DEOs to the most modern management and leadership knowledge base, hoping to inspire them to find alternate ways of addressing their challenges. The USAID funded project through ED-LINKS at AKU-IED was one such initiative.

These and many other debilitating contextual problems pose enormous limitations on the execution of DEOs' duties. In this context, we, the researchers, wanted to listen (not just read the literature) to these officials as to how they see and interpret their roles in their particular contexts so that we know them and their roles better, and develop insights about their challenges and how they meet them. The report, it is hoped, would add to the knowledge about educational management and leadership in Pakistan, an almost barren area and a less travelled road thus far. We now move on to research methodology followed by other components of the reporting of the study findings and their analysis.

RESEARCH METHODOLOGY

The study used a qualitative exploratory method (Bodgan & Biklen, 1998; Eisner, 1998; Merriam, 1988; Creswell, 1998) which provided the opportunity to engage in a dynamic epistemology that helped explore the beliefs and perceptions, strategies, and methods of applying leadership and management practices in the governance of education at the district level. The qualitative research design provided a template that helped respect the research participants and approach them with a pedagogy that encouraged them to share their ways of looking at leadership and management practices before and after the programme. The researchers approached the research participants with an open mind in the sense that we did not seek to see what we wanted but saw what the research participants wanted us to.

Since the qualitative research offers valuable ways to explore the qualitative world of human beings, which offers a better and more suitable template for exploring the beliefs and practices of people in their real-life situations, it therefore suitably matched the purpose of this study and became a preferred choice. Within the qualitative framework, we selected the case study method, because we were focusing on key individuals, or important players in the area of educational leadership and management of the targeted districts. The following interlinked key questions were explored.

Research Question(s)

How do the DEOs perceive and practice their roles and responsibilities as educational leaders and managers in Pakistan? And, how does this influence their performance? How do the headteachers view their managers' roles and responsibilities? To what extent is their role helpful?

Research Participants (RPs)

The primary subjects of this study were the DEOs who benefited from the ED-LINKS programme during 2008–2009. However, this study was not exclusively meant for them, as was said in the beginning of this chapter. The secondary participants of the study were the headteachers, so that we could understand whether they perceived the contributions of the middle management education officials as a source of support and inspiration or as an obstacle.

The number of primary participants with secondary participants from each site of selection is given in Table 2.1. These were selected based on the criteria mentioned below out of the total participants who joined the programme at the AKU-IED.

SELECTION CRITERIA

The selection criteria of the RPs were the following:
- The RPs have attended the ED-LINKS sponsored AKU-IED course;
- are willing to participate in the study;
- are able to communicate fluently either in English or Urdu; and
- are able to spare time for the interview and subsequent discussion.

Table 2.1: Research Participants against each Province/Territory

Research Participants (RPs)	Balochistan	Sindh	ICT	Total
EDOs	2	2	1	05
DEOs	2	2	1	05
Headteachers	2	2	1	05

DATA COLLECTION

The data collection was based mostly on semi-structured interviews with the research participants. Though it was seen desirable to observe their work in their natural settings, security issues and natural adverse circumstances (huge floods in Balochistan and Sindh) made it difficult to travel to their districts and observe them. However, the ICT was visited and interviews taken in Islamabad. Data collection tools included cassette recorders and researchers' personal notes. The interviewers were very candid; DEOs shared their perceptions freely but at the same time they were protective as well. They may not have wanted to reveal too much, so as not to annoy their superiors; however, they were frank in many ways in identifying their problems. We have no illusions that they said everything their hearts wanted; but, they as in many such situations, did reveal what was required in a measured and calculated manner.

FINDINGS

This section of the chapter, due to word limit, discusses only the first part of the question related to DEOs' perceptions about their roles and responsibilities. The second question regarding headteachers' perceptions of the DEOs' roles and responsibilities, and their learnings from the IED course, is not reported here.

Perceptions of their Roles and Responsibilities

A. Bridge between two layers of governance

Very generally, the DEOs of all the three regions (Balochistan, Sindh, and ICT) perceived their roles as a bridge between the Executive District Officers (EDOs) and headteachers, meaning thereby that they are responsible to share and implement the policies that their seniors devise and to convey to their seniors the problems of the headteachers for resolution. Reflecting on this role, one of the DEOs from Balochistan said, 'Basically we...work as a bridge between EDO and headteachers of the schools....' The quote reflects their image of themselves as a bridge between the upper and lower echelons of the bureaucracy. This respondent further added, 'The governance structures are based on bureaucracy and appeasing the seniors who behave like demagogues'. The statement reflects their negative perception of the upper bureaucracy, perceiving their seniors as authoritarian figures. Since the DEOs are unable to challenge their high-ups, they then tend to model their own behaviour on them.

B. Follower vs Leaders

The DEOs interviewed saw themselves more as followers than leaders. They reported that the DEOs are supposed to follow the policies and have no real say in their formulation. One of the directors of the ICT argued that his and his colleagues' job was implementation of the policies. They can at best give advice but they have no say in framing the policies. This implies that they see themselves as mere 'followers' and not 'leaders'. One of the DEOs commented, 'The important thing (in their job) is to do whatever you are assigned to do effectively'. This officer perceives his job as given and thus the point is to do it effectively (as we say in management literature, managers do things right). 'Doing things right' emerges as the key consideration from their perception. The role is seen as 'given' and performing it effectively seems to make the job important. Thus, it leads to what was seen as a compliant culture.

C. Trouble-shooters vs Problem-solvers

Some DEOs thought that their job description is relatively unclear; their roles are often defined by external forces, including political leaders.

They respond to these external demands and try to survive in a relatively hostile environment. Describing their roles, one of the DEOs from Balochistan stated, 'We should visit and inspect schools frequently and identify and solve issues such as students' lack of interest, issues related to feudalism etc.'. Another DEO reported, 'They (DEOs) should visit every school and arrange programmes. It all depends on funds but sadly, they don't have enough funds (to meet the expenses such as petrol for their vehicles) to make proper visits. This and many other issues can be resolved by providing them sufficient budgets'. The citation shows some of the problems that we have already discussed in the contextual background review.

D. Inspectors vs Facilitators

DEOs visualise themselves more as inspectors than facilitators. They think their job predominantly is to provide basic things to schools and oversee what they are supposed to do. One of the DEOs articulated their central role in these words:

> We provide and ensure the regular provision of free books to students of class one to ten. We make sure that teachers complete the syllabus in the due course of time, we visit every class for the same and we try our best to guarantee that students are being taught according to syllabus and that they maintain their daily diary.

This, in a nutshell, is reported by DEOs as their key responsibility because their bosses often keep on telling them that these are the sorts of duties they are supposed to perform.

E. Psychologists vs Politicians

DEOs have to deal with all sorts of people in their role set. They have to deal with, not only the personnel inside the schools, but also the people outside. Elaborating how they perceive their role, a director from ICT said, '[Their job is] understanding different kinds of nature, temperaments, abilities, capabilities, talents, attitudes, and aptitudes of staff; and [appointing] the right man for the right job. People believe that running the management is a one-man-show, but it is not'. The official argued that his organisation is an outdated one and there are no clear-cut rules and regulations developed to follow. In such an uncertain situation, it is difficult for them to execute their duties. He further elaborated by arguing that in Pakistan 'we have no system in place, we have no defined sets of procedures and, where we have any, they are outdated'.

F. Political Pressure and Corruption

While discharging their duties, DEOs face many challenges but the most daunting is political pressure leading to corruption for one favour or another. One of the DEOs from ICT went on to say, 'Another challenge was that people used their authority in wrong ways on political grounds. I, being Director Administration, people expect the same from me, but I don't believe in using my authority unfairly, which make people turn against me sometimes'.

Citing corruption as one of the major issues, another DEO complained, 'One of the major issues we are facing is like this: if we have 100 teachers, only 20 among them are on duty at a time, while the remaining have their representatives for just signing the attendance record. The teachers hire them for Rs. 2000 per month for appearing in the school in their place'.

This problem appears to be common in both Sindh and Balochistan but was not reported from ICT. Such teachers, we are told, are called '*ewazi*' teachers, persons who are not teachers, but a relative of theirs who is sent to the school while the real teachers actually do some other business. Alluding to the level of corruption, one DEO frankly told us that everyone (i.e. DEOs) was involved in some kind of corruption. 'Recently, in our district…the Deputy DEO had given Rs. 120,000 for his transfer. In the new place he would first recover this amount…and then only he would do anything for education'.

Another DEO from Balochistan reported that, due to lack of follow up by the DEOs, even good work is being spoilt. Citing an example, he went on to say, 'Ninety-nine per cent of the 16 fully furnished computer labs that were constructed in 101 schools of Balochistan in 2003 remain non-functional because of teacher negligence. Proper follow-up should be done in this regard'. Thus, malpractices, lack of efficacy, and helplessness are recurrent themes most DEOs referred to in their interviews.

DISCUSSION AND RECOMMENDATIONS

The study of the DEOs revealed the well-known patterns of perceptions and practices which are characterised by the roles of administrators who do confine themselves to doing the normal chores that many district officers in this country proverbially do. These findings are consistent with what we had found about the headteachers in public schools in many of our studies (Khaki, 2005; Khaki & Safdar, 2010; Simkins et al., 2003).

During the interviews, DEOs were frank and straightforward in analysing their contextual realities. Despite all good intentions and efforts, they thought they were unable to remedy the situation because of the inhibiting contextual realities. Their perceptions of their job were mainly administrative, dealing with the day-to-day school issues, teaching staff (i.e. their attendance, disbursement of salaries, and covering of syllabus), and students (i.e. their attendance and exams). They (DEOs) also deal with academics but since most academic dimensions are given, such as the official curriculum, textbooks, and even prescribed pedagogies, all that is left to them to do is to monitor what goes on in schools, based on this entire official template. They can only monitor, not alter much (Takbir Ali chapter in this volume). Thus, they are expected to be good administrators, at best managers, but never academicians or instructional leaders. Their education, training, and orientation also do not enable them to be more proactive and play leadership roles. Before coming to the programme, they hardly thought they were leaders of their institutions; they would also argue that they are administrators, and never saw themselves as instructional leaders because they are hardly familiar with the modern literature on educational management and leadership. This leads us to conclude that our education officials over-manage and under-lead the process of education.

The foregoing analysis illustrates that the DEOs' role has an overbearing focus on administration. However, their roles are also characterised by many other factors, including those related to the typical government bureaucracy, local customs, cultural norms, and tribal conditions. It is easier for the EDOs to issue orders but much more difficult for DEOs to implement them in such situations. Also, the complexity is that these officials come and live among closely-knit communities and, therefore, would naturally be afraid of taking drastic, radical, or unwelcomed actions that could easily invite reprisals from tribes or local lords, or political leaders who feel affected by such decisions. Transfers, for example, very often end up even as court cases, as was highlighted above. The district officials are often unable to even account, move, or terminate the lowest ranking employee, known as the '*chaprasi*' (peon or messenger), let alone taking any significant action against a teacher or headteacher or overall, for the improvement of the schools. Even senior officials, like the Secretary of Education, could face embarrassing situations in their jurisdictions, as we saw above in the case of a Secretary of Education (being manhandled).

The role perceptions articulated by the research participants tend to be more homogeneous, traditional, conventional, and symbolic. Their perceptions of their roles are mostly defined by their inadequate sense of efficacy, low self-image, feelings of powerlessness, and a sense of siege and defeat. They seem to feel that their contextual, not just departmental, problems are too daunting and overwhelming. Political interference, particularly, seems to sap their energies or, maybe, it is an excuse to shelter their own shortcomings. However, we know in other contexts in Pakistan, that political interference *does* matter in the execution of official duties. It may be idealistic to expect these officials to rise above these debilitating contextual limitations, and act as they should. Nevertheless, they do act and to the extent possible, they do what they can do; and that is why they are able to keep these schools open, no matter how disabling the situation may be.

This general perception of seeing themselves as administrators has been the overall attitude of the district officers in many government offices for a long time, which can be characterised in Hofstedian terms as a 'compliant culture' (Hofstede, 1993). This culture survives, even thrives, on following the orders of their seniors and striving to keep them happy by becoming 'good' and 'obedient' subordinates. They like what Hofstede calls 'power distance' (Hofstede, 1980; 1984; 1991), which means that they accept and like the distance between themselves and their bosses. These attitudes have led to what we may call 'bureaucratic inertia'.

However, these officials do seem to have made efforts, no matter how small, to bring about some change in their contexts. They do, according to their view, *struggle*. Their stories, though perhaps somewhat understated or exaggerated, do tell us about their enthusiasm and willingness to do something more than what they had been doing before the course started at IED. There might not be a paradigm shift in their practice, but their stories do assure that they are trying to do what it is possible for them in their difficult circumstances with caution and prudence as the path is perceived to be risky. This analysis can be summed up in what Memon (2010), one of the pioneering researchers, educational practitioners, and writers, has said about educational administrators, 'Educational leadership positions are…no longer exciting in Pakistan due to a number of factors including political interference, teacher union pressure, lack of professional autonomy- and accountability measures, and increased expectations' (p. 284). In his view, the entropic conditions need systemic, not just cosmetic change; one could hardly disagree with his analysis.

RECOMMENDATIONS FOR RESEARCH

Lastly, we would like to make some recommendations for future research studies:

- Undertake in-depth studies of educational administration, taking an ethnographic approach to document interesting stories of DEOs who sometimes fulfil their duties in very complex circumstances;
- Do some survey studies to explore a much larger sample to see the common and differentiating patterns of educational management across the provinces;
- Examine life histories of many of the aging DEOs, whose stories may provide interesting data from which young leaders could learn a lot.

This study did not specifically look at the male and female styles of leadership. This is a potentially very rewarding area to look at in future studies as we could see some remarkable differences between the two approaches to school administration.

We conclude this chapter with a quote (writer unknown) that reflects the mood of this study: 'Not everything that is faced can be changed; but nothing can be changed unless faced'. More or less the same spirit has been expressed by a verse from the Holy Qur'an which says, 'Allah does not change a people's lot unless they change what is in their hearts' (Surah Ar-Ra'd, 13: 11). An Urdu language poet conveys the same message so well:

خدا نے آج تک اس قوم کی حالت نہیں بدلی
نہ ہو جس کو خیال، آپ اپنی حالت کے بدلنے کا

Translation: God never changed till today the condition of a nation unless it thought of changing its condition itself.

Note

1. 'Links to Learning: Education Support to Pakistan' (ED-LINKS) project, funded by the US Agency for International Development (USAID).

3

School Supervision: A Tool for Effective Governance or an Institutional Burden?

TAKBIR ALI

INTRODUCTION

School supervision is an age-old practice used worldwide for ensuring quality in education. It is an important arena of action for school leaders and a lifeline for an efficient and effective educational system. In Pakistan, school supervision is considered as part and parcel of educational governance. A research study was undertaken at AKU-IED under its Strengthening Teacher Education in Pakistan (STEP) Project to explore the complexities of school supervision as a tool of educational governance. The study collected data from selected public schools in Sindh, Balochistan, and Gilgit-Baltistan (GB). This chapter presents and critically reflects upon some of the key findings of the study and their implications for policy and practice. The key highlights of the chapter include: contesting the notion of 'school supervision' in the context in which it was studied; structure of the supervision system; supervisory activities; conflicting conceptions of supervision; decision-making authority; standards, model behaviour, work practices; supervision and accountability; and supervision for change or reinforcing the status quo. The chapter ends with key recommendations.

OVERVIEW AND BACKGROUND

Supervision is a core activity which enforces accountability and ensures quality in delivery of educational services. It is considered a lifeline for an efficient and effective educational system. Supervision is not only about monitoring and inspection, it is also a process through which teachers are supported and encouraged to pursue their professional development (Onoyase, 1991). It is a tool that ensures effective governance in education (Ali & Babur, 2010).

Supervision serves two intertwined purposes. First, supervision entails the collection of credible information from schools which informs decisions and improves policy and practices of school governance. Second, it provides support to teachers and headteachers who make efforts to induce change through supervisory activities (Institute for Educational Planning (IEP)-UNESO, 2007). Education officials can exert pressure on teachers and schools to initiate the much needed structural, cultural, and pedagogical changes and to sustain those changes to improve students' learning and achievements (Onoyas, 1991). Supervisors are the key government officials who link schools with other administrative bodies of the government (IEP-UNESCO, 2007).

In Pakistan, various reforms have been introduced at different periods to enhance the quality of supervision. However, their impact has been negligible (Jaffer, 2007). Although, structural changes of school supervision were introduced at different stages, they were not able to facilitate change at the functional level. The only major difference was assigning district education officers (DEOs) the tasks of professional development, trainings, and planning whereas during the colonial era, inspectors were mainly entrusted with the responsibility of administrative inspection (Ali & Babur, 2010).

The concept of supervision in education consists of two distinct but complementary tasks. First, it includes the task of control and evaluation, and second, it offers support and help to teachers and headteachers. To carry out these tasks, supervisors are based at local, regional, and district levels (Merchant & Ali, 2003). Having accepted school supervision as the cornerstone of educational governance, one would like to know how supervision is perceived and practiced by supervisors amidst complex realties surrounding education system in Pakistan. Very few studies have looked into the processes, practices, and issues involved in school supervision in Pakistan. There is a need to assess the circumstances which either help use school supervision as an effective tool of educational governance or make it as a mundane activity with no substantive purpose attached to it. This study attempts to provide evidence-based explanation to the questions concerning effectiveness of school supervision.

Overview of Literature

School supervision is a widely-used concept in the realm of education. Due to its linkage with school improvement and school effectiveness, it has become a distinct field of study. Internationally, there exists a great deal of literature on educational supervision. The literature discusses various aspects of educational supervision. It is therefore pertinent to have a look at the historical background of school supervision in Pakistan, and how it looks like, what developments and reforms have been introduced, and then discuss perspectives from internationally available literature in order to situate analysis in the broader framework. Keeping this in mind, a brief, selective overview of the literature is presented, with specific reference to the history and current status of school supervision in Pakistan, definition of educational supervision, the importance of academic supervision, types of supervision, effectiveness of academic supervision and supervisors, and obstacles to effective academic supervision.

Historical Perspective on School Supervision in Pakistan

The history of school supervision in Pakistan is traced back to the British education system in the subcontinent. Pakistan inherited its education system from British Colonial rule (Ali & Babur, 2010). Since independence in 1947, various governments in Pakistan have tried to improve educational supervision system, albeit with more emphasis on structural and administrative aspects of supervision. Supervision, as a tool of effective governance, in fact, remains one of the most important components in national education policies including the most recent draft National Education Policy 2017. Various reforms have been introduced at different occasions to enhance the quality of school supervision; however, little has changed as a result (Jaffer, 2010). This might be due to the fact that reforms in school supervision system have been directed at strengthening administrative capacity of district offices (for example, adding another layer of supervisory staff called 'Taluka Education Officers' in Sindh) and other structural changes rather than aiming at academic improvement (focused on teacher development leading to improved student learning outcomes).

Hence, despite various superficial changes brought in the school supervision, the system, in terms of practices and outputs, continues to function in the same manner as it was inherited from the British at the time of independence (Merchant & Ali, 2003). As Jaffer reports, although new structures of supervision have been developed, ToRs of various supervisory staff remained same or merged without any significant functional changes. The only major difference has been assigning DEOs the tasks of professional development, trainings, and planning (Jaffer, 2007). Jaffer further explains that, at policy level, the government has tried to move away from the terminology of inspection and rather use the terms such as monitoring and evaluation system. All policies after 1979, for example, do stress upon the need for improvement of monitoring and evaluation system, as Jaffer reports. The reasons for the shift, from the idea of inspection to supervision, according to Jaffer, was motivated by the role of Inspector as a more administrative figure than supporting and assisting teachers and headteachers in education. However, the change in nomenclature made little difference in terms of practice on the ground.

In a nutshell, at the policy level an attempt has been made to restructure and improve the system of school supervision in Pakistan. However, in practice, many issues related to the structure of inspectors still exist in the so-called reformed supervisory system.

Defining Supervision

Broadly defined, educational supervision is '…the facilitation in what teachers and students do in teaching and learning programmes of schools…supervision involves those activities that school leaders perform as supervisors in building relationships with teachers' (Tomal et al., 2015: 5). Conforming to the broader definition of educational supervision, the notion of 'academic' or 'instructional' supervision (the two words interchangeably used in the literature) frequently used in the literature aims at enhancing teacher instructional efficacy which should result in increased student achievement (Woolfolk & Hoy, 2009). These definitions suggest that supervision in education is not an end in itself rather a means to improving the quality of instruction and other aspects of classroom environment which ultimately result in improved students learning outcomes.

The Importance of Supervision

Supervision occupies a central place in educational governance. According to Bruce and Grimsley (1987), 'Supervision in education has as its central mission the facilitation of effective instruction' (p. 1). The authors go on to explain that supervision provides supervisors and school leaders with an opportunity to work with teachers and other staff members to help improve instruction, develop curriculum, and promote the professional growth of all staff members. Supervisors provide leadership for change in schools—in teaching practices, curriculum, and in other areas (school development planning, science and math instructional improvement) that affect the quality of the instructional programme. Contrary to evaluation, academic supervision focuses on professional development and growth. It helps generate useful data for academic planning (simultaneously taking into consideration improvement in the quality of both teaching and learning). Supervision is about '…supervisors helping teachers build their teaching skill and addressing the need for ongoing improvement, and evaluation is a related function that addresses the decision about performance' (Tomal, 2015: 11).

Types of Supervision

As discussed in the literature, school supervision generally takes two forms. First is the *administrative inspection* by authorities (e.g. ministers, trustees, and other administrative officials from district and provincial management). In *administrative* supervision, mostly district and provincial officials as well as principals at school level get involved in supervisory activities. As explained by Bruce and Grimsley (1987), administrative supervisors visit schools, observe teachers, and quiz students to ensure that order is kept or discipline is maintained in terms of teachers' and students' attendance and teachers are performing their duties. The second form of supervision is academic or instructional supervision which seeks changes in the attitude aimed at improving teaching and learning through in-service and school-based teacher professional development. The school-based teacher development is intended to train teachers to use the best methods of teaching (Bruce & Grimsley, 1987).

As underscored in the literature, for maximum output, academic supervision should be carried out along scientific lines. As McNeil (1987) defines, 'Scientific supervision' '…involves understanding about what occurs in classroom to get better ideas about what is involved in effective teaching' (p. 17). Elaborating on the concept, McNeil asserts that it (academic supervision) takes a form of practical action research whereby practitioners (teachers) and researchers (supervisors) together try to resolve limited problems in particular school or classroom situation by searching for procedures that work best for the teachers. Thus, in scientific supervision, supervisors perform two basic tasks: guiding teachers in the selection of methods and preparing for and renewing teaching (i.e. updating or upgrading teachers' knowledge and skills). To accomplish this, supervisors themselves need to discover the best practices and procedures for performing teaching tasks and to help teachers acquire these methods in order to ensure maximum student achievement. This requires identification of teacher weaknesses (in both content and pedagogy) first before planning for provision of supervisory support to teacher by measuring teachers' knowledge of subject matter, understanding of methods, and teaching processes.

Overview of the literature suggests that the meanings, theories, schemes, and practices of academic supervision have undergone changes in response to increasing standardisation and accountability measures directed at school districts, school leaders, and teachers. There is an abundance of literature that discusses these changes with particular reference to the context, processes, and models of effective academic supervision. One of the widely discussed models of academic supervision is 'clinical supervision'. This concept comes primarily from Western literature and it frequently appears in the literature from developing countries as well. In the literature, the concept of clinical supervision is traced back to Goldhammer (1969, cited in Smyth, 1984) who has been the most ardent, passionate, and articulate proponent of clinical supervision, as a model of teacher professional development. According to Goldhammer (Ibid, cited in Smyth, ibid.), the purpose of clinical supervision is to liberate the concept of academic or instructional supervision from its 'threatening, autocratic, and administrative-sanctioned meaning, and positioning in its place a process that is enlightening as well as being intellectually and professionally liberating for teachers' (p. 3). Thus, the underlying assumption of clinical supervision is its belief in the importance, dignity, and worth of individual teacher, unlike other forms of supervision that rely largely on methods of rating or evaluating teachers. Also, clinical supervision emphasises the importance of supervisors and teachers, working collaboratively to uncover, and attend to the hidden messages implicit in classroom teaching. In this way, teaching processes can be improved when the teacher is provided with timely, critical, constructive, and relevant feedback on various aspects of his or her teaching.

Effectiveness of Supervision and Supervisors

Supervision, as an important tool of educational governance, may be effective as it helps facilitate continued improvement in teaching and learning by motivating teachers, enhancing their technical capacity, and creating conditions within school and classroom essential for instructional improvements aimed at improved student learning outcomes. Although the literature discusses several attributes of effective academic supervision, yet at the core of these attributes lies the focus on 'instructional improvement', intended at improved student learning outcomes. Tomal et al. (2015) presents a summary of the factors that essentially account for effective academic supervision. According to Tomal et al. (2015: 50), effective supervision includes: active coaching and mentoring, mutual collaboration and sharing of ideas, provision of constructive feedback, multiple classroom visits (informal and formal), active supervisors, conflict mediation when needed, measurable and relevant goals, and monitoring, recording, and analysis of the outcomes. Above all, effective academic supervision depends largely on the qualities or abilities of the supervisor.

Obstacles to Effective Supervision

Overview of the literature suggests that most of the challenges to academic supervision arise from the supervisors' level of preparedness to undertake the task. Other issues, that hinder effective supervision, emerge from teachers' perception about supervision and supervisor. Tomal et al. (2015: 3), for example, identify four types of obstacles to supervisors' work: first, most supervisors may lack the resolve and competency; second, teachers may resist because they lack a clear understanding of the process involved; third, there may be a lack of uniform practices within schools and districts; and fourth, there may be a lack of training for supervisors. Tomal et al. (2015) further argue that if supervision is not important to the supervisors (school leader), there is very little chance of supervision having an effect on teacher growth and increased student learning. Supervisors not having the knowledge, skills, and disposition to be effective supervisors may raise the issues of quality professional learning for teachers. Also, teachers may not see value in supervision and may resist it. Some teachers may argue that, since supervision has made no difference in their teaching in the past, there is no point considering it now.

To sum up, supervision is all about supervisors helping teachers build their teaching repertoire and addressing the need for ongoing improvement in teaching and learning. Linking supervision and student learning is what makes supervision an academic activity of primary importance. The professional learning and growth model of supervision is aimed at development of a relationship in which the supervisor and teacher work together to build increased teaching and learning experiences for the teachers as well as for the students.

METHODOLOGY AND RESEARCH QUESTIONS

The findings reported in this chapter came from a relatively large-scale research study conducted with funding from Strengthening Teacher Education in Pakistan (STEP) project. The study was undertaken to understand the decision-making processes and structures in educational governance in Sindh, Balochistan, and GB. This research study used a quasi-ethnographic approach within qualitative research paradigm to examine decision-making processes in educational governance. For this study, thirteen districts were selected from the provinces of Sindh, Balochistan, and GB. The primary data collection sites were the primary schools located within each district and the corresponding district government offices (for interviews with government stakeholders). In total, there were thirteen primary schools (i.e. five boys' primary schools, eight girls' primary schools) from the three provinces. In order to make this selection more representative and inclusive, special consideration was given to ensuring regional diversity and gender parity, and to maintaining an urban/rural balance. Regional diversity (i.e. the selection of schools from three different provinces) ensured that districts with diverse geographies, low income levels, multiple ethnic communities and language groups were included as part of the research. The sources of data included semi-structured focus group discussions and interviews of teachers, parents, students, headteachers, government district officials, local notables and influential members of each village/community. From each school, the headteacher, five teachers, six students, six parents, at least three government officials, and several local notables were selected either for an interview or for participation in a focus group discussion. However, the data used for analysis in this chapter is limited to the respondents chosen for the study including: Directors (n=9), DEOs (n=11), ADOs and Supervisors (n=21), headteachers (n=13), and teachers (n=59) from selected districts in Sindh, Balochistan, and GB. The participants included both men and women.

Within the broader framework of the study on school governance, data was collected to help understand the current policies and practices pertaining to school supervision. It also reflected on the challenges of improving supervisory practices and proposed a way forward for improvements. The specific questions which guided the data collection with particular emphasis on school supervision included:

- What is expected of school supervision?
- How are the expectations met?
- How and in which areas do supervisors provide services to schools?
- How is school supervision carried out at district and school levels and by whom?
- What structures (provisions and resources), practices and processes are involved in school supervision?
- What key issues are involved in effective school supervision?

FINDINGS

The data suggests that supervision involves extensive individual and institutional efforts, time, and material resources. However, in the observed 13 districts (eight in Sindh, two in GB, and three in Balochistan), supervision in the public system is carried out as a mundane, mechanical, and rote activity. A supervisor's routine visit in a school generally entails a cursory glance at the attendance register, a brief conversation about teachers' leaves, and a discussion around examination dates and student assessments. The role of supervision seems to be reduced simply to a procedural and inspectorial process rather than an academic engagement. The supervision system, in its current state, is not being used to achieve the desired goals of supervisory practices highlighted in the literature review above. Rather it is becoming a burden on institutional resources. There is a huge gap between school supervision and school outputs in terms of students' achievements measured through end-of-term/year examination in particular. The resources spent on school supervision largely go wasted. Analysis of the evidence gathered in this study reveals flaws or pitfalls in the technical aspect of the school supervision system and explains how the practices of school supervision are subverted and corrupted.

STRUCTURE OF THE SUPERVISION SYSTEM

Supervision at the district level is the responsibility of district officials. The education system at district levels has designated supervisors and assistant district officials, who are primarily responsible for supervision at the primary school level. For conducting supervisory activities, the district is divided into tehsils and union councils (i.e. the administrative units within a district). The Assistant District Officers of Education (ADOEs) are responsible for school supervision at the tehsil level. In one typical tehsil in Sindh roughly there are 50 primary (Grades 1–5), elementary (Grades 1–8), and secondary schools (Grades 1/5–10). While the supervisors, on the other hand, are responsible for supervision of schools at the union council level. In one tehsil, on an average, there are 4–6 union councils. A designated male and one female ADOE are responsible for supervising schools in two union councils and one supervisor (also known as the Learning Coordinator in Balochistan and the Assistant Inspector of Schools in GB) are responsible for supervising ten schools in a union council. Recently in Sindh, a new cadre of supervisors named as 'Taluka Education Officers (TEOs)' has been introduced.

The responsibility of supervision proceeds upwards from headteachers to supervisors, to the assistant district officers education, deputy district officers education, and Executive District Officer Education to directors, divisional directors, and lastly to the Secretary of Education.[1] Authority, in turn, passes downward through the same chain. Communication between a school and the district office is channelled through the headteacher.

SUPERVISORY ACTIVITIES

Typically, supervisory processes and practices are supposed to include periodic visits to schools by supervisors and maintaining a functional channel of communication between schools and district offices. Due to the shortage of supervisory (particularly female) staff or restrictions on female mobility, supervisors do not frequently conduct school visits. In practice, the school-based supervision activities are limited to collecting or updating demographic information, i.e. student enrolment, teacher and student attendance, fixture, and furniture. A supervisor, describing the activities he usually carries out during his school visits, said:

> I check classes, copies and student textbooks to know the syllabus coverage. I also check the attendance of teachers and students. I write a report of the visit and send one copy of it to the ADOE and give one copy to the DEO and keep one for my record.

Sharing his experiences and views on the above issues, one of the ADOEs stated that making decisions and solving issues related to teacher transfer should be the prerogative of headteachers. In some schools, for example, there are many teachers and few students. In others the opposite scenario prevails: there are only two or three teachers for over two hundred students. Due to such situations, the ADOE proposed that decision-making regarding teachers and students, leaves, holidays, admission and examination schedules should be delegated to the headteachers because they are more aware of the school needs and the local conditions, and could more effectively influence teaching and learning in the classroom. As a matter of fact, primary schools in Sindh, Balochistan, and GB do not get properly trained, empowered permanent headteachers and their appointments are made on an ad hoc basis. Senior teachers—in fact, in many instances even junior teachers—due to their family/tribal influences or personal connections and relationships with district officials are designated as in-charge (headteachers) to run primary schools. The practice of appointment of an in-charge teacher in primary schools based on nepotism and violation of rule of seniority and merit is pervasive, which is often condemned by primary school teachers who believe in merit and transparency.

When asked what she does when a teacher is not regularly attending school or takes long leaves without informing the school headteachers, another female ADOE responded:

> This is a difficult question [with a meaningful smile]. Actually the problem is that there is political influence which plays a huge role here. Some teachers, who have support of political persons or landlords, they come and go according to their wish and if we ask them to be regular, they pressurise us. We receive calls from influential persons telling us not to disturb those teachers.

This statement, an illustration of the uncontrolled autonomy enjoyed by some teachers, also points to a critical challenge in educational supervision.

Key Issues

A closer look at the policies, structures, activities, and outcomes related to educational supervision suggests that public sector schools in both urban and rural areas are poorly supervised or are not being supervised at all. The menace of corruption in terms of financial misappropriation and political nepotism has rendered the whole system of public schooling inconsequential. Due to the corrupt practices in the upper echelons of administration and politics, it is difficult for supervisors to make the teachers and headteachers at the school level accountable. This is because the headteachers and teachers often have direct contacts with senior education officials and political representatives who provide undue support for corrupt practices. Consequently, supervisors become ineffective.

Hence, it can be concluded that the supervision of schools and teaching in Pakistan remains an issue of great concern. In the past, claims have been made to reform the education system in the country to leave behind the legacy of colonial rule. However, most of these claims have proved to be trivial rhetoric. Supervision of public sector schools still follows the old philosophy and practices of inspection. Supervisors (ADEOs and TEOs) reported that they continue doing clerical jobs of gathering demographic data which is used for a limited purpose to update the district data base, suggesting that their visits to schools are not aimed at addressing issues that hinder improvement in the quality of education.

Nevertheless, the titles of officials responsible for school supervision have been changed without changing their functions and attitudes. In Sindh and Balochistan, the impoverished school supervision system seems to be one of the major elements responsible for the deteriorating state of education. The collapse of educational supervision is attributed to convoluted governance structures, leading to the lack of interest shown by public officials in both political institutions and educational administration. Moreover, a lack of motivation is also seen among the supervisory personnel. From the analysis of the data, key issues involved in effective supervision of schools are discussed below:

Supervision Reinforces the Status Quo

The teachers, headteachers, and supervisors interviewed in this study discussed various other issues involved in school supervision. The teacher respondents opined that supervisory visits are intended to maintain the status-quo. They ensure the smooth continuation of existing routines and do not facilitate change by interacting with the school staff to provide motivation and inspiration to them to do their work with due diligence. The teacher respondents believe that the officials' sporadic supervisory visits aim at finding their weaknesses. They argue that supervision should instead stimulate school improvement through observation of teacher work, constructive feedback, and provision of professional and support material.

Many officials and administrative staff in the hierarchy embrace this normative proposition of educational management. The teachers feel that it is hard, if not impossible, to bring about change while working under people 'who fear and ignore change' because it is inevitably accompanied by challenges. A problem identified by a teacher respondent was that the supervisors do not model good behaviour. In other words, teachers feel that supervisors do not practice what they preach. Teachers do not find educational officials as inspiring role models, whose good practices or behaviours could be emulated by them. One teacher stated:

> Sometimes senior education officials in public forums talk about education reform and what needs to be done to reform the education system. What the officials tell the public or the education stakeholders is hollow rhetoric because practical actions do not follow what is said.

The headteachers, teachers, and community representatives emphasise the importance of senior officials in developing processes, procedures, standards, and practices for effective supervision because in the absence of an effective school supervision system, the people responsible for monitoring and supervision of school activities continue to operate according to their own convenience.

Supervision and Accountability

The evidence collected in this study suggests that teachers and headteachers underscore the need for keeping academic and ethical standards at the forefront while attempting to reform the existing system of school supervision. One of the headteachers, for example, argued:

> Until and unless we all agree upon academic, professional, and moral standards, and clearly outline the negative and positive implications of living up to or violating these standards, obliging all those who work in schools and those who work at district and other offices to strictly comply with these standards, we will not be able to bring about any improvement in the culture of teaching and learning in schools, which we have inherited as a legacy of our failing education system.

In the above excerpt, the headteacher tries to make a connection between school supervision and individual accountability and how these concepts play out to have an impact on teaching and learning culture in schools. Teachers and headteachers believe that the typical sporadic inspections and supervisory visits by senior district officers are purely mechanical. Overall, the typical supervisory visit does little to improve teaching and learning practices in schools.

According to one of the teacher respondents, supervision should not only be a part of the accountability system but should also be an integral part of the support system for teacher professional learning. In the teachers' view, the existing supervision system rests on authority delegated to the headteacher, whose key responsibility is the management of daily school routines. As one of headteachers said, 'The authorities issue orders which are communicated to school staff through the supervisors and ADOEs'. In the teachers' and headteachers' opinion, the current supervision system offers little, because it is not directly connected to educational improvement and school reform. It neither recognises the need for in-service professional development of teachers nor does it address the co-operative development of school improvement goals and change strategies. Supervision is, therefore, not geared towards the development of children, teachers, or schools.

In addition, the teachers and headteachers further report that supervisory school visits by senior level district officers do not occur regularly in the education system. A secretary or director level official rarely conducts visits to familiarise him/herself with the progress and changes in schools and issues facing them. One of the headteachers said, 'Our senior officials rarely visit us because due to their engagement in administrative chores and political activities, it is hard for them to spare time for school visits in order to get familiarised with school activities'.

Absence of Standards, Model Behaviour, and Proper Work Practices

The respondent teachers frequently discussed their teacher colleagues' negative behaviours, stating that the latter's conduct was generally not held accountable. They explained their viewpoints using examples of practices, which inter alia, included: resisting change, violating organisational discipline (e.g. lateness, nonattendance), reinforcing traditional practices (e.g. merely lecturing or having students memorise from the textbook), and using corporal punishment. These behaviours not only affected the teachers' own classrooms but also caused inconvenience to those taught by their colleagues. A headteacher stated:

> Hardworking teachers in the school get discouraged and gradually lose motivation. Slowly, the enthusiasm they bring to their work is diminished. And, the neglectful teachers, who shirk their work, are not subjected to accountability. Consequently, the hardworking teachers get demoralised.

These remarks reflect the headteachers' frustration and dissatisfaction with the faults of the supervision system, which lacks checks and balances and has no provision for rewards and punishments. In her view, this system is responsible for a mediocre, self-indulgent work culture. The teachers who work hard do not get rewarded, and the teachers who do not act responsibly are not held accountable. It is believed that this poor work ethic can be attributed to the negligence of the education department and the compromises made by the district office staff.

Another headteacher shared her frustrations in the following words:

> As a matter of fact, the administrators and supervisors do not hold themselves accountable. So how can they ensure accountability from others? The officials are not committed to or mindful of their responsibility to enforce the rules and regulations and implement policies. They shy away from problems and tend to ignore teachers' indulgence in unwanted practices.

The headteacher further reveals that senior officials yield to expediencies and override the disciplinary actions taken by headteachers. It is common for a headteacher to report to the district education authorities issues related to absence or violation of other organisational rules and regulations. If they (district education officials) do not pay heed to these complaints and take no appropriate corrective action, the headteacher's agency or authority to enforce accountability in the school gets weakened, which deeply humiliates her/him. At the same time, the lack of action reinforces poor and undesirable behaviour. More often than not, on the request or demand of the headteacher, the district education officer transfers the offending teacher reported by the headteacher to another school as a punitive measure. However, the transfer order is not abided by the authorities superior to the district officer, thereby cancelling the transfer order and asking the teacher to return to the original school, against the district officers' (DEO, ADEO) or the headteacher's will. As a result, the headteacher loses the limited moral and administrative authority he has over the school management. Such common occurrences jeopardise the headteacher's and like-minded educators' hope for bringing about change in school's functions.

Conflicting Conceptions of Supervision

The teachers' and headteachers' reflections suggest that teachers and administrators differ fundamentally in their conception of the supervisory function of the district office. The district officials are neither interested in knowing how the headteacher manages the school nor are willing to learn about what the teachers do inside their classroom. This suggests that they consider improvements in school management and classroom practices as exclusively the responsibility of headteachers and teachers, respectively. Teachers, on the other hand, feel that they need help from supervisors and other district officials to work cooperatively on how best to help students learn and progress. Teachers are of the view that training opportunities alone are not a guarantee for change; and that they need consistent follow-up support from officials. The teachers stated that they need to continue working on and actively utilise newly learnt pedagogical techniques for some time before these techniques are embedded in their daily teaching routines. However, they also feel that they require additional follow-up support from officials to enter into such a transition. They emphasise that classrooms should be the primary focus of supervisory activities conducted by supervisors and other government officials.

Supervisors' Lack of Decision-Making Authority

The information and data that ADOEs and supervisors collect from school is rarely, if ever, used in decision-making processes by higher level management officials. One of the ADOEs, for example, reflecting on this situation, expressed his frustration:

> We cannot make decisions over transfers of teachers. In some schools there is enrolment of only 50 students and there are 15 teachers and somewhere 15 teachers are for 500 students. There should be a balance. If one teacher is enough for 30 students, then the education standard would be better. I shared this data with my management but there was no action on this information. The reason is that influential people like member of the National Assembly, the Provincial Assembly, the Senate, and other influential people in the community strongly leverage decisions about teachers' appointments, placement, and transfers.

The information collected from schools by the supervisors, ADOEs, or other district-based academic and management staff during their routine school visits does not practically feed into the decision-making and planning for improvement and change in schools.

Ambiguity in Terms of Reference (ToRs), Roles, and Responsibilities

The data suggests that there is little or no clarity amongst teachers, the headteacher, and government officials regarding the lines of authority, their responsibilities, and their respective roles in providing quality education. The majority of teachers, headteachers, supervisors, and even senior level district management (EDO and DEOs) stated that they never received any ToRs (Terms of Reference) when they were appointed. The majority of interviewees stated that they learnt about their roles and responsibilities by observing and following the performance, behaviour, and techniques of their predecessors. One teacher stated: 'We did not get any ToRs when we were appointed. Our responsibilities and duties were not detailed by the government to us before we started our work'.

This statement is consistent with observations in other districts of Sindh and Balochistan, where teachers, headteachers, and government officers did not receive ToRs for their respective positions either. The few respondents who said they had received ToRs were unable to produce any such document for the research team. When asked why they had not distributed ToRs, some government officials claimed that they had given ToRs to teachers and headteachers. Other government officials, in response to the same question, claimed that they were unaware that they were responsible for formulating and distributing ToRs. In the case of the former, where ToRs had been allegedly developed, the research team again requested the district government officials to show a sample ToRs document for a teacher, supervisor, or a district government official (i.e. ToRs for their own job). In all cases, whether or not the ToRs existed, not a single respondent was able to produce any single document listing his or her responsibilities and duties.

Although members of school management committees (SMCs) were delegated the task of working with schools and improving school performance, however, they did not have a clear understanding of the purpose of the SMC. Furthermore, they were unaware of each SMC members' specific role within the committee. When asked who from their community is supposed to participate in the SMC, the members and other parents were unaware that the SMC is meant to include parents as well. At times, the chairperson was equally ignorant regarding the SMC's purpose and responsibilities, and thus could not provide guidance or leadership to the remaining committee.

Budgetary Issues

The failure in information governance was clearly evident around financial matters and budgetary issues. The teachers and district officials openly stated that they did not know where the money for schools came from, who developed the budget, and how the budget was developed. They were similarly unaware of which expenses the government offices were responsible for paying, and how much money schools were allowed to request each year. In some cases, teachers and headteachers either paid for furniture, books, notebooks, pencils, and other school materials from their own salaries, or they collected money from the students to cover school expenses. In one school, when asked how she would pay for school material, one headteacher explained that she would list textbooks under the category of 'sports equipment'. Then instead of purchasing sports equipment, she would utilise the money to purchase school books. Though this may be characterised as a 'misuse' of funds, the headteacher's decision needs to be appropriately situated in the context she was operating in. Though her intention of purchasing learning materials for her students was honourable, she was unaware of how to proceed appropriately to acquire the materials she needed. The research team brought up this incident with the ADOE responsible for this particular school. The corresponding ADOE stated that though she was aware of this headteacher's situation, she was unaware of the appropriate channels through which the headteacher could potentially work through to purchase school material.

Ambiguity around financial matters also hindered SMCs from fulfilling their duties. At the time of data collection in this study, SMCs would receive 22,000 PKR annually (approximately $220). This money could be spent on small renovations in the school or on purchasing minor equipment or materials for children. The SMC is authorised to spend the money as it deems fit. However, in the majority of cases the SMC members were under the impression that they needed the approval of district government officials to utilise the funds. In one school, the headteacher stated that she was unable to access the funds in the SMC bank account because the district government official had not given her permission and had placed a 'block' on the utilisation of funds. This headteacher was unaware that the government official's decision to put a block was in fact illegal because district government officials are not allowed to intervene in the affairs of SMCs. Interestingly, when the research team informed the headteacher about her misconception regarding SMC funds, the headteacher responded by saying that this new information was useless for her as the district official was a powerful individual in the community, therefore she was helpless in taking any action against the district official's decision.

Access to clear information is a prerequisite for informed decision-making. It is a self-evident truth that individuals can only act (or choose not to) according to the information they receive. If they do not receive any information, they either do not act, or act in sub-optimal ways which does not guarantee the best chance of achieving the desired outcomes. Therefore, access to information is a necessary but not sufficient prerequisite for decision-making. The scenario given above indicates that decision-making requires the power and authority to take action in light of the information.

Asymmetries in Information Management

Effective decision-making and supervisory management require easy access to accurate information. Information asymmetries are rampant throughout the education system. The result is imbalance of power in transactions and information monopolies. The asymmetries of information can also be evaluated in terms of the principal-agent framework. Without the appropriate information about what the schools, teachers, communities, and students require, education officials at the upper tiers of management are unable to act appropriately (if they in fact desire to do so) on behalf of their constituents. The education departments and governing bodies at each level lack systematic procedures for capturing, developing, sharing, and making effective use of information within the education system. However, this failure in information governance is more easily remediable through simple and concrete systems. By disclosing information more widely and publicly, and establishing avenues and mechanisms for the dissemination of information, schools and government offices can counteract governance failures that result from poor information management.

Overlaps and Gaps

Institutions, organisations, committees, and individuals in education are largely unaware of their own and each other's respective duties and responsibilities. The result is duplication of activities in some areas, and a complete dearth of activity in others. At times, one will observe individuals and institutions performing the same activity simultaneously, but without being aware of the other's proceedings. In other cases, an individual may absolve him/herself of a responsibility, (incorrectly) believing it to be another's, and in the end, the task is left incomplete. Instances such as these were most apparent when the SMCs were unaware that it was within their jurisdiction (and their responsibility) to undertake certain tasks which had to be done for the sake of school's development.

Sharing information and making it accessible is a prerequisite for effective cooperation and collaboration between education stakeholders. Without the necessary information, institutions and individuals cannot identify areas for collaboration. For example, at the provincial level in Sindh, there exists the Sindh Textbook Board, the Reform Support Unit, the Bureau of Curriculum of Sindh, the Department of Education and Literacy, Divisional Directorate, Provincial Institute for Teacher Education, Sindh Teacher Development Authority, and several other provincial educational institutions. Though all these institutions are operating within one province and with one overarching goal i.e. educational development, there is little collaboration between these agencies, as far as effective implementation of policies and programmes is concerned. In fact, there appears significant duplication in their activities. In 2013, the STEP Project undertook a capacity building initiative with the Bureau of Curriculum of Sindh, and invited the directors/heads of several of the aforementioned institutional bodies for a collaborative meeting. It is worth noting that representatives of the institutions stated that the meeting which STEP conducted, was the first time they had all sat together in one room to work on a common objective.

Looking at the situations of impoverished schools and taking into account the experiences and perceptions of education stakeholders interviewed in this study, it may be suggested that poor or ineffective supervision is considered to be one of the major elements responsible for deterioration of education. The roots of corrosion of supervision exist due to the lack of interest shown by the people holding public offices in political institutions and educational administration. Moreover, lack of funding for the professional development of supervisors, incoherent and inconsistent education policy, dissatisfaction and lack of motivation of supervisory personnel due to inappropriate financial rewards and undue political influence in appointments, promotions, and transfers of personnel in education department are some of the factors impeding efficient supervision.

In order to improve the quality of education system and its supervision, it is highly important to change the existing malfunctioning practices and philosophy of public sector education. It requires re-examining and understanding the trajectory of educational supervision in Pakistan and comparing it with countries, where the school supervision system has successfully contributed in improving the quality of education. In a nutshell, Pakistan needs a complete overhaul of its policies and practices in the context of improving school education in order to improve students learning and education.

Conclusions and Recommendations

The school supervision system, an essential part of school and education governance, is facing critical gaps and loopholes in its implementation. The respondents' reflections also point to gaps in the relationships between teachers and school supervisory and management staff. The findings discussed above, present conflicting views amongst teachers and supervisors concerning the process of change, the role and purpose of supervision, and the expected outcomes of supervisory visits. Though teachers, headteachers, and parents interviewed in this study agreed that supervision is an integral part of the education system, they emphatically expressed their frustration towards the supervision system. They felt that supervisory practices were not adequately directed towards supporting teachers, students, and promoting school improvement (Jaffer, 2010). The teachers felt that the supervision system did not respond to the teachers' needs. It did not integrate teachers' perspectives in educational decision-making nor empowered headteachers. Instead, the system functioned as an ineffective, useless tool that burdened and hindered teachers' efforts to deliver quality education. The overarching conclusion is that the investments (in terms of deployment of human resources and engagement of financial and material resources) made into school supervision is not necessarily linked to school improvement. School improvement in the context of public schools in Sindh, Balochistan, and GB should be understood in terms of improved student and teacher attendance, punctuality of teaching and other staff, school discipline (adherence to school rules and regulations, i.e. time timetable, ethical protocols, etc.), availability and effective utilisation of resources and facilities. It also includes maintenance of facilities, qualitative school management, and teaching and learning practices. It may be concluded that supervision is not used as an effective management tool towards good governance. It is carried out as a legacy of old-aged management practices without a purpose, and has become a burden on resources. It is believed that significant successes can be achieved by improving the provisions, policy, practices, and processes of education supervision.

The importance of effective and efficient supervision and monitoring of schools is emphasised to ensure delivery of quality education to children. Drawing on this conclusion and the deliberations throughout the chapter, some important recommendations are made with regards to improving school supervision in the public sector for better school outcomes.

- School supervision should not be made a mundane activity. It should be connected with school improvement (monitoring of execution of school development plans) and students' learning outcomes in the sense that students participate in activities inside and outside the classroom.
- The supervisors often face the issue of little or no action regarding the suggestions or feedback they provide to their seniors for improvement of conditions in schools which impacts the quality of teaching and learning. This discourages them from taking new initiatives and prevents them from being assertive and innovative in their supervisory practices.
- New job descriptions or terms of references (ToRs) for supervisory staff (e.g. TEOs, ADEOs, Learning Coordinators, etc.) should be developed and existing job descriptions should be revised radically to make them compatible with the needs of school improvement programmes initiated by schools as part of their annual school development plans. ToRs are highly important because outdated ToRs or in the absence of which it would be difficult to make supervisors accountable for what they do in their supervisory role and evaluate their performance.
- In the current situation, supervisors spend a great deal of time (estimated time 68 per cent) in administrative activities whereas they spend little time (estimated time is only 3 per cent) in building community relationships and approximately 32 per cent of their time

in academic support. It is highly important to reorient supervisors/ learning coordinators towards provision of academic support and to maintain a productive balance between administrative and academic matters.
- Generally, teachers are appointed as supervisors without any training in school supervision and monitoring. Therefore, they lack the required knowledge, skills, and tools of effective supervision and monitoring of the schools. It is highly important to train supervisors, ADOs, and other administrative officers in the areas of supervision, monitoring, and leadership skills so that they can become effective and efficient along modern lines. Institutional arrangements should be put in place for the pre- and in-service professional trainings of the supervisory staff of the district offices. Supervisors are appointed without consideration to their preparedness to undertake the responsibility. Normally, supervisors do not receive in-service training; they lack professional expertise and technical skills to effectively perform roles and responsibilities. Therefore, at various levels of their career ladder, supervisors require specific trainings to meet the requirement of effective and efficient supervision. In the absence of institutionalised training, it is very difficult to expect quality performance according to the criteria established by the relevant education departments.
- One of the major issues is the appointment of people at supervisory level (ADE, TEO) by sabotaging merit and without following any defined criteria. Usually, teachers from secondary schools or even from colleges are appointed as ADOs which creates frustration among deserving and meritorious candidates for being deprived of promotions and professional development opportunities. It is suggested that the appointment of administrative positions should be made through the Provincial Civil Service Commission (PCSCs) by conducting competitive exams which ought to be given by the interested candidates of the education department for various administrative positions. This process will ensure the appointment of meritorious candidates for these positions only, and will also reduce the political interference phenomenally.
- There are pervasive irregularities in posting and transfer of supervisors. Supervisors at district offices are frequently transferred on a short notice and to places where it is practically difficult for them to perform their duties due to geographical and contextual challenges. These logistical issues often create a lack of consistency

in the implementation of procedure and operational plans as well as frustration and a lack of ownership among the supervisors to improve the quality of the education system.

- Interference of political figures in school affairs or undue exertion of influences and practice of nepotism on part of influential personage make the supervisors' work more complex. The rampant political influence in the appointments, transfers, and promotions, coupled with pressure from the teachers' unions, severely damages the integrity and quality of effective supervision in school education. Through appropriate policies and mechanisms, these people's influence on supervisors' work should be reduced.

- Public education in Pakistan continues to remain as one of the most underfunded sectors. Unavailability of adequate funds required for supervisors' in-service training and other supervisory activities such as transportation for school visits, compensatory allowances, etc., adversely affects the quality and the outcome of supervision. The absence of transportation facility hampers female mobility because in the given social, cultural, and security situation, it becomes difficult for them to travel on public transport over longer distances.

- Safety and security are considered to be one of the major concerns of supervisors, TEOs, and ADOs, particularly women working on these positions. Supervisory staff is threatened by teachers with political affiliations in case any disciplinary action is taken against them for absenteeism or non-fulfilment of their duties. There is little or no security assurance from the government or the education department in such cases. This prevents the supervisory staff from enforcing accountability of teachers. The government should ensure the security of the supervisors and protect them from the negative influence of teachers' unions and other pressure groups.

- Supervisors, TEOs, and ADOs are responsible for reporting to and providing the district education department with data about school demographic as well as performance of headteachers and teachers. However, generally there exists a poor data management system at the administration level. The supervisory staff is asked repeatedly to provide the same information which is a waste of time and resources for them. The education information management system should be strengthened at all levels by the streamlining process, which uses standardised monitoring and evaluation tools and use of Information and Communications Technology (ICTy) in data management.

- The education system is governed by bureaucrats who often do not have the required qualification, training, or experience to lead and manage the education system. These bureaucrats not only lack in understanding of the system of education but also succumb to expediencies. This allows erosion of supervisory practices from top-to-bottom. People should be appointed on top level management (secretaries, deputy secretaries, additional secretaries, divisional directors, etc.) who have proper training in educational management and a strong relevant background.
- It is very important to develop an independent school monitoring and evaluation system at provincial and district levels to ensure smooth functioning of schools. This will help reduce and stop interference of the education department or political forces in the monitoring and evaluation system to ensure transparency and validity of the process.
- Considering the current level of high engagement of the supervisors in the administrative activities, it is highly desirable to develop a cadre of subject specialists as mentors at the Union Council (UC) level who could provide ongoing academic support to teachers in the area of their subject specialisation. These mentors/subject specialists will concentrate only on the academic development of teachers in school, which could be highly beneficial in terms of improved teaching and learning at the school level.

If the supervision system in public sector is reformed in line with the above recommendations, visible improvements can be seen in school management and governance practices, which can lead to improved school performance outcomes in terms of increased student enrolment, decreased student absenteeism and dropout rates, enhanced performance of teachers and headteachers. The authorities sitting at the helm of affairs should realise that the meagre resources in the education system should not continue getting drained. These resources should be utilised purposefully so that supervision becomes a productive, purposeful, and outcome-bearing activity rather than a burden on the education system.

Note

1. Slightly different titles are used for these positions in different provinces. The titles used here are the ones used in Sindh province.

4

Pedagogies for Developing Pedagogical Leaders

Mir Afzal Tajik

Introduction

This chapter discusses some of the innovative pedagogies developed in various academic programmes for educational leaders, such as school principals, teacher educators, and education managers, at the Aga Khan University Institute for Educational Development[1] (AKU-IED), based in Karachi, Pakistan. It also delineates how these pedagogies helped the educational leaders re-conceptualise their leadership philosophies, approaches, and practices as they were exposed to and engaged in more innovative and interesting ways of learning about leadership in general and 'pedagogical leadership' in particular. The chapter enunciates the rationale, relevance, and effectiveness of the pedagogies employed in various academic programs to help the participants not only learn about pedagogical leadership but also develop their skills as pedagogical leaders through engaging in practical activities. It also highlights the challenges of developing and implementing such pedagogies in the context of Pakistan and other developing countries. It concludes with a discussion on the implications of these pedagogies and recommendations for policy and practice.

The Context

The education system in Pakistan has suffered due mostly to poor governance and management, changing education policies, lack of financial resources, ad-hoc planning, lack of sustainability of new initiatives, and a fragile law and order situation and security threats (Tajik, 2012). As a result, the quality of education continues to decline, particularly in the public sector schools. According to a survey, 30 per cent school-age children are out of schools; about one-third of children enroled in primary schools are lost after Grade 5; only 42 per cent children at Grade 5 could hardly read a sentence of Grade 2 level in English; and only 43 per cent children at Grade 5 could do simple division of Grade 3 level (ASER, 2014). This rather dismal situation indicates that there is a kind of 'education emergency' in the country (*Dawn*, 2014[2]). The standards of education in rural areas are more depressing, with many more children out of schools, higher drop rates, poorly qualified and undertrained teachers, and poorer quality of teaching and learning in schools (ASER, 2014). Despite the political claims for increasing education budget, Pakistan has failed to achieve both Millennium Development Goals (MDGs) and Education for All (EFA) targets. Although some efforts have been made to devolve educational governance and management to the provinces through the 18th Constitutional Amendment, the eroding public trust in the public sector schools seems to be an unabated challenge, which has also resulted in the mushrooming growth of private schools in the country.

Despite a number of education reforms (such as devolution of education governance and management to provinces, establishment of Higher Education Commission, revised draft Education Policy 2017, adoption of public sector schools by private education providers and so on) in the country, quality of education in Pakistan has not improved much, especially in the public sector schools (ASER, 2014; Ali & Niyozov, 2018; Ashraf, Tajik & Niyozov, 2017).

The low quality of students' learning outcomes is often attributed to the lack of pedagogical leadership in schools (Memon, 2010). The school principals lack the capacity and motivation to improve the teaching and learning processes in schools. Most principals assume their roles more as administrators and managers who are primarily concerned with the day-to-day operations than as leaders who are able to transform the teaching and learning practices in their schools (Khaki & Safdar, 2010; Tajik 2008, 2012). One of the reasons for this dominant managerial leadership prevalent in the public sector schools is the lack of sound theoretical base and inadequate awareness about more effective leadership styles on the part of school principals and educational leaders. According to Khaki and Safdar (2010), there was hardly any research study on educational leadership conducted in Pakistan until the late-1990s when some faculty members from AKU-IED Pakistan and Sheffield Hallam University, UK, conducted studies on school principals (Simkins, Garrett, Memon & Nazirali, 1998). These ground-breaking studies on school leadership, as

Khaki and Safdar (2010) argue, 'had emerged as a result of a pioneering course [for school principals] initiated by the AKU-IED in collaboration with Sheffield Hallam University, UK, in the late 1990s' (p. xi). Thus, an increasing interest was created in researchers, educational managers, and school leaders to understand the theoretical underpinnings and practices of school leadership. As a result, further studies were conducted by Kunwar (2000), Simkins, Charles, Memon and Khaki (2001), Shafa (2003), Safdar (2006), and Tajik (2008, 2010, 2011). All these studies revealed that most of the issues faced in schools in Pakistan were mainly due to absence of effective leadership and management. Thus, in an attempt to respond to this acute shortage of qualified and trained leaders in schools, the Aga Khan University, Institute for Educational Development in Karachi, Pakistan has been offering a number of academic programmes informed by research in the area of educational leadership and management. Before discussing the programmes at AKU-IED, a brief theoretical framework is provided to situate the study as to why educational leadership has increasingly become so important.

Theoretical Context

The concept of leadership is not new. It can be traced back to as far as the earliest human history (Bass, 2008; Gronn, 2010; Lingard & Christie, 2003). Leadership existed not only among human beings but also among animals, birds, bees, etc. For example, we see enormous levels of coordination and synchronised movements of flocks, herds, bees, and other creatures for locating food sources, nesting, resting, avoiding collisions, and protecting themselves from threats, even if there appears to be no centralised leader or controller in the flocks or herds (Gronn, 2010). A form of leadership is exercised by more experienced members who transfer information to less experienced members through sensory modalities such as vision, temperature, pressure, sound, and smell (Couzin et al., 2005). Gronn (2010) identifies that human beings have genetic predispositions to dominate and a social hierarchy has existed throughout human history with 'heroic' fixation of problems by an individual. Thus, the concept of leadership existed in individuals, families, tribes, and groups. Early leadership theories (early part of the 20th century) focused mostly on what distinguishes between leaders and followers, while subsequent theories have looked at what makes a successful leader (Bass, 2008). Four major theories of leadership, as a result, emerged in the 20th century (Bass & Avolio, 1997; Gronn, 2010). These include:

1. The *Trait Theory* or the *Great Man Theory*, which assumes that leaders are born—not developed. In other words, leaders are different from the average persons in terms of innate qualities and traits such as intelligence, vision, perseverance, and ambition. Thus, people who become great leaders are the ones who have certain traits or the right combination of traits required for a leader. If other people could also be found with these traits, then they could also become great leaders.
2. The *Behaviourist Theory*, which is based on research into the behavioural patterns of successful leaders, assumes that successful leaders are not always born but developed through education, training, exposure, and experience. According to this theory, there are certain behaviours and skills required to become an effective leader and everyone can become a leader provided that he/she develops the required skills and behaviours; hence the exponential growth of leadership 'training' programmes across the globe.
3. The *Situational Leadership Theory*, which argues that one person can not be a successful and effective leader in all situations, nor can there be a single style of leadership that can work in all situations and environments (Bass & Avolio, 1997; Greenleaf, 1977). Therefore, this theory assumes that for leaders to be successful there must be a match between the needs of the situation/context and the knowledge and skills of the leader. A person who is able to choose the best course of action and decisions in a particular situation based on the nature and needs of the situation is a more successful leader as the saying goes, 'cometh the hour cometh the man'.
4. The *Participatory Leadership Theory*, which is based on the assumption that an individual leader, however capable and knowledgeable he/she might be, cannot lead alone and bring about a positive change; he/she needs inputs and contributions from other people in the group. This theory has evolved into other leadership concepts such as democratic leadership, consultative leadership, distributed or shared leadership and others (Harris, 2004).

These theories have been subjected to further investigation and undergone further evolution. Therefore, other theories of leadership have emerged in different disciplines. Thus, it can be considered that each theory of leadership is emergent, dynamic, and subject to further investigation and evolution (Bass & Avolio, 1997; Michelle & Santamaria, 2016).

Although people have long been interested in leadership throughout human history, it has been only relatively recently that a number of educational and school leadership theories have emerged (Bogotch, 2011; Covey, 1992; Sergiovanni, 1992). Drawn largely from commerce and business management principles, the theories of educational/school leadership have been adopted and adapted for use in educational settings around the globe. According to Michelle and Santamaria (2016), 'the theories of educational leadership have been derived from a diversity of interdisciplinary conceptualisations and models over time' (p. 1). An analysis of these theories reveals the characteristics (traits and behaviours), styles, practices, and conceptual frameworks of leadership. Some of the contemporary theories and styles of educational leadership include instructional leadership, learning-centred leadership, managerial leadership, transformational leadership, distributed leadership, situational leadership, ethical leadership, and pedagogical leadership (Bush & Glover, 2014; Bogotch, 2011; Davies & Davies, 2011; Glatter & Kydd, 2003; Harris, 2004; Leithwood & Jantzi, 2011; Male & Palaiologou, 2012; Starratt, 2011). Table 4.1 provides an overview of the theoretical premise of each leadership style, the core function of the leader subscribing to the leadership style, and the strengths and weaknesses of each leadership style and associated theory.

A close look at these leadership theories and styles reveals that each theory and style is subject to further scrutiny and investigation. For example, there was a time when the instructional leadership and learner-centred leadership (which is an extension of the former) styles were preferred by school principals assuming that students' learning outcomes will be enhanced by influencing teachers' instructional strategies and close supervision of teaching (Hallinger, 1992, 2009). Therefore, school principals in the USA 'extended their roles beyond managerial tasks in order to affect the quality of teachers' performance in the classroom' (Alameen, Male & Palaiologou, 2015: 7). However, further research into these theories of leadership revealed that the leaders applying these styles had a narrow focus on students learning outcomes. They were more concerned about the mechanics of raising students' outcomes than on students' experience and holistic development. They also had a rather top-down approach to supervising and monitoring teaching processes and teachers' performance in the classroom (Bush, 2015; Leithwood, Harris & Hopkins, 2008; Male & Palaiologou 2012). Therefore, researchers 'sought to re-conceptualise "pedagogical leadership", which has often been promulgated as a desirable approach for education, as such a style appears to focus on the fundamental process of supporting learning' (Male & Palaiologou, 2012: 8).

Pedagogical leadership essentially is the study of teaching and learning process and understanding how learning takes place and the philosophy and practice that support that understanding of learning. Male and Palaiogou (2012) state that pedagogical leadership is 'a construct which places knowledge creation and management ahead of knowledge transmission' (p. 107). Thus, pedagogical leadership can be considered as an alternative leadership style to provide effective learning environment for enhancing student learning outcomes. Sergiovanni (1998), a strong proponent of this model, describes it (pedagogical leadership) as it 'develops human capital by helping schools become caring, focused, and inquiring communities within which teachers [and others] work together as members of community of practice' (p. 37) for improving student learning outcomes.

Alameen et al. (2015) argue that pedagogical leadership is not just supporting teaching and learning but it is a 'praxis' that 'is concerned with theory, practice and a set of social axes' (p. 8). These authors further argue that there is no one best way of leading or practicing leadership but leadership action and practice should be appropriate to the particular situation and social context in which it is applied. Consequently, pedagogical leadership becomes an ethical approach, which respects socio-cultural values and benefits the ecology of a community rather than benefiting an individual. School principals as pedagogical leaders work for the promotion of learning communities and environments in which interactions and relationships are strengthened among learners, teachers, family, and community in order to jointly construct knowledge (Male & Palaiologou, 2013; Memon, 2010; Shareef, 2010; Tajik, 2017). Therefore, there is an increasing emphasis on school principals as pedagogical leaders, who treat teachers as intellectuals and acknowledge complexity of the interplay between teaching and learning (Khaki, 2010; Khan, 2010; Shafa, 2010; Male & Palaiogou, 2012; Tajik, 2010). Keeping in view these theoretical underpinnings of education leadership, AKU-IED has designed and delivered a variety of programmes to develop both current and prospective school principals and education managers as pedagogical leaders.

DEVELOPING PEDAGOGICAL LEADERS

From its very inception, AKU-IED realised the fact that educational leadership plays one of the most critical roles in building capacity and improving the performance of educational institutions. Therefore, it created a number of innovative and contextually responsive programmes, ranging from short seminars to certificate courses, Advanced Diploma to a Specialisation in the MEd Programme[3], for developing educational leaders. AKU-IED developed these programmes in collaboration with the faculty of Education, Oxford University, UK, The Ontario Institute for Studies in Education, University of Toronto, Canada, and Sheffield Hallam University, UK. These programmes were delivered through a number of innovative pedagogies such as unfreezing participants' conceptual frameworks of leadership, using metaphors to describe a leader, comparative analysis of leadership models and their relevance to students' contexts, practical demonstration of various leadership models through action research projects, and studying cases of successful leaders etc. These pedagogies were underpinned by the philosophy that educational leaders, especially school principals, must play their role as 'pedagogical leaders' to develop human capacity by 'helping schools become caring, focused, and inquiring communities within which teacher [and others] work together as members of community of practice' (Sergiovanni, 1998: 37). Thus, the pedagogies used in the programmes aimed at enabling the participants to focus more on knowledge creation and management than on knowledge transmission (Male & Palaiogou, 2012). Within the pedagogies of developing pedagogical leaders, emphasis was placed on the value of 'learning' for and by everyone, and that the headteachers (leaders) being the role models of active learners who not only contribute to the learning of others (teachers, students, community members) but they also become self-directed learners themselves (Leithwood & Jantzi, 2011; Leithwood, Harris & Hopkins, 2008). The following section discusses the pedagogies used in the different leadership programmes offered at AKU-IED.

1. UNFREEZING PARTICIPANTS' MENTAL MODELS

The participants in the Educational Leadership and Management Specialisation of the MEd programme were principals, headteachers, education officers/managers, and teachers aspiring to become school leaders. They came from both rural and urban backgrounds, different school systems, and had varied experiences. They all came, understandably, with certain preconceived images and 'unquestioned' beliefs with which they exercised their positional leadership and teaching leadership. Obviously, the way they believed what leadership is, and how a leader should behave and act, had largely shaped their approach to and practice of leadership. To explore their deep-rooted beliefs and mental models of leadership, they were engaged in reflective practice and critical analysis of how they had understood their role as leaders; how they had approached and practiced it; and why they had preferred certain leadership styles and practices over others. Through such discussions and analysis, they began to *identify* the elements of the conceptual frameworks that had shaped their views and images of leadership in schools/educational institutions. Once they became aware of their deeply entrenched beliefs and views of leadership, then they began the next phase of *unfreezing* their conceptual frameworks as they were exposed to more innovative and research-based leadership models and practices.

After being introduced to the key concepts and elements of different leadership styles and particularly the 'pedagogical leadership', the participants were given the opportunity to visit schools/educational institutions and explore how the theories of pedagogical leadership actually worked and were practiced in the field. The participants, organised into small groups, spent two days in schools during which they interviewed, observed, and interacted with principals, vice principals, and teacher leaders who practiced at least some aspects of pedagogical leadership in order to improve teaching and learning processes in their schools. Interestingly, the principals and vice principals of some of these schools were more or less familiar with pedagogical leadership through seminars and workshops attended at AKU-IED. The MEd participants were asked to keep the following questions in mind during their school visits:

- How is pedagogical leadership understood, developed, and practiced in the school they visit?
- What are some of the examples/evidences of pedagogical leadership facilitating teaching and learning processes and students' learning outcomes at the school?
- What are some of the challenges faced by the pedagogical leaders at the school and how are they being addressed?

Each visit to the schools was followed by a debriefing session within each small group once they came back to their classrooms at the campus on their observations and learning about different aspects of pedagogical leadership. Each group would then develop a detailed presentation in response to the above guiding questions. The presentations made to the larger group would generate more in-depth discussions and reflection on how the theories of pedagogical leadership are translated into actions in the schools; what works and what does not and why. Through these discussions and reflections on the school visits, the participants started realizing that leadership itself is a 'pedagogy' (Sergiovanni, 1998) of engaging in reflective thinking and inquiry for creating community of learners in schools. As they observed how the principals and other leaders (including those at AKU-IED itself) played their leadership role to improve teaching and learning processes and students' learning outcomes in the schools, they started *reconceptualizing* their own leadership models, as one of the participants in the MEd Programme (2016) stated:

> Our long-held beliefs about leadership did conflict with the new leadership models and practices introduced to us at IED, but through constant reflection, experimentation with the new leadership practices, group discussions and feedback from the faculty, we began to *reconceptualize* our beliefs and internalize the new leadership models and approaches (Course evaluation survey, July 2016).

Another participant expressed his views, 'I had a very different notion and image of a good school principal before coming to the MEd programme. I always thought a good principal is the one who controls the whole school and commands over teachers' (Course evaluation survey, July 2016). She went on to say:

> I began to question and reflect on my preconceived image and model of a leader when I saw the directors and faculty with leadership roles standing at the queue behind their secretaries, drivers, and cleaning staff and waiting for their turn to take food in the cafeteria. This is not how leaders behave in the organisations I know. The peon in my school is like a personal servant to the principal. But here, there is no hierarchy and bureaucracy at IED. The faculty members who teach us in the leadership course actually demonstrate outside the classroom what they teach inside the classroom (Course evaluation survey, July 2016).

These citations suggest that pedagogy adopted to introduce the pedagogical approach to leadership development was useful as it helped both theoretically and practically how to demonstrate leadership pedagogy both inside and outside the classroom.

2. Using Metaphors to Understand Leadership

A very useful pedagogy used in most of the leadership programmes at AKU-IED was asking them to use metaphors to describe their notions of school/leadership. Since educational leadership is a complex and multidimensional concept, metaphors are powerful tools to explain the personal, cultural, and contextual dimensions of leadership. As Virtanen (2007) explains:

> Metaphors of leadership are strong instruments in describing the culture of leadership in organisations. Their descriptive power is based on their inherently evaluative content. Single metaphors can illustrate many dimensions of culture and they are efficient tools for communication (p. 14).

Since the use of metaphors to describe different personalities, places, and objects is quite common in the socio-cultural context of Pakistan (Bana, 2010), it was a very relevant and effective pedagogy to be used in the leadership programmes at AKU-IED. The faculty members teaching the leadership courses would ask CPs at the very beginning of the course to think of a metaphor from their own cultural context to define and describe their own leadership style or a leader they were most inspired by. The students would think individually and come up with a metaphor that would best describe their ideal leader and his/her leadership style. The metaphors of leader as a 'guide', 'gardener', 'orchestra master', 'coach', 'facilitator', 'mentor', 'sun', 'commander', 'captain', and 'eagle' were most commonly used by the participants. Each student would make a poster depicting their metaphor of leadership. The students would then present and discuss their metaphors in groups and examine the relevance, strengths, and limitation of each metaphor in relation to their understanding of leadership. They would also learn more about leadership metaphors through the readings and input provided by the faculty as well as from their own reflections, which they would write on weekly basis. Towards the end of the course, the faculty would ask students again to choose a metaphor to describe who is a leader. The purpose of repeating this activity was to see if the students had changed their notions and beliefs about leadership, and consequently their leadership metaphors, as a result of their learnings from the course. The majority of students would choose a metaphor different from what they had chosen earlier in the course, as one of the students states:

At the beginning of the course I chose 'guide' as a metaphor to describe leadership and my ideal leader because I thought it was the leader's job to show the followers which directions to go. As I learnt more about leadership in the course, I realised that a good leader is not the one who walks in front and directs everyone which way to go but the one who walks along and encourages everyone to find the way, I mean the one who believes in shared vision. I now use 'snowball' as a metaphor because it starts as a small ball but gets bigger and bigger as it rolls. The same is true for a leader who starts something with a few people but gradually he/she is joined by many others and he becomes one of them rather than staying above them (Course evaluation survey, December 2015).

Students would then work around different metaphors to understand pedagogical leadership keeping in mind the unique context of their schools. This pedagogy of describing leadership and the characteristics of effective leaders works well as it stimulates students' creative and critical thinking about choosing a metaphor from their cultural context to describe their notions of leadership and the characteristics of the leader they are inspired by. It also helps the faculty to see how students' notions of, and beliefs about, leadership change as they are exposed to different notions, theories, and styles of leadership.

Engaging in Action Research

As the participants began to re-conceptualise their conceptual frameworks, beliefs, and perceptions about leadership they were engaged in developing small-scale action research projects on leadership related topics in order to help them better understand, appreciate, and internalise the concept and practices of pedagogical leadership. Since all students had already taken an 'Educational Inquiry' course, they had developed an understanding of action research. To refresh and further deepen their understanding of action research, they were asked to review a few action research reports. Guided by the faculty, each participant would design a miniature action research project on a topic related to his/her role as a pedagogical leader and presented the project plan in the class. With the feedback from the faculty and peers, he/she further developed the action research plan before going to the field for implementation. Throughout the action research cycles in the field, the students remained in close contact with the faculty to share their reflections and seek feedback/input from the faculty. Twice during the fieldwork, debriefing sessions were conducted in smaller groups in which the students were able to share their reflections on the action research processes in the field. The students found these sessions very useful as they were able to share with each other their excitement, accomplishments, challenges, and frustrations from the fieldwork. They completed their fieldworks and developed action research reports. They also made poster presentations to faculty, peers, and other students for their feedback and critical comments. The whole process of action research allowed the students to engage in self-reflective enquiry in real school context in order to improve the rationales and justifications for their own social, educational and leadership actions, decisions and approaches as well as their understanding of these actions, decisions and approaches, and the context and situations in which these actions, decisions and approaches were taken (Kemmis, 1993). When the students were first introduced to the concepts, approach, and practices of pedagogical leadership at the beginning of the programme, they were all excited about it but at the same time uncertain about how it would actually work in their schools. Therefore, the action research projects allowed them to practically implement pedagogical leadership style and practices and see what works and what does not and why. Research has revealed that it is not easy to convey a concept, an idea, a problem, or a thought from one person to another. In fact, one needs to wrestle with the concept or problem and think deeper to make meaning of the nuances of the concept and conditions of the problem at first hand (Dewey, 1938, 1929). The programme conductors knew right from the beginning that giving brilliant ideas, and theories about pedagogical leadership to students will not make them good pedagogical leaders unless they put those ideas and theories into practice, wrestle with the challenges, and experience how it feels and what it means to be a pedagogical leader in the context in which they work. Therefore, the pedagogy of developing leaders, particularly pedagogical leaders, must engage students in not only learning about a particular theory of leadership but also in testing the theory, its relevance and applicability by translating the theory into practice in the local contexts.

3. Comparative Analysis of Leadership Models and their Relevance and Application

Once the students had developed an understanding and appreciation for the pedagogical leadership style, it was important for them to compare and contrast it with other leadership styles mentioned above (such as Instructional Leadership, Transformational Leadership, Distributed

Leadership, Situational Leadership). So, the students were divided into small groups and engaged in the comparative analysis of the various leadership styles and models discussed in the literature in order to see: (a) how the various leadership styles are different from each other in terms of the philosophical and theoretical underpinnings, core functions, approaches and practices; and (b) how each style fits and is responsive to the realities of the contexts in which the students work. Each group studied two leadership styles focusing on commonalties and differences in terms of the philosophy, theoretical position, overall approach, and key practices underpinning each style and its relevance to, and applicability in, the local context. The students were provided with focused readings and case studies on each style and they also looked at online resources, such as success stories of leaders adopting a particular leadership style, presentations, lectures, and videos on leadership styles on YouTube. Each group presented its comparative analysis of the leadership styles through role plays, power-point or poster presentation, or panel discussion. Each presentation was followed by discussions and questions and answers aimed at providing constructive feedback on the presentation to the group for further reflections. The group members would then submit, individually, in pairs and/or trios, their comparative and analytical essay as a course assignment.

This strategy was found useful in that it allowed students to choose any two leadership cases and critically analyse them in the light of the questions provided by the faculty. The CPs found the whole process of the case analysis (i.e. identifying and choosing leadership cases, reviewing articles, case studies, and other electronic resources about the cases, developing and making presentations on the comparative analysis, receiving feedback from fellow students and faculty and responding to their questions, and writing the essay) engaging and interesting. As one of the students stated, 'many questions and confusions I had about pedagogical leadership and how it actually works in school were addressed during the process of reviewing and presenting the cases'. Another participant commented, 'This was a very systematic and comprehensive learning experience (about leadership) for me' (Course evaluation survey, December, 2015).

Thus, these multiple ways of approaching and exposing the CPs to pedagogical leadership styles were found quite useful and rewarding. It was the employment of a variety of teaching methods by the faculty that fostered meaningful engagement of the CPs in exploring pedagogical leadership at the level of both theory and practice.

Conclusion

Developing pedagogical leaders requires not only innovative pedagogies informed by empirical research but also practical demonstration of such leadership by the university management and faculty. The pedagogy of developing pedagogical leaders should not be confined to the classroom and course instructions only but be seen in the larger culture and ethos, from classroom practice to real field experience to practical demonstration or teaching by example, across the campus. Adults as well as children learn more from the behaviour, actions, and relationships demonstrated by the university or school leadership and faculty, as it is said that action speaks louder than words (Memon, 2010; Tajik, 2010). As the study conducted by Alameen et al. (2015) finds that for developing pedagogical leaders it was crucially important that 'formal leaders of each setting were corresponding their behaviour to internal pedagogical axes, rather than being solely driven by external agendas' (p. 19). Pedagogical leaders emerge and grow out of 'pedagogical community' established in a 'pedagogical environment' (Sergiovanni, 1998). It is not so much of what is taught in a pedagogical leadership course but what really matters is the larger pedagogical environment and community that nurture leaders— the community where individuals feel respected, trusted, empowered, and self-accountable for their learning and growth (Khaki, 2010; Tajik, 2010). This, according to Male and Palaiologou (2012), is the 'epistemic nature of pedagogy', which allows for a wide range of methods, materials, technologies and other resources to be used to promote a pedagogical environment conducive to developing pedagogical leaders. Therefore, the approach taken at AKU-IED towards pedagogical leadership programmes for developing pedagogical leaders, places huge emphasis on modelling leadership so that CPs relate the concepts and theories of leadership they learn inside the classroom to the (leadership) practices they experience outside the classroom. Indeed, pedagogical leaders lead by example and role modelling to demonstrate that actions speak louder than words.

Table 4.1: Summary of Leadership Theories and Styles

Leadership Style	Philosophical/ Theoretical Premise	Core Functions	Strengths	Weaknesses
Instructional	The leader's expertise, power, and authority influences teachers and others to work and achieve targets	• Defining goals, objectives • Giving clear instructions • Monitoring progress • Managing tasks and people	• Influencing quality of school outcomes • Employing hands-on supervision • Contributing to school effectiveness	• Top-down approach • Leader is the source of knowledge, expertise, and authority • Talents of others remain untapped • Narrow focus on students' learning outcomes
Managerial	The leader's positional power in combination with formal policies and procedures is the source of influence	• Defining policies, functions, behaviours, tasks, and procedures • Managing day-to-day activities • Maintaining status-quo	• Efficient in achieving objectives by following procedures • Clear focus on tasks in hand • Rational thinking	• Top-Down approach • Danger of value-free management • Developing more technicians than practitioners
Transformational	The leader's trust and focus on members' commitment and capacities and the creation of a stimulating environment influences change	• Providing individual support • Shared goals and vision • Intellectual stimulation • Culture building	• Creating conditions for success • Enhancing members' capacity and motivation • Bottom-up approach to change	• Can ignore immediate needs/issue • Can lead to change for the sake of change • Ensuring individual accountability can become an issue

Moral & Authentic	The leader's values; integrity, and moral and ethical standing influences change	• Inculcating moral and ethical values • Role modelling • Defining what is right and wrong	• Develops moral confidence in people • Focuses on principles, values, and ethics • Inspiring members through role modelling	• Too focused on the leader's character than on his/her vision and capacity • Difficult to measure success • Lack of diversity in thinking, values, and practices
Pedagogical	Leadership itself is a pedagogy of engaging in reflective thinking and inquiry for creating community of learners	• Facilitating learning at all levels • Creating a culture of inquiry • Developing communities of learners/practice	• Builds individual and institutional capacity • Focus on teaching and learning processes • Develops collaborative culture and team work • Incremental changes leading to transformation of structures, culture, and practices	• The heavy emphasis on academics/learning can weaken management practices • The leader's visibility and influence through authority gets blurred • Managing workload becomes an issue

Leadership Style	Philosophical/Theoretical Premise	Core Functions	Strengths	Weaknesses
Distributive	The source of influence is the collective wisdom and expertise of people working in an institution	• Distribute power, authority, and responsibilities to members • Coordinate, mentor, and facilitate members in fulfilling their responsibilities	• Shared leadership leading to greater synergies and ownership of change • Development of 2nd line leadership • Broad-based leadership that strengthens networking and coordination • Less hierarchical structures	• The role of leader gets blurred • Everyone tends to lead—many leaders • Can create negative competition for resources and score making • Those not having leadership role will feel excluded
Contingent/Situational Leadership	There is no single 'best' type of leadership that can fit all sizes	• Responds to evolving/emerging situation • Leadership approach changes according to changing situations	• Works on the principle of what is best in a particular situation rather than using 'one size fits all' style • Continuous review of situations and adapting responses • More appropriate leadership style for unpredictable contexts and situations	• More reactive than proactive • No long-term vision and plan • Unable to forecast future trends and take calculated risks • Not fully prepared for emerging situations

Notes

1. The Aga Khan University is a non-profit, non-denominational private university offering academic programs in Pakistan, Kenya, Tanzania, Uganda, Afghanistan, and the United Kingdom for preparing young men and women to succeed in the global knowledge economy, to lead change in their societies and to increase understanding and respect in a pluralistic world (www.aku.edu)
2. Published in *Dawn*, 29 October 2014, http://www.dawn.com/news/1141039.
3. AKU-IED offers a two-year MEd programme to serving teachers, headteachers, teacher educators, and education managers. The programme offers three specialisations: Teacher Education, Educational Leadership and Management, and Assessment and Evaluation.

5

A Leadership Development Programme: Challenges, Opportunities, and Lessons Learnt

DHANI BUX SHAH

This chapter is aimed at sharing the insights of the writer, who has been part of a team of faculty and Professional Development Teachers (PDTs) involved in a leadership development programme entitled Certificate of Education: Educational Leadership and Management (CE:ELM). The programme or the project (used here interchangeably) was designed for capacity building of in-service school headteachers working in the government secondary schools of two provinces—Sindh and Balochistan. The programme was funded by USAID/ED-LINKS. There were three key stakeholders: (i) the governments of Sindh and Balochistan (ii) the host university, well known for its quality of teaching and learning; and (iii) the USAID-ED-LINKS project. These three created a synergy to offer a relatively unusual programme of professional enhancement for the leaderships in these provinces. Episodic in structure, the programme spanned over three phases for a period of three months each spread over a year, and offered to over 800 current/potential and acting headteachers. The author was responsible for developing and implementing this innovative professional development programme for school leaders.

This chapter is primarily a reflective paper that shares my observations and insights regarding the project in the hope that it will help all those who may conduct such programmes gain deeper insights regarding in-service professional development programmes. The chapter outlines the challenges faced in the project and the key learnings gained from my engagement in the processes of planning, development, and implementation of the programme at a premier private university in Pakistan. This chapter follows Schon's (1991) model of reflection on actions, which involves reflecting on an experience that one has already gone through and what could have been done differently. It tells the story of a leadership development journey by first setting the scene, explaining the why and what of this programme. Later on, the writer encapsulates his key learnings, and reflects on each of the components of this programme under several headings, including selection of participants, accommodation and transport arrangements, the cultural shock generated, changing patterns of teaching and learning, and the monitoring and evaluation mechanisms of the programme. Each section of the chapter is developed to respond to three key questions for reflection: What happened? Why did it happen? And what were the learnings of the writer? The chapter culminates in a brief conclusion.

This certificate programme participants consisted of assistant or potential or actual headteachers, who were managing elementary schools (grades 1–8), middle schools (grades 6–8), high schools (grades 6–10), and higher secondary schools (grades 6–12) in the rural and urban areas of Sindh and Balochistan provinces.

Various education policies in Pakistan reveal that the government has recognised a need for the professional development of headteachers proposing the recruitment of trained and qualified headteachers in public sector schools. However, these policies have mostly remained on paper and could not be actualised in practice for various reasons (Simkins, Sisum & Memon, 2003).

It is a common practice in Pakistan, as evidenced by my own experience over a decade as a teacher/headteacher, that in general, and specifically in Sindh and Balochistan provinces, headteachers are selected on the basis of seniority rather than on academic and professional experience. For example, the senior-most teacher is appointed as the headteacher of the school, and before his/her appointment as a headteacher, s/he seldom gets any opportunity to learn about school leadership and management practices in any pre-induction professional development programme. Memon (2000) has a point when he argues that on the basis of their experience the teachers promoted to headship may be good teachers but not necessarily good headteachers. Thus, generally, untrained headteachers, who have been hired on the basis of teaching experience rather than based on management and administration knowledge and skills, manage most government-sector schools in Pakistan. This situation still continues as I write this chapter (in 2018). Currently, this practice is in-progress specifically in Sindh and Balochistan and generally in Pakistan. For example, in Sindh, 25 per cent seats for the direct selection of secondary school headteachers are allocated to the Sindh Public Service Commission, while 75 per cent seats are reserved for the selection of headteachers through seniority basis (personal communication to a senior education officer of Sindh, 15 October 2018).

Furthermore, nearly a decade ago, the Government of Pakistan realised the need to improve schools and school systems by investing in the capacity building of school headteachers. They should perform their responsibilities, it was felt, not only as managers largely responsible for routine day-to-day activities at schools; but also should be visionary leaders, providing a clear and shared vision for the sustainable development and improvement of their schools benefiting students, teachers, and other stakeholders (parents, community) of the society (The Government of Pakistan, National Commission for Government Service Reforms, 2008).

In 2008, in response to this reconceptualisation, the governments of Sindh and Balochistan entrusted one of the prominent universities of Pakistan to offer a ten-week certificate course in Educational Leadership and Management (CE:ELM) to the serving headteachers and deputy headteachers of secondary schools from both provinces. Funding was provided by United States Agency for International Development (USAID) under its ED-LINKS project.

I am inclined to believe that this initiative of both provincial governments (Sindh and Balochistan) was a wise and well-thought-out decision, a need long felt, and found necessary. Literature on educational leadership and management emphasises that, considering the importance and breadth of the school headteachers' roles and responsibilities, in-service professional development has become a mandatory requirement. For example, Darling-Hammond et al. (2010) suggest that in-service professional development facilitates headteachers to perform their duties more effectively and efficiently, in a time of rapid change and increasing expectations. Darling-Hammond and colleagues suggest that in-service professional development programmes should be based on a combination of theory and practice. Browne-Ferrigno (2007) advocates a more cyclical pattern of classroom learning and field application as the optimal in-service learning mechanisms for headteachers.

For a long time, in-service professional development in the education system was reserved only for teachers, and hardly any in-service professional development opportunity was provided to headteachers. However, better sense prevailed and, having realised the importance of school headteachers, it was soon recognised that headteachers also needed effective management and leadership skills. By exposing them to the most modern theories of school management, it was hoped that they would be able to meet the challenges of a rapidly changing world and the increasing expectations of parents, communities, and governments (Skrla, Erlandson, Reed, & Wilson, 2001). In fact, different institutes and universities in almost every part of the world were designing several school leadership development programmes for those who wished to be school headteachers; and in-service professional development programmes for serving headteachers. In the context of Pakistan, a realisation began to emerge in the late 1990s as a result of studies in the MDCs that leadership does matter (Memon, 2010). Hence, the government was looking for an institution that would help it design a capacity building in-service course for headteachers. The provincial governments of both Sindh and Balochistan approached a premier private university to help them to undertake this gigantic task, owing to the university's prior experience of successfully undertaking such programmes for teachers.

A. Structure and Philosophy of the Programme

A team, including the experienced professors and the university's own MEd graduates (called the PDTs) designed the programme. Based on their experience of the Pakistani education system, specifically in the government sector, review of the relevant local and global literature, and earlier experiences of offering similar programmes for serving headteachers, a programme handbook that included the course's rationale, philosophy, the andragogy, implementation, and follow up mechanisms were developed, which served as a 'curriculum' for this leadership programme. During this phase, as part of the faculty team, I learnt how important it was to think meticulously through all the stages and phases of a programme with shared understanding among all involved in the preparation and implementation of the offering through their collective wisdom.

The certificate course was guided by a philosophy of school improvement through the development and up-gradation of school leadership, which requires (a) developing a school leadership that is sensitive to establishing a clear, shared vision and mission that focuses on student learning; (b) identifying the areas for improvement;

(c) developing plans by engaging in the specified sessions of plans to address the identified areas of improvement at school; and (d) implementing those plans or programmes effectively.

The programme comprised 300 contact hours, of which 66 per cent were devoted to face-to-face contact, including time for Information and Communication Technology, educational visits relevant to their work, CPs' time spent in independent learning and completing assigned tasks; and 34 per cent to the fieldwork (practicum) where the CPs were to apply newly acquired knowledge and skills at their work places.

There were two cohorts, each comprising 30 participants from the selected districts (Sindh and Balochistan). The programme was planned in three phases (details as below): an introductory phase in the beginning, followed up by fieldwork and, finally, a face to face component to conclude it. The advantage of this three-phase structure allowed the heads to attend their necessary duties in their schools while also doing their field-work in their own schools. The structure of the three phases was as follows:

Phase	Number of Weeks
I: Face-to-face at AKU-IED	Four weeks (126 hours)
II: Field work in CPs' work place	Spread over approximately eight weeks (102 hours)
III: Face-to-face in District (Hyderabad for Sindh and Quetta for Balochistan CPs)	Two Weeks (72 hours)

The course was organised under the following five interconnected themes:

Theme One: Headteachers as educational leaders
Theme Two: Developing management skills
Theme Three: Managing educational change and improvement
Theme Four: ICTy in educational management
Theme Five: Mobilizing parents and community for school improvement

(Source: CE: ELM, Programme Handbook, 2009)

B. Reflections on the Programme: Conception to Implementation

Having given a brief introduction of the structure and philosophy of the programme, as well as the background and institutions involved, I now identify challenges and issues addressed, and insights gained during the programme, starting from the reception on the first day to the conclusion of the programme.

1. Selection of Participants

The university offering CE: ELM was not entitled to select the CPs. Senior management of the education and literacy departments from both provinces, and the ED-LINKS project management had entitled the local District Education Officers (DEOs) to select the participants due to various reasons including the spread of both provinces, and time involved in such a possible exercise. The DEOs' nominations were based on their criteria of nominating the senior most headteachers and deputy headteachers in their jurisdiction. It seems that the DEOs selected the participants keeping in mind their own practical limitations.

In this scenario, the project team at the university took the task of organising this leadership programme as a challenge. They worked harder to ensure a contextually relevant programme that was tailored to the participants' needs and exposed them to the very basic concepts of ELM, such as defining educational administration, management, and leadership, before moving on to more advanced concepts and taking them to a position where they could be engaged in devising school development plans (SDPs). In addition, the CPs were helped to learn the skills of Monitoring and Evaluation (M&E) frameworks to be used in their respective schools. They were given opportunity to develop the SDPs and M&E formats, and were asked to make presentations of the way they had done them to get the feedback from their colleagues and facilitators. The reflections, responses, and discussions of CPs, and the post-test results alluded to indications that the course had reasonably positive impact on the way they now conceived their roles and how to enact them in their schools. The possible influence was evident in the way they did their fieldwork as well as the way they developed their school development plans which were shared in the class and displayed on the walls for feedback from their colleagues and faculty.

My personal view regarding participant selection suggests that ideally the university could have been given the mandate of selecting headteachers and deputy headteachers from the targeted 22 districts of the ED-LINKS project. In this way, there would have been better chances of the CPs selection being on pure merit. On the other hand, since this was a need-based programme for in-service leadership therefore selection by a distant university would have made little sense. It was not just a degree programme open to all, but a specific one. I realise how important it is to be realistic about ground realities and adjust accordingly so that universities serve the needed segments as best as they can. The good part is that all involved in the development and implementation of the programme were familiar with the existing contexts of the participants and therefore could meet their expectations by empathizing with their issues and concerns. In many developing countries like Pakistan, the realities, rather than ideals, dictate what needs to be done. As a headteacher, I have learnt this. As an educator/PDT, I have learnt this. Currently, working as a full-fledged university faculty leading educational improvement programmes myself, I recognise this reality.

2. Scene at the Registration Desk: Surprises and Shocks

As mentioned earlier, I was working as a PDT in the programme, which meant facilitating, and where necessary, taking over, the role of the faculty. One of my roles included welcoming the CPs of the programme. Since the university site was in Karachi, Sindh, CPs came from far flung areas of both provinces. On the very first day, a reception desk was put up right at the entrance of the university, situated in a beautiful setting, and some of the faculty assistants, including myself, were supposed to welcome the CPs. Having reached the reception desk early in the morning, before the arrival of the CPs, with many uncertainties in my mind, my eyes looked towards the gate to spot the visitors. Around 9 a.m., a group of CPs appeared at the gate, the men and women clad in their local style clothes. As I welcomed them, they spoke in their own language that luckily I knew well. I could converse easily with them although the university had advised us to use English as much as possible to enable them to read the most up-to-date leadership literature.

As the morning progressed, more and more participants—the men, mostly in their 50s, sporting heavy moustaches, some with beards and some without, and the women, as well, mostly in their 40s and

50s, wearing head scarves, while others wearing local dupattas—were converging on the registration desk. These were the secondary school head and deputy headteachers who often enjoy high respect in their villages and towns. For many of them, it was their first time visiting the venue of professional development at a reputed and prestigious university.

Observing students, staff, and faculty members of the university (predominantly dressed in shirts and trousers or fashionable urban ladies' attires), the CPs did display some anxiety and awkwardness. I sensed that they felt some unease largely owing to language divide; they spoke largely their own mother tongues, while the official medium of instruction at the university and the language used by most students was English. Another factor that must have amazed them is that the overall culture of the university encourages free intermingling of both genders, while these CPs' background was largely gender segregated. Also, the relatively greater interaction between faculty and students than these officers were used to, was yet another surprise for them. I noted that the CPs were frequently whispering or sometimes loudly saying to one another in their own languages (which I happened to understand), 'We feel like aliens here, although we are also from the same country'. This was, as one can imagine, a culture shock. Interestingly enough, this was both an amazement as well as a shock because, by the time they graduated, they started appreciating what they had learnt here about the overall culture of the university.

I, along with other facilitators, made every effort to help them bridge this gap, by explaining the cultural diversity of the university and its ways of teaching and learning and the overall culture prevalent here in terms of respecting the diversity and pluralism as it was an international university and a multi-cultural milieu prevalent across the globe. Luckily, the programme leadership had already thought about these possible issues and had appointed on the programme PDTs like me from the cultures these participants were coming from, in order to minimise the cultural gaps and maximise their learning from them. I learnt from this approach that learning could be maximised and made more relevant if cultural sensitivities are taken care of, particularly when there are language barriers. When I now lead programmes at my own university, I am particularly sensitive to these issues, making sure the newcomers feel at home to be able to open up to the teaching and learning culture.

3. Accommodation and Transport: A Source of Contentions

The management of the university made accommodation arrangements at a 4-star hotel in Karachi during the first four-weeks phase of the programme, as was the usual practice in such programmes. The university also made arrangements for pick-and-drop in the official transport. However, on the very first day, the majority of CPs said that they were not willing to stay at the hotel booked for them, and they wanted to receive a daily Transport Allowance (TA) and Daily Allowance (DA) as per the fixed approved rates of the governments of Sindh and Balochistan. They said that they would manage their accommodation and transport themselves. Some of the CPs were very vocal and started protesting against the management of the university. The senior management met with the CPs and, although some agreed to avail the transport as well as accommodation arrangements made by the university, the majority did not agree and again started protesting. This created an un-easy atmosphere on the campus. So, to avoid any further disturbance, the university management agreed to pay TA and DA after consultation with the government officials dealing with the project. Thus, the programme started with some tension, not so much academic, but administrative.

The lesson I learnt here was that pre-emptive thinking is important if conflicts have to be avoided. In a politically volatile environment in Pakistan, and especially in the education system, where unions and other pressure groups tend to become difficult at times and earning more than learning becomes a priority, it is all the more important that such untoward issues be settled right at the beginning before the programme starts. If the university management had already discussed these administrative arrangements for the accommodation and transport with the education management authorities of both provincial governments, then such issues could have been avoided. Both the provincial governments could have informed their respective district governments that the accommodation and transport will be arranged by the university and the District Education Officers could have informed the participants of the programme in advance. Although no prior or pre-emptive planning can pre-empt all potential situations, leadership is all about foreseeing possible issues and addressing them as early as possible. In my current responsibility, I use this learning as much as possible and attempt to list all possible issues before launching a programme.

4. Acculturation and Sense of Alienation

When the contentious issues were settled, the inauguration day went smoothly. After lunch, all CPs were guided to the Social Area.[1] The rule of the Social Area was to form a queue and the lunch was self-served. Initially, some of the senior headteachers complained about these arrangements, including forming a queue, and self-service, as in their culture this did not happen because they were very respected officials. However, when they saw that the Director of Institute, faculty members, students, and staff were forming queues and getting their food for themselves, and putting their plates back in the required place, they gradually got used to it and started appreciating the culture of treating all equally and in the same manner. In fact, reportedly, they started helping in home chores as well when they went back for fieldwork—a habit not very common in these cultural contexts.

Having myself grown up in rural Sindh, I see and interpret their complaints about the self-service food arrangements in their certain cultural contexts, where normally food is served by someone else, such as waiters in restaurants, and younger family members (generally females) at home. Thus, self-service food arrangements were new to them. However, I interpret it positively that almost all of them got accustomed to it, although I observed that some of them, after eating, often used to leave the plates on the table and forgot to take them back to the empty dishes' rack. But, overall, they got accustomed to the new 'culture'.

5. Re-conceptualizing Teaching, Learning, and Leading Cultures

Teaching, learning, and leading practices in most developing countries tend to be authoritarian, top down, and transactional (Khaki & Safdar, 2010). In the absence of any professional development courses, the teachers and headteachers practice what they have learnt from their own teachers and heads. The university, on the other hand, with modern, up to date approaches to all these dimensions of education, has a more participatory, activity based, computer intensive, reflective practice orientation, adopting a more transformational paradigm that helps the participants to re-conceptualise the mental scopes of the learners, whether they be teachers or senior leaders. Obviously, the CPs found it difficult to reconcile their existing theory and practice with what the university was aiming at, particularly in the early days. For example, it was difficult for them to be treated equally with their juniors when working in groups. But, gradually, they began to be more accepting as the course progressed. The transition of their learning from traditional to more current practices and overall progress can be summarised in the following phase-wise discussion.

First Phase of the Programme

Overall, the focus of the programme was to provide enough self-learning opportunities to the participants to enable them to re-conceptualise their roles by emphasizing that they can initiate, maintain, and sustain the change process at their respective schools. Interactive lectures of the professors included several examples and evidence of how headteachers in developing as well as developed contexts are working as educational leaders, serving their communities by providing quality leadership in teaching, learning, and assessment related services. This idea, that they were educational leaders, was difficult for them to accept as they were used to regarding themselves as mere policy followers, i.e. 'obedient servants', thus epitomising what Hofstede (1991, 1980) calls the 'compliant culture'.

Teaching activities were designed to engage the CPs in the process of self-reflection by identifying issues in their particular contexts, seeking suggestions from their fellows, and reviewing the examples related to the solution of similar type of issues in other similar contexts. Thus, at the end of an activity or activities, participants used to come to the resolution of their issues that hindered their work as educational leaders in their own schools.

Throughout the face-to-face sessions in the first episode of the programme, the focus of classroom sessions had been on the revisiting of their own conceptions of school management and their analysis of the advantages and disadvantages. Also, the key areas of school management, including school improvement, leadership, and management were examined. In addition, they were also exposed to literature, such as, the instructional leadership, resource management, including both human and material, conflict management, professional conduct of meetings, and time management. Keeping in view their roles, effective communication skills, and mobilizing parents and community by involving them in the decision-making process were also part of the areas dealt with. The programme also provided opportunities to the CPs to learn the basic ICTy skills, as need assessment revealed that most of the participants lacked in these. The lack of ICTy awareness can be gauged by the fact that majority of the CPs had reportedly switched a computer on/off for the first time. Moreover, the CPs were also sensitised to their roles related to health and inclusive education. Sessions on human resource management and financial management were also included in the programme to develop participants' skills in the areas of staff appraisal, understanding the roles and responsibilities of Drawing and Disbursing Officer (DDO) of schools, understanding the financial rules related to schools, school audit procedures, and the rules related to retirement and pension (Certificate in Education: Educational Leadership and Management: Programme Handbook, 2009).

My entire education is from the rural public-sector schools and colleges of Sindh. Hence, generally, I viewed the participants as my teachers, headteachers, and elders because of our cultural habits and values. Conducting co-teaching in the programme along with my professors, I felt blessed that the MEd degree from the same university enabled me to teach my (past) teachers and elders (of the villages). Hence, in a very short time-span, the participants and I jelled well. Our relatedness brought great opportunities to learn from each other, and to continue to learn creatively from the sessions in a relatively more enabling learning environment.

The participants engaged in different sessions of the programme with great interest. They were usually positive and volunteered easily for different activities. They listened attentively to the interactive lectures of professors with great interest and participated enthusiastically during group activities, and presented their group work with seriousness and enthusiasm. They appreciated that they had received a unique opportunity to benefit from senior professors as well as the PDTs in a modern university that integrated both traditional and modern wisdom of teaching and leadership (Memon, 2010).

The seating arrangements (group seating), the air-conditioned environment of the classes, the interactive teaching strategies of professors, the ample opportunities for discussion with their fellows and professors were generally a novel experience for the majority of the CPs. They appeared to be enjoying themselves during the learning process in a relatively comfortable environment, and could see the benefits of the programme. During classroom discussions and informal interaction in the Social Area, during tea and lunch breaks, many of the CPs described to me in great detail how the programme had served them as an eye-opener to understand effective administration, management, and leadership strategies to help them manage their schools collaboratively, effectively, and efficiently. One of the CPs commented at the concluding session that the programme had done a great 'disservice' to him because 'I used to sleep peacefully before the start of the programme, but now, I cannot sleep, having become restless to bring about changes in my school'. The vignette speaks well about the way these CPs felt the impact of the programme on them. Many suggested that such programmes should be offered to all the headteachers, not just the chosen ones.

By the end of the first phase of the programme, most of the participants were eager to go back to their schools, share the details of the programme with their teachers, staff, and community, and commence initiatives for change at their schools. They were excited about the newly learnt knowledge with regard to, for example, the strategies to effectively engage community and parents in the school affairs, leading the school with a collaborative and distributive leadership approach, and providing avenues to students, teachers, staff, community, and parents to share their views about school improvement.

The reading of participants' reflections, listening to their positive comments and informal discussions, one could sense the efficacy of the programme. Participation in the programme for me proved to be a truly rewarding experience and it always motivates me to offer more such programmes to many others who have not yet had any such opportunity. There are thousands out there waiting for such an opportunity in the whole of Pakistan, not just in the two provinces fortunate enough to participate in this programme.

Second Phase—Fieldwork

After the four-week face-to-face sessions at the campus, the participants returned to their particular schools for a further eight-week fieldwork. They were given a fieldwork booklet wherein it was explained how to work in the fieldwork in pairs (headteachers and deputy headteachers of the respective schools), write different assignments, and record their reflections concerning their roles and responsibilities as educational leaders, and also to reflect on their school management, and find areas that needed improvement. All activities mentioned in the fieldwork booklet were in line with different topics that had been covered in the face-to-face sessions. For example, the fieldwork booklet began with the school's introduction, followed by questions about teachers and students, such as the teaching and learning environment, competency, interest, relevance, needs, coordination, and future plans. Furthermore, different reflective activities were also included, like the school's working environment, their role as educational leaders, and their management practices. The last activity of the fieldwork booklet contained developing and implementing a SDP. The CPs were advised to develop an SDP in coordination with other stakeholders of the school and discuss it with the faculty member in the sessions in the third and final phase of the programme. They were facilitated in their fieldwork by some PDTs who supported on the field in understanding and applying what they had learnt at the university in the first face-to-face component.

This second programme phase was a bridge between theory and practice. The beauty of in-service professional development programmes is that the CPs have the capacity of connecting theory to practice because the participants are from a real working environment, with their schools as contexts for their fieldwork. Being alive to this reality, the programme developers had embedded the fieldwork portion into the overall offering of the programme.

Third and Last Phase: Recoup, Internalisation, Reflection, and Take-Home Learnings

The third and last phase of the programme was conducted for two weeks. In this phase, the CPs submitted their fieldwork booklets to faculty members, who reviewed the work of participants and provided detailed feedback on their school-based fieldwork, including the challenges and lessons learnt for future action.

One of the tasks I was responsible for during the programme was also to assess the fieldwork assignments of CPs to give the feedback on their written work. Most of them had responded to different questions asked in the fieldwork booklet. They had also reportedly conducted many practical activities in their respective schools, such as conducting meetings and taking steps for community involvement or developing SDP. They felt they had made an effort, however small, to bring about change in their schools. However, it is difficult to judge exactly what they actually achieved, as opposed to what they reported. I for one kept my fingers crossed hoping all had reported their work honestly. We did not have any means to check but were obliged to trust them. It may be safe to say that majority of them tried their best to do something or the other as their enthusiasm reflected.

The question that stuck in my mind at the time and remains there until now is: Did all these headteachers and deputy headteachers continue their efforts at their respective schools after the completion of the programme?

What were the steps taken by the university and governments of both provinces to ensure the application of learned knowledge? These questions are in fact difficult to judge as the funding concluded with the end of the programme, and no follow up programme could be added to it. The work should have ideally been carried out or followed up under the Public Education Department. Soon after the programme, I came back to my original school to assume my own duties and have had no formal contact with the programme managers/leaders.

The lesson I learnt from this is that when I plan a professional development programme, I should make sure that a research component is embedded in the programme to gauge the follow up work by the CPs and the impact of the programme on the improvement of student learning and improvement of the school. No programme should be designed without a study of its impact. Practical realities may not always allow this important step but for those for whom it is possible, the impact study to me seems an important indication to show the long term sustainability of such donor funded projects.

The focus of the third phase of CE: ELM was on discussing the SDPs, prepared by the headteachers and deputy headteachers in the field, and refining to them. The faculty and assisting faculty, including myself, held sessions on SDPs and M&E plans and through interactive activities engaged the participants in discussion, review, and refinement of the SDPs. The sessions were focused on sharing the importance of school SDP and M&E, as these were geared towards their school issues. Professors and PDTs/project faculty engaged with the participants to identify the crucial problems of their particular schools, prioritise the five most crucial problems, and develop 1–5 years SDP and M&E for these identified problems. All participants presented their school-specific SDPs and M&Es on the last day of the programme. The CPs were advised that they should share SDPs and M&Es with the relevant stakeholders of their particular schools, seek their feedback, incorporate it, and initiate the implementation of SDPs at their respective schools.

Throughout this phase of the programme, I played an active role in supporting the CPs in performing their tasks. For example, I facilitated participants in the sessions of SDP and M&E, and assessed fieldwork booklets. Theoretically speaking, this phase concluded the certificate programme with strong expectations of the university, as well as of the provincial governments that the CPs will apply the learned knowledge and skills at their respective schools. Nevertheless, I have always questioned myself as to how, in the absence of an effective follow-up system to monitor the application of learned knowledge as well as to measure the impact of the programme, the participants would apply the learned knowledge and skills at their respective schools. I have discussed the M&E of this programme in the next section.

C. Monitoring and Evaluation of the Programme

The M&E responsibilities of the programme were assigned to the District and *Taluqa* (a local administrative unit) education officers working in the respective districts of Sindh and Balochistan. For this purpose, the university's project team provided detailed orientations and training workshops to these government education officials about the design, development, aims and objectives, and monitoring mechanism of the programme. The underlying objective of these orientations and workshops was to enable Education Officers to monitor, evaluate, and effectively follow up the programme in the respective schools of the participants. It was anticipated that these DEOs would ensure the application of learned knowledge and skills in the actual contexts of the head- and deputy headteachers.

The ED-LINKS project management team at the provincial level also appointed two district managers to monitor the project activities at the respective districts. The programme also provided orientation and workshops to these district managers. However, as the headteachers and deputy heads informed me during my school visits, that most of these managers were engaged in administrative activities of the project rather than monitoring the academic activities of headteachers and deputy headteachers at their particular schools. Since there was no one to follow them up, the buck stopped with them.

Informally, the university's project team remained in contact with the graduating heads and deputy heads of the schools. Moreover, the project team also remained in contact with the district-based project managers of the ED-LINKS project. The purpose of these contacts was to learn about the progress of school heads at their respective schools, and to know and understand how they were applying their newly acquired knowledge and skills from the professional development programme at their schools as well as their progress related to the implementation of SDPs.

The information collected from different sources revealed that, although a reasonable number of participants were applying the learned knowledge at their work places, there were many others who could not because of many issues, including lack of funds and stakeholders' support.

Many of them did not opt to share the developed SDPs in the training programme with their teachers and other stakeholders, and thus not all could implement SDPs at their respective schools. Nevertheless, there was also good news from some of the headteachers and deputy heads, who told us that they had held workshops for their school teachers and staff, and told them about CE: ELM, and they had also shared the SDPs developed during the training programme with their district level officers, teachers, staff, and other stakeholders, and received their feedback for improvement in SDPs. They had made serious efforts to implement SDPs at their respective schools. These headteachers and deputy heads were in constant contact with the project team of the university through telephone and emails, and shared their success stories with us. Such outcomes were obviously a great sense of satisfaction for the project team, and we were happy that a reasonable number of headteachers and deputy heads were making a positive impact on their communities as a result of the inspiration and the learnings from the professional development programme.

I personally feel that, during the professional development programme, all participants should have been clearly informed about a systematic accountability mechanism for the leadership programme. This accountability mechanism should have been devised collaboratively by the ED-LINKS project team at provincial level, the university, senior provincial level officials from the Education and Literacy Departments of the governments of Sindh and Balochistan, and the consultants. The accountability system should have contained clear instructions for reward for those who would implement the learned knowledge and skills at their schools. Either a third party, the ED-LINKS project, or the university offering CE: ELM, could have been given the responsibility to implement the accountability mechanism in the targeted schools. All those head- and deputy headteachers who participated in the programme should have been made responsible to bring about positive changes at their respective schools, and their performances objectively evaluated.

One of the headteachers in the programme had shared his views about the follow up, suggesting an accountability mechanism for the programme, and I paraphrase his suggestion below:

> If headteachers and deputy headteachers were implementing the SDPs, and applying their learnt knowledge and skills at their schools successfully, then they should have been given rewards and recognitions, and one additional allowance/increment in their monthly salaries. However, if they were

unable to do so, then they could have been made responsible, and could have been asked why they were not applying their learned knowledge and skills at their schools. As a penalty, the amount of TA/DA that was given to the headteachers and deputy headteachers during the CE: ELM could have been recovered from them along with deducting one increment amount from their monthly salaries.

Whether this is possible or even desirable to follow is another matter, but it does show that training programmes must always be followed by accountability for their application. This, again, is easier said than done. Teaching and learning takes place on the basis of trust and commitment of all concerned. I, for one, feel that educational leadership must inspire rather than coerce good work and dedication and, therefore, should not be treated lightly. Particularly, in the context of a resource-starved country like Pakistan, all those related to education must do everything possible to get maximum benefit from the resources. Additionally, when donor agencies fund such programmes, the moral duty doubles and those who take daily allowances for learning and are well looked after during the programme must go the additional mile to justify the spending on them. Anecdotal stories abound regarding committed teachers and school heads who do their best in a difficult world.

It is heartening to note that, recently, a Pakistani teacher (from a private school, admittedly) was awarded the 'Best Dedicated Teacher Award' by Cambridge University (*Dawn*, 2 February 2019). As we hear reliable stories, we know that there are many such teachers and heads who even risk their lives (in many vulnerable regions) and use personal resources to ensure their students do succeed. Research on headteachers in Pakistan tells us that '...heads strive to invest their lives in making the world of the young a little better or happier... They want to give their students something to stand on in life, whether a good career, ...life skills or the tools of (better) communication, ...or the bedrock of ...values'. The lives of these heads, '...tell us that a high vision (for the excellence of schooling) can motivate people to accomplish things, generally seen as difficult' (Khaki, 2010: 123).

Note

1. Breakfast, lunch, and tea prepared in the self-managed kitchen were served in a well-furnished hall, called the Social Area.

6

The Nature of School Administrators' Support of Beginning Teachers in Kyrgyzstan

DUISHON ALIEVICH SHAMATOV

This chapter is about education in Kyrgyzstan, a former USSR Republic in Central Asia, which is experiencing dramatic changes (Niyozov, 2001; Shamatov, 2014). The chapter presents the school administrators' support to beginning teachers in Kyrgyzstan. Beginning teachers' initial experiences are the most challenging and influential in their future careers (Bullough, 1997). School administrators are reportedly the most significant professionals in a beginning teacher's initial experiences at a school (Brock & Grady, 2001). This chapter is based on the findings of a qualitative case study which explored beginning teachers' initial work at schools, and in particular what challenges they face and how they get support from school administrators. The study demonstrated that the main participant of the study, a young female biology teacher in the town school, got a lot of professional support from the school principal and the assigned mentor who helped her adjust well to a new workplace. The study findings offer significant policy and practical implications.

INTRODUCTION

I would like to begin this chapter by presenting a brief background of my country. Kyrgyzstan, officially the Kyrgyz Republic, is a small, landlocked, and mostly mountainous country in Central Asia. It encompasses 198,500 square kilometres, bordering China to the east, Tajikistan to the south, Uzbekistan to the west, and Kazakhstan to the north (Shamatov, 2005). Kyrgyzstan was previously one of the 15 union republics of the former

Soviet Union. After the breakup of the Soviet Union in 1991, Kyrgyzstan began experiencing serious problems in the field of education (DeYoung, 2004; Shamatov & Niyozov, 2010). For example, preschool enrolment declined catastrophically during the 1990s. Out of 1,604 preschool institutions existing in 1991, only 416 remained by 2000 (DeYoung, ibid.), and overall preschool enrolment in Central Asia was only 14 per cent in 1999 (Open Society Institute, 2002). According to the Ministry of Education and Science (MoES) statistics in 2009–2010, there were 2,134 public schools in Kyrgyzstan: 1,379 were Kyrgyz-medium schools, 162 were Russian-medium schools, 137 were Uzbek-medium schools, and seven were Tajik-medium schools. Four hundred and forty-nine schools had two or more languages of instruction (interview, staff of Ministry of Education and Science, 5 July 2009). Some 83.6 per cent of the population of Kyrgyzstan completed secondary education in 1993; this decreased to 76.4 per cent in 1996 and 1999 respectively (DeYoung, 2002).

This chapter describes how school administrators provide support to beginning teachers in their initial period of adjustment at a new workplace. It is widely documented internationally that new teachers face many challenges in their initial periods of work at schools, and their initial experiences are described as the most challenging and influential in their future careers (Bullough, 1997). Therefore, they have a need for support and belonging (Shamatov, 2013; Watkins, 2005), and if their ideas and experiences are recognised and valued by the members of school community, it is more likely to help new teachers survive their initial period and adjust more successfully (Hahs-Vaughn & Scherff, 2008). Without a strong support, it is more likely that new teachers may leave the school, or even the teaching profession in general causing further problems including exacerbating teacher shortage adding to the worsening quality of education (Davis & Higdon, 2008). When a large number of teachers leave schools, it causes serious problems for school administrators. Thus, retaining teachers is often the priority of school administrators. The school administrators reportedly use different approaches and strategies to support new teachers to help them adjust well and become effective members of school community (Brown & Wynn, 2009; Price, 2012). Thus, this chapter explores, using the qualitative study method, how the school principal and the mentor provide support to a beginning teacher of a secondary school in Kyrgyzstan. The study explored what challenges beginning teachers face and what kind of support they get from their school administrators in dealing with the challenges.

Literature Review

School administrators are reportedly the most significant persons in beginning teachers' initial experiences at school (Brock & Grady, 2001; Shamatov, 2013; Veenman, 1984). They make the final decision about hiring new teachers and supervising them (Brock & Grady, 2001; Duckworth & Carnine, 1987). They monitor beginning teacher practices, provide them with professional support, and help them adjust to a new workplace (Aspfors & Fransson, 2015). They also make decisions about distributing resources to beginning teachers, allotting assignments and schedules, and deciding on beginning teachers' promotion or dismissal. Ideally, beginning teachers need to be provided with preferred assignments which may include a reduced workload, a greater distribution of resources and facilities, and regular supervision (Thiessen & Kilcher, 1993). Ongoing direction and assistance (induction) from administrators and experienced colleagues play an important role in helping beginning teachers to adjust successfully (Gold, 1996; Kilbourn & Roberts, 1996). Professional support for beginning teachers can make their experiences less traumatic and more positive and at the same time continue to develop their teaching skills. Beginning teachers may manage to cope with their challenges more effectively and improve their practices significantly when they are provided with adequate and systematic support from school administrators and experienced colleagues. Without the induction support and assistance, many beginning teachers experience serious challenges during their initial period of work and many potentially good teachers become discouraged and abandon their teaching careers (Cole, 1996).

School administrators organise staff meetings to communicate mostly their expectations for teacher behaviour, to reinforce official definitions, and to exert their control over teachers (Blase, 1997; Brown & Wynn, 2009). Some school administrators may force teachers into passive political roles as recipients of information during meetings; as Ball (1987) reports, 'The teachers are not so much participants in, as subjects of, the meeting. The meeting is a camouflage, a diversion. The ritual of information-giving and consultation is asserted over any substantive involvement in decision making' (pp. 239–240).

School administrators make decisions regarding beginning teachers' practices by observing them conduct lessons and control their pupils. Veenman (1984) observes that school administrators may judge beginning teachers' abilities according to how the latter handle discipline and control their pupils. Therefore, beginning teachers experience self-concerns, feelings of uncertainty, and self-doubt while interacting with their administrators. They face pressure to show their administrators that they are in full control of their classes.

Among school administrators, principals play the most crucial role in beginning teachers' adjustment at schools. Blase (1997) argues, 'Principals are the ultimate authority on student discipline and make decisions about the allocation of space, materials, and equipment—decisions that strongly influence teachers' working conditions' (p. 948). They establish the climate and vision for their schools; they play an important role in helping beginning teachers develop a sense of membership in their schools (Le Maistre & Paré, 2010). Goodlad (1984) contends, 'Principals establish and maintain the academic tone of their schools and are extremely important to faculty morale' (cited in Bullough, 1989: 12). Brock and Grady (2001) assert that the school climate the principals create can be pleasant and welcoming for beginning teachers or unpleasant, even threatening, for them. They further comment:

> Principals have the power to praise or criticize teaching, offer or withhold resources, determine schedules and assignments, provide or refuse support, and recommend or not recommend continuing employment. Their comments and body language speak loudly about their pleasure or displeasure. (p. 41)

On the basis of their observations, principals make decisions regarding teachers' performance, renewal, promotion, and disciplinary measures. They critique and provide feedback to beginning teachers about the latter's practices. They attend beginning teachers' lessons to monitor the teachers' instructional and classroom management strategies or to observe how well pupils are learning and behaving in the teachers' classes. Beginning teachers are aware of their principals' role; therefore, they attempt to meet their expectations. They may feel uncomfortable, apprehensive, or fearful until they receive feedback and affirmation from their principals (Brock & Grady, 2001; Brown & Wynn, 2009; Shamatov, 2013).

Beginning teachers rely on their principals for professional support and induction at school. Supportive principals 'organise and orchestrate induction activities, share their philosophy of education with newcomers, and provide information and encouragement' (Brock & Grady, 2001: 45). Such professional support makes beginning teachers' experiences more pleasant and less troublesome. Those beginning teachers who receive adequate, effective professional support and a welcoming induction in the new workplace adjust better (Blase, 1997; Brock & Grady, 2001; Hong, 2012; Kilbourn & Roberts, 1996; Thiessen & Anderson, 1999). Professional support for beginning teachers can make their experiences less traumatic and more positive. Moreover, beginning teachers can improve their practices significantly during and after effective induction. For example, Feiman-Nemser and Remillard (1996) showed how a small number of beginning teachers remarkably improved their practices through professional support during their induction. These teachers improved their use of instructional time, classroom management techniques, blackboard use, record-keeping systems, voice inflections, eye contact, and questioning strategies. They began paying attention to every pupil individually rather than paying attention only to those who were active and interested in learning. They also encouraged pupils to understand concepts rather than merely memorise facts.

Brock and Grady (2001) add that beginning teachers can feel more comfortable and freer to innovate if their principals treat them as competent professionals and support new ideas. However, critical and punishing principals create an unhappy and unhealthy climate which alienates beginning teachers, making them afraid of experiments, and creates frustration. Many beginning teachers want their principals to support them in their practices, and especially in pupil discipline matters. They also want principals to support and protect them from outside pressures, such as pupils' parents, education board administrators, and other community members (Feiman-Nemser & Floden, 1986).

As stated above, school administrators make decisions about beginning teachers' hiring, supervising their practices, evaluating, promoting, sanctioning, allocating space, materials or equipment to them (Brown & Wynn, 2009; Duckworth & Carnine, 1987). Therefore, beginning teachers are usually cautious in interacting with their school administrators though they want to remain on good terms with them. They experience self-concerns, feelings of uncertainty and self-doubt while interacting with their administrators. They feel vulnerable to external criticism and feelings of personal failure (Borich, 1995; Bullough et al., 1992). They worry about being accepted by the school community. 'The experience of professional success inside and outside the classroom proves to be essential in the development of professional self-confidence to beginning teachers' (Kelchtermans & Ballet, 1999, p. 1). Beginning teachers thus seek self-affirmation and try to demonstrate to their administrators that they *can* cope with the tasks they are assigned to do.

Beginning teachers worry that their professional competencies may not be accurately assessed by those limited, partial observations. Therefore, they do not want to expose any possible weakness, instead they try to camouflage doubts and show their best practices to their administrators. Teachers come to terms with their administrators' expectations and definitions of good classroom management and good discipline; then they try to demonstrate that they can control their classrooms and impose discipline on their pupils (Bullough, 1989).

Blase and Anderson (1995) point out that teachers' relations with their administrators are determined by what kind of principals they have. They categorise principals broadly into 'open' and 'closed' and explain how these types of principals and teachers influence each other (Table 6.1).

Table 6.1: Principals' Characteristics and Teachers' Responses

Principals' Characteristics	Teachers' Responses
'Open' principals: • honesty • collegiality • non-manipulation • supportiveness • communicativeness • participation	'Open' political responses: • diplomacy • conformity • extra work and visibility • greater proactivity • two-way (bilateral) communication and influence • complexity
'Closed' principals: • Authoritarian, inaccessible, inflexible • Manipulative, control-oriented • Use of sanctions, harassment • management of personal access	Accommodative, reactive, and protective political responses: • Anger, confusion, depression, insecurity, and sense of resignation • Avoidance and ingratiation • Covert and indirect responses • Individualised, privatised, and reactive responses • Passive political orientations • Survival considerations

Source: Blaze & Anderson, 1995

The authors further elaborate that when principals are open, honest, and supportive, beginning teachers implement these political tactics:

- They exhibit diplomacy to create a good image of themselves in the eyes of principals and colleagues
- They may disagree with some of their principals' demands.

However, when principals are 'closed' and authoritarian, beginning teachers may often use conformity as a strategy to avoid criticisms and sanctions as well as to gain certain benefits. Zeichner and Tabachnick (1985) argue, 'Conformity is essentially an adaptive response without the corresponding value basis on which the behaviour rests' (p. 9). Blase (1997) argues that an effective principal also plays an important role by establishing a teacher culture that may either enable or impede beginning teachers' relating to their colleagues. An effective principal encourages teachers to interact with one another with respect, to cooperate, and to support each other. Beginning teachers, who join schools where there is an ineffective principal, encounter a teacher culture in which flaunting, gossip, spying, criticism, tensions, and aloofness are common.

In many schools, principals assign mentors who provide beginning teachers with continuous direction and assistance, guiding them in their most difficult period of adjusting and learning to work as teachers (Borman & Dowling, 2008; Brown & Wynn, 2009; Little, 1987). Brock and Grady (2001) define mentor as 'an individual with experience and expertise who has assumed primary responsibility for providing support and guidance for a beginning teacher' (p. 71). Mentors are usually assigned from amongst experienced teachers, often teachers of the same class (grade) and subject, to help beginning teachers with their problems, including instructional and classroom management issues (Brown & Wynn, 2009; Hannam et al., 1984; Roehrig et al., 2002). Beginning teachers without mentors' support face far greater challenges and are more likely to quit teaching (Brock & Grady, 2001).

Research Design

The study employed qualitative research approach to explore the beginning teachers' initial period of work and the kind of support the school administrators provided them (Creswell, 2014). Qualitative research involves an interpretative, descriptive, and naturalistic approach to the world (Bell, 2005; McEwan & McEwan, 2003). The qualitative approach enabled me to learn first-hand about the beginning teachers' experiences through my participation and involvement in their social world (Creswell, 2014).

Working within the qualitative paradigm, I conducted an in-depth case study (Creswell, 2014; Merriam, 1988; Yin, 1989). The main and secondary participants of this study are the beginning teachers who worked at secondary schools (Classes 6 to 11) of Kyrgyzstan for less than three years. I thus selected two main participants: Ainura (pseudonym), a biology teacher from an urban school and Kanybek (pseudonym), a history teacher from a rural school. They were teachers of two different subjects (social science and natural science). I also had 28 secondary participants, whose input was used to supplement and verify data from the two main participants. All these participants were selected with the help of a purposive sampling strategy (Cohen & Manion, 1997; Creswell, 1998; McMillan & Schumacher, 1997).

Data were mainly collected with the help of individual interviews, group interviews, and observations. I conducted ten semi-structured in-depth interviews with each of the main participants. Each interview took from one to two hours and was arranged at a mutually convenient time and place. I conducted these interviews prior to and following field observations and at any opportune times (e.g. break, lunch, preparation periods) during the course of the school day. Also, I did group interviews with the secondary participants (Fontana & Frey, 2000). With 28 secondary participants, I conducted overall twelve group interviews (6 to 8 participants in each group interview). I conducted these group interviews 'to test a specific research question about consensus beliefs; to obtain greater depth and breadth in responses than occurs in individual interviews; to verify research plans or findings; and, more speculatively, to enhance the reliability of interviewee responses' (Hitchcock & Hughes, 1995: 161). These group interviews yielded additional data with wider perspectives (Cohen & Manion, 1997); they also helped to corroborate the findings from the main participants' interviews. In addition to interviews, I also used observation as a data-gathering tool with my main participants. Observation is systematic, deliberate, and question-specific means of gathering data (Everton & Green, 1986). I observed them in their classrooms, schools, and communities while they interacted with their pupils, colleagues, school administrators, parents, and other community members.

Data analysis is a rigorous continuous process of systematically searching and arranging the accumulated data in order to increase one's understanding of them (Creswell, 2014). This process involved making sense of the data by arranging them into coherent and plausible arguments. I developed coding categories and kept different categories in separate files (LeComte & Schensul, 1998; Niyozov, 2001). I arranged data by using the following process codes: sequence of events, changes over time, and participants' chronological experiences, namely, childhood and school, university (pre-service), and joining a school.

In the next section, I present the findings of the study. Unfortunately, due to shortage of space and word limit, I cannot present the findings of both of the main participants. Instead, I present the findings from one of them only, Ainura, a young female teacher of biology from Osh town school.

FINDINGS OF THE STUDY

The findings of the study demonstrated that when Ainura joined the town school as a biology teacher, she faced many challenges but she also got a lot of support from school administrators, in particular from the principal of the school and a mentor assigned to her.

Initial Encounters with the Principal

In Ainura's school, the school leadership comprised the principal and four vice-principals. Kanyshay (pseudonym), the principal of the school, was a very serious woman of around 60 years old. She was a very strict principal and she tightly controlled all the teachers. Ainura noticed immediately that all the teachers were compliant and did not talk back to Kanyshay. Kanyshay demanded discipline from all teachers and she discouraged teachers from disobeying or talking back to her. In fact, some teachers warned Ainura to avoid getting into trouble with the principal. A senior teacher advised, 'If you get into trouble with her, the principal can make your life miserable. Your name will go into her "blacklist", and she will chase you. She will attend your classes, and will discuss your problems in a staff meeting'. Ainura thus was very careful in her relations with the principal. She tried to avoid conflicts with her and did not want to get on Kanyshay's blacklist. She often tried to avoid meeting the principal at school and she did not spend much time in the staff room, where the principal would be able to see the teachers.

The Principal's Unexpected Visits

The principal regularly attended teachers' lessons to assess and appraise. The teachers were generally afraid to have the principal as an observer. They were especially worried when the principal made visits without prior notice. The principal would come and sit in the class, and check whether the teacher had a lesson plan and was following it, whether the teacher used visual aids or other teaching resources, and whether the pupils were active in the class or not. Based on those visits, the principal would usually make a judgement about the teachers' work, who should be promoted, and so on. Ainura was usually well prepared for her lessons. Nevertheless, she always worried about the principal's dreaded visit to her classes for observation. She feared that the principal would negatively judge her teaching on the basis of a particular lesson and that she might not be able to show what she could do in just one lesson. Ainura started working hard on her teaching practices; she would often remind her pupils that they should not let her down when the principal came to observe.

Then, one day, the principal came to her class. Ainura was very nervous when the principal attended her lesson. She had prepared a detailed lesson plan which she followed, the pupils seemed to understand what she explained in the class, and she also had colourful visual aids to explain the concepts. When the observation was over, Ainura thought her lesson went well; she was confident that the principal would praise her teaching. Instead, the principal commented that Ainura should encourage the pupils to be more active and should involve them in their learning, rather than pouring out information on them. Later, the principal attended Ainura's lessons again. She was pleased that Ainura was putting a lot of effort into improving her practices; particularly, she noted that Ainura was now asking more questions of her pupils and was trying to engage them in talking. The principal told other teachers that Ainura was trying to improve and that she liked Ainura's interest in self-development. Ainura observed, 'She did not praise my lesson to me personally. Maybe that is her strategy. She does not want to praise people in their presence, but it was still good to know from my colleagues that she liked my lesson'. During one of the staff meetings, the principal spoke about the necessity of hiring more teachers in several subjects because the teachers of those subjects could not do a good job due to their overload of teaching commitments.

However, the principal was positive about the biology teachers and said that she was pleased with them, 'We have few Biology teachers, but they are enough for us because they work well, they are doing a good job'. She also referred to Ainura's teaching, saying that Ainura conducted her classes well despite her lack of experience. She encouraged the other teachers to attend Ainura's lessons, saying, 'Ainura is a young teacher, but she teaches better than many experienced teachers. You should attend and learn something useful from her'. Ainura was very pleased to hear this kind of comment in front of the whole staff and this really encouraged Ainura and raised her self-esteem as a teacher. The more Ainura got to know the principal, the more she started feeling good about her. Contrary to Ainura's initial fears, the principal proved to be a very sympathetic, fair, and objective administrator. What we learn here is maybe that often the beginning teachers regard their heads to be more worrisome than they actually are out of their sheer fear. Therefore, beginning teachers need to be more open to feedback and do not necessarily entertain apprehension from their heads.

Growing appreciation towards the principal

As mentioned above, Ainura had thought initially that the principal was an overly strict and perhaps an authoritarian administrator, but by the end of the academic year, she had more respect and understanding for the principal. She associated the school's successes with the principal's leadership, stating:

> The school is good because of her. She maintains good discipline. With our large staff, we need someone like her; otherwise, there could be a lot of conflicts and fights among teachers over various issues. I think our school is far better than many other schools because of her.

Ainura also thought the principal was doing a good job because her school had a reputation of being one of the strongest in Osh town. Many pupils were regularly winning various regional and national Olympiads in different subjects, and many graduates were entering higher educational institutions. Because of the principal's proactivity, the school had established contacts with foreign educational institutions and many pupils visited other countries for study trips and exchange programmes. The principal made sure that teachers developed collegial relationships with each other. She did not tolerate teachers who were involved in gossip, blackmailing each other, or fighting to burnish their images or establish their own positions. She was strict, but she was also a motherly figure. She often would say that the school staff members were a family, and she insisted that anything that happened should stay in the family. When teachers quarrelled with each other, she would immediately remind the teachers that 'those were internal family issues' and that no one should air them outside the school 'as dirty linen'.

Ainura improved her relations with the principal and increasingly she developed a lot of appreciation for her. She felt that her classroom performance helped her to gain more recognition from the school administrators. Ainura says, 'Kanyshay is a role model for me. I want to be like her'. The principal too noted that Ainura was a promising young teacher and started sending her to attend various in-service teacher education programmes, such as seminars, workshops, and conferences. For example, the principal chose and sent Ainura to Bishkek (capital city) to attend professional development courses. Kanyshay was also pleased with Ainura's commitment and interest in self-development. She explained to Ainura that she wanted to prepare her to become a vice-principal of the school; therefore, she encouraged her to participate in professional development courses.

Support from a Mentor

The principal assigned a mentor to help Ainura adjust to teaching at the school: Kalys (pseudonym), an experienced Biology teacher. Ainura's mentor guided her carefully during the initial period of her work at the school. Ainura got a lot of help from her mentor with school documentation and planning. She learned how to manage documents such as the class register, calendar plan, and other teacher records. Kalys also shared teaching resources with Ainura, including illustrations and other visual aids for teaching Biology that she had collected at the school for many years. Kalys also advised Ainura on personal and professional matters. She explained that the school was large and that there were different problems with various teachers; in addition, some teachers did not get along well with each other. She told Ainura to be aware of those groups and individuals and not to get involved in any conflicts. She also advised her to 'stay away from other teachers' and spend less time in the staff room in order to avoid becoming involved in gossip or conflicts. She also helped with classroom management issues. An important lesson that Ainura learned from her mentor was to be consistent in applying strategies of classroom management. Kalys told her, 'Whatever you do, do it with consistence. Pupils can get confused if they get mixed messages, and they may revolt if you do not follow what you do consistently'. However, Kalys could not always be available for offering support to Ainura, because she was often busy teaching her own classes; she had 28 hours to teach per week instead of the usual 18. Whenever she could, the mentor also helped with class management. However, Ainura, at times, felt that the mentor's help was sometimes more negative than positive, as one example of her interference with Ainura's teaching showed. She actually undermined Ainura's authority in front of her pupils (Box 6.1).

It was the beginning of the lesson and Kalys Ejeke entered Ainura's classroom while the pupils were greeting Ainura.

> **Box 6.1: Lesson Episode**
>
> **Ainura:** Good morning.
>
> **P:** [greeted her in chorus] I am strong. I am clever. I love my country and I will make my country prosperous. [The pupils did not speak in unison, and several were talking to each other. At that time, Kalys entered the room to get teaching materials. She noted that the pupils were not greeting 'properly' and that there was noise in the room. When the pupils saw her, they grew quiet. Kalys then intervened with a loud and firm voice].
>
> **Kalys:** What happened to you? You are not greeting your teacher properly. You forgot how to do it? Now greet again [emphasis hers]. Repeat once more… Again… Again… [Ainura became visibly uncomfortable…. Pupils repeated the greeting several times…. Kalys Ejeke was finally pleased that she had succeeded in organising the class to greet in chorus, and she looked at Ainura as if to say, 'That is the way they should greet you'. She took her materials and left the room.]

Even after Kalys left the room, Ainura felt uncomfortable, because Kalys had intervened in her practices in front of her pupils, rather than guiding her with classroom management strategies later outside the class:

> I was upset because it was not professional of her. I did not say anything. But she should have told me how to address such issues in private and not to embarrass me in front of you and more important in front of my pupils. What will my pupils think of me now? They'll think I cannot handle things on my own.

Ainura also often substituted in her mentor's classes because Kalys was a very senior person and often used to get sick. She had taught at the school for more than 35 years and had already passed retirement age; she was still working because she needed the salary. At first, Ainura complied with her mentor and took over her classes. She said, 'I can't say "no" to her because of my respect towards her and other senior teachers'. She did not mind teaching the mentor's lessons, especially because she thought she could gain more teaching experience and thus improve her practices. While substituting for her mentor, Ainura worried about whether she could do a good job and whether the pupils would appreciate her teaching because she was inexperienced. After substituting for her mentor several times, Ainura became very disappointed with the pupils' lack of knowledge and lack of interest in studying. There were many disciplinary issues; most of the pupils did not do their assignments and just sat in the classes looking indifferent. Ainura said: 'These pupils just waste their time, come to school, sit in class and hope to get a school leaving certificate one day. When I began teaching them I asked very simple questions, but they could not answer them'. Ainura then realised that her mentor did not teach her pupils well. Ainura was disappointed because often Kalys would tell her how to teach, how to attract the pupils' interest in lessons, how to engage everyone in lessons, and how to help pupils learn well. Now Ainura saw how poorly the mentor's own pupils performed.

Ainura planned her activities well, tried to engage the pupils in question-and-answer sessions and discussions, and provided additional information about the course content. As a result, after several lessons, the pupils started appreciating her teaching. The pupils were happy that they were learning more when Ainura taught than when Kalys did. They told Ainura that Kalys conducted 'boring lessons'; therefore, they had lost all interest and their knowledge was poor. They said to Ainura, 'Kalys comes to classes with her old notes, sits on her chair and tells us to study on our own. We read the text and go home. Her classes are boring'. Ainura was pleased at the improvement in the pupils' attitudes towards their studies. She said, 'Many pupils became more interested in learning Biology. They listened attentively in classes and asked questions. When I questioned them, they tried to respond'. The pupils liked her teaching so much that they wanted to write a letter to the principal, requesting her to assign Ainura to them on a regular basis instead of the mentor. But Ainura refused because she feared that it could hurt her mentor; she did not want to create a conflict with her. Ainura recalled an incident when the pupils wanted to change one of her colleagues because they did not like her teaching. They wrote a letter of complaint to the principal, requesting she change their teacher. The principal put in another teacher. She also brought up the issue during a staff meeting in front of the whole staff; she cautioned the teachers to improve their teaching practices in order to avoid such embarrassing situations. The teacher who was changed became very upset that the principal had brought the issue up in public and she left the school soon after. Hence, Ainura did not allow the pupils to write the letter to the principal, though she was pleased that the pupils recognised her efforts and preferred her teaching to that of the more experienced teacher.

As a new teacher, Ainura faced many challenges. For example, she did not have a classroom when she started teaching. Instead, she used any classroom which was available for her classes. The older teachers had already distributed the available classrooms among themselves before the academic year started. These senior teachers usually locked their classrooms when they did not have lessons, because they feared other teachers' pupils would damage their classroom furniture if they are opened without their supervision. Ainura thought she would have fewer troubles and feel much more relaxed if she had a permanent classroom. Instead, she had to teach in small, uncomfortable rooms and move from room to room for her lessons. Therefore, she faced difficulties in conducting her classroom activities, demonstrating experiments, or arranging visual aids and illustrations.

Ainura preferred conducting her classes in the Biology classroom which was used by Kalys. This classroom had colourful pictures of animals and birds, as well as a large hand-drawn diagram of the theory of evolution displayed on the walls; most of these illustrations were from Soviet times. 'Illustrations are helpful for pupils to understand Biology concepts better,' Ainura explained. She believed, 'If I stay at school longer, perhaps next year I may get opportunities to choose better classrooms, better classes and an easier schedule in the future. Besides, Kalys promised she will leave this classroom with me when she leaves the school in a couple of years'.

Thus, by the end of this study, Ainura had developed a lot of confidence and her adjustment at the school has been going well. She is gaining the respect of her students, and trust and support from the principal and the mentor.

Conclusion

This study explored how beginning teachers in Kyrgyzstan are supported in their new experiences at schools and how different systems, such as the support of school leadership and assigning mentors, are in place. The chapter presented the findings as one example of a young female teacher in Osh town of south Kyrgyzstan. The study found out that this new teacher had, as expected, different perceptions of school heads and general nervousness about this experience. Interestingly enough, her experience was not that horrifying, instead she had a growing admiration towards her strict principal who, after some initial introductory challenges, supported her in full to the extent of seeing Ainura as a model teacher. In fact, the young teacher wanted to emulate the strict but fair principal.

The study demonstrated that the school administrators provided support to the new teacher. This is similar to what is widely documented in international research literature. Effective professional support enables beginning teachers to continue to develop their teaching skills and helps them confront the adjustment difficulties of the first year (Gold, 1996; Kilbourn & Roberts, 1996). The study showed that the beginning teachers need a lot of support, not only in their teaching work or disciplinary matters but also in working with other people such as colleagues, pupils' parents, and education officials.

The study also showed that the findings are consistent with other studies where the role of the principal of the school is a critical factor for the success or otherwise of the school. Ainura reports that her principal is the key to the success of her school. This leads us to the conclusion that the school principals can ensure a steady career selection for teachers if they provide conducive, enabling, and empowering environment particularly for beginning teachers.

7

Supporting Students Affected by War and Terrorism: School Leadership Challenges

NEELOFAR AHMED

This chapter explores the role of Pakistani school leadership in supporting students affected by war and terrorism. It also looks at the prospects of cross-cultural collaboration among communities and countries that can come together with similar problems to address the possible issues effectively. The chapter is largely drawn from a (comparative) study, which I conducted for my major research paper at Brock University and presented at the International Study Association on Teachers and Teaching conference, Kazan Federal University, Kazan, Russia, in 2018.

Pakistan's public schools are multi-cultural, and this diversity includes children coming from different religious, social, ethnic, and economic backgrounds, as well as children from refugee families. Currently, more than 1.4 million refugees live in Pakistan, half of whom are children under the age of 18 years (UNHCR, 2019). The NEP (2018) is promising and pledges to provide an inclusive and equitable education to all. However, in terms of policy and practice, it does not provide much guidance to school leaders as to how to support refugee students or to foster parental engagement to improve their social integration and academic achievements. It is essential that stakeholders in education recognise the needs and address the challenges of refugee students as research reveals that children who are exposed to life-time traumatic events often suffer Post-Traumatic Stress Disorder (PTSD), and, therefore, their socio-psychological needs differ from those of their peers (Feuerverger, 2011). Contextual to the challenges of students affected by war and terrorism, this chapter aims to examine the supporting role of school principals using Bronfenbrenner's (1999) bioecological model of child development. It also highlights the importance of parental engagement from refugee families as their children transit into schools. Finally, this chapter explores the prospects of bilateral collaboration between countries like Canada and Pakistan to enhance the capacity building of local practitioners by learning and sharing the experiences of school leaders who support war and terrorism affected students in their schools. Although in Pakistan, the directors of education, superintendents, headteachers, and school principals are all considered as 'school leaders', I explicitly use this label to describe the school principals or headteachers working in public schools in Pakistan.

The Background Context

In the past two decades, history has witnessed a series of overwhelming events emerging from war and war-like situations in Central and South Asia as well as in the Middle East. The United Nations High Commissioner for Refugees (UNHCR, 2019) claims that the global population of war and terrorism affected people had grown substantially from 33.9 million in 1997 to 70.8 million in 2018. The report further highlights that this population includes people who are directly or indirectly affected by war, terrorism, armed conflicts, airstrikes, as well as 'internally displaced persons' (IDPs) who are forced to flee from their homes and remain at the borders of their native or host countries. This report also estimates that children under the age of 18 years account for more than half of the total refugee population. A new wave of terrorism has emerged that has dramatically affected various countries. The unfortunate event of 11 September 2001 was a major instance of terrorism that killed close to 3,000 innocent people and instigated an enduring 'War on Terror', that has fostered war and war-like situations in many countries, including Afghanistan, Iraq, Libya, Syria, and Pakistan.

Pakistan has been settling and supporting Afghan refugees since 1979 and currently hosts a large population of registered/unregistered Afghans whose second and third generations are born and raised in Pakistan. Geographically, Pakistan shares a more than two thousand miles long border with Afghanistan and has been hosting Afghan refugees since 1979—the year when the Soviet army first invaded Afghanistan. Until 1989, when the Soviet army left, Pakistan remained the top Afghan refugee country in the world. The Soviet Union's withdrawal created a civil war situation in Afghanistan until the mid-1990s when the Taliban regime took control of Afghanistan and announced their government (Hussain & Latif, 2012). Taliban continued to govern Afghanistan until after the incident of 9/11, when American President George W. Bush announced a 'War on Terror' in Afghanistan, which later on spread to all parts of Pakistan and to other Middle Eastern countries. Besides war, the drone attacks, airstrikes, and landmines killed thousands of people in the conflict-affected and border-sharing countries. Crawford et al. (2020) observe that, since President George W. Bush announced a 'War on Terror', more than 800,000 people have been killed in Iraq, Afghanistan, Syria, Yemen, and Pakistan. This count, however, does not include millions of other civilians who lost their lives due to the damage caused by the war, including destroyed hospitals, lack of healthcare facilities and frontline workers, medicines, poor nutrition, and contaminated water. In Iraq, about half a million people were killed and thousands displaced during and after the war. In Syria, it has been more than seven years that the conflicts have created a war-like situation. The UNHCR High Commissioner, Filippo Grandi, calls the Syrian conflict as the 'biggest humanitarian and refugee crises of our times', which is causing millions to suffer from the tyranny of war and armed conflicts (UNHCR, 2018).

According to a recently published report of the UNHCR (2019), since 2011, there are more than 6.6 million people who are internally displaced in Syria, whereas over 5.6 million people have taken refuge/asylum in host countries like Lebanon, Turkey, and Jordan. Whereas in Pakistan (which is not directly in a state of war), it is estimated that at least 80,000 Pakistanis have been killed, thousands are missing or displaced, and hundreds are directly or indirectly affected by terrorism, especially children (Haider, 2014). Crawford (2016) recognises Pakistan as 'a hot, albeit underreported, war zone' (p. 10). She further asserts that the actual number of Pakistani civilians killed by (direct or indirect) Afghan war is likely much higher than reported in the media. Much higher is the suspected count of causalities and those injured during airstrikes, drone attacks, and landmines explosions in North Waziristan.

Pakistan has also witnessed terrorist attacks on schools and the killing of innocent school students and staff all across the country. One such horrific incident was the terrorist attack on the Army Public School (APS), Peshawar, Pakistan, on 16 December 2014. BBC (2014) reports that the terrorists killed more than 140 students and school staff. The school principal of APS, late Mrs Tahira Qazi, was also shot dead by the terrorists as she was trying to rescue her students.

International and Pakistani scholars and researchers have paid attention to the plight of students' resettlement in schools after the traumatic events of war and terrorism. Research indicates that the resettlement of students who are once exposed to lifetime traumatic events of war and terrorism may instigate a challenge to school leaders as the socio-psychological needs of these students are different from their peers. For instance, Ayoub (2014) reports that students who suffer from trauma find it difficult to socialise and thrive academically in schools. Stewart (2012) highlights that the experiences of students, affected by war and terrorism, are observed to be unique, and many students are reported to have suffered severe personal trauma, violence, and loss. UN reports (2016) suggest that the impact of conflict on young people cannot be estimated by statistics alone and that children suffer from long-term psychological trauma.

Internationally, researchers have paid particular attention to the issues of post-traumatic academic and social challenges of students affected by or exposed to war and terrorism. Stewart (2012) conducted a study in thirteen high schools in Manitoba, Canada, to document the post-settlement experiences of refugee students. The study revealed the likelihood of refugee students who suffer from trauma to leave the schools if their unique social and psychological needs are not met. It is also observed that besides trauma, a lack of support from school principals, administrators, staff, and teachers could further aggravate students' challenges as they struggle to transit smoothly in schools. Ratković et al. (2017) imply that this happens because at times, school leaders lack cross-cultural competencies and social justice focus in their practices.

In Pakistan, several studies have been conducted to determine the consequences of terrorism on students' learning and academic outcomes. Bilal, Inamullah, and Irshadullah (2016) conducted a study in fifty-six schools in Khyber Pakhtunkhwa, the most terrorism-affected province in Pakistan. They performed this study in several districts, including Peshawar, Kohat, Bannu, Swat, Malakand, Abbottabad, and Nowshera. The study revealed that the repeated events of terrorism make students feel unsafe and insecure. The trauma negatively impacts students' cognition and academic achievements. Moreover, students affected by terrorism feel fear which eventually leads to lower student achievement. The study also showed that repeated terrorist attacks made students intolerant, undisciplined, aggressive, and disheartened. While the academic achievements of these students substantially declined, they were reported to be least participative in extra and co-curricular school activities.

Rationale for the Study

Pakistan is the second-ranking refugee-hosting country in the world, having received more than 1.4 million refugees from Afghanistan, Bangladesh, Bosnia, Burma, and India (Rafi, 2015; Rashid, 1993). Crawford (2016) investigates that Pakistan became the most terrorist-attacked country in the world following the 9/11 incident in the United States. Moreover, Usman (2016) reports that there have been more than 850 attacks on schools and universities in Pakistan since 1970. This implies that Pakistani schools embrace diversity, comprising students affected by war and terrorism, as well as students who are marginalised due to disabilities, ethnicity, or socio-economic status. To make students, who come from marginalised families, thrive in the classroom, the school leaders must understand the challenges of the past traumatic experiences of their students. Researchers agree that the trauma of war and terrorism affects the cognition, social behaviours, and psychology of the affected children, and leads them to low academic achievements (Bilal, Inamullah, & Irshadullah, 2016). Moreover, due to psychological isolation, students consider themselves as outsiders (Kilbride, Murphy, & Paul, 2003; Oxman-Martinez & Choi, 2014; Oxman-Martinez et al., 2012; Stewart, 2012).

School leaders can support these vulnerable groups of students to overcome their social, psychological, and academic challenges by making their schools inclusive and equitable (Ahmed, 2018). However, in terms of policy and practice, the education policies in Pakistan do not guide school leaders to effectively address the challenges of having children in their schools that are affected by war and terrorism. The NEP (2009, 2017) recognises that Pakistan has been affected by terrorism, but it does not provide guidelines to school leaders as to how to support students who are affectees of such unfortunate situations. Nor are there any special training programmes for the teachers and school leaders to manage such situations and make their schools inclusive for their students. This study, therefore, intends to contribute to the existing body of knowledge about the way school leadership can meet the challenges of war and terrorism affected children's inclusive education. The study will help to develop more awareness among different education stakeholders and policymakers about the issues and the way of handling these human tragedies.

SIGNIFICANCE OF THE STUDY

In the context of forced migration due mainly to terrorism or war, increased diversity, and multiculturalism in schools, this study contributes to the existing body of literature. The recommendations made in this chapter have implications for policy, theory, and practice. The implications suggest improvements in existing educational policies concerning the issues of children affected by war and terrorism, by considering the UN's policy guidelines on equity and inclusion in schools and by developing cross-cultural learning partnerships to mobilise knowledge across the globe.

Besides, this study reveals the evolving role of school leaders in bringing students, their families, and teachers closer, especially the students who have suffered the trauma of war or terrorism. The study further suggests that educational leaders can make schools more inclusive and enabling spaces for students by employing Bronfenbrenner's (1999) bio-ecological model of human development (discussed below) within and across schools, countries, and cross-cultural contexts. The study will add to the existing literature on the much-needed subject of how to support war and terrorism affected students in different settings.

RESEARCH QUESTIONS

1. What are the current practices of the Pakistani school leaders of dealing with war and terrorism affected children as revealed in the literature?
2. What guidance does the National Education Policy (NEP) provide to school principals about the students affected by war and terrorism?
3. How can cross-cultural educational partnership between Canada and Pakistan help school principals to strengthen their leadership practices in supporting students affected by war and terrorism?

CONCEPTUAL FRAMEWORK

This study is positioned within Bronfenbrenner's (1999) bioecological model of child development to examine the role of school leaders in supporting students affected by war and terrorism. For the past few years, researchers and educators have paid particular attention to this model to understand the underpinnings of child development. Some researchers, such as Stewart (2012) in Canada, have used this framework to conceptualise the relationship of refugee students with their surroundings as they transit into schools. Similarly, Hirani (2014) in Pakistan has used this framework to identify the connection between vulnerable children living in disaster camps and their surroundings. Considering the complexity of the relationship between students affected by war and terrorism and their surroundings, Bronfenbrenner's (1999) model of child development hypothesises the importance of school leadership in bridging gaps between students and their families with teachers, school, and community. The purpose of using the biological model of child development as the conceptual framework is first to conceptualise and then to illustrate the relationship of a child with his environment. According to Bronfenbrenner's (1999) bio-ecological model, child development is a set of complex interactions between multiple stakeholders and environments:

> [Child development] is a pattern of activities, social roles, and interpersonal relations experienced by the developing person in a given face-to-face setting with physical, social and symbolic features that invite, permit or inhibit engagement in sustained more complex interaction progressively with, and activity in, the immediate environment. Examples include such settings as the family, school, peer group, and workplace. (Bronfenbrenner, 1999: 39)

Originally, the bio-ecological model proposed by Bronfenbrenner (1999) constituted several layers representing various individuals or groups that a child interacts with in his lifetime. These entwined layers work with each other and consist of the microsystem, mesosystem, exosystem, macrosystem, and chronosystem. Positioned at the core, a child first interacts with the inner-most layer, the microsystem, represented by parents, immediate family members, and teachers and friends at school. The next interacting layer is the mesosystem, which is exemplified as a connection between the microsystem and the exosystem layers; it also reflects the influence of these individuals on a child. The people in this layer, however, are the same, including parents, teachers, and friends. The next layer is the exosystem, which comprises people from extended groups, such as friends of the family, social agencies, and workplaces.

The final layer in this model is the macrosystem, which represents the community and its culture, norms, and values that have a direct influence on an individual.

Variations to the Bio-ecological Model

Since the onset of this theory, researchers, scholars, and educators have used this model to explain the relationship of a child with the surroundings. In the context of forced migration, some researchers have paid attention to this model to propose a framework for school leaders to understand child development. Stewart (2012), for instance, uses Bronfenbrenner's (1999) bio-ecological model to suggest how a school could be used as a safe space to support refugee students. In her proposed model, Stewart (2012) introduced the nanosystem which exists between a student and the microsystem. This system comprises people who take time and personal interest 'to connect with the student and who exhibit perseverance, patience, and kindness' (p. 184). Stewart emphasises that, contrary to the relative nature of the microsystem, the nanosystem is more interpersonal and positions its members uniquely to foster diversity, equity, and social justice within schools and the communities. She underscores that the member who create a nanosystem is one who supports and cares for the individual and 'who fosters their development, and makes a marked difference in the outcomes of their lives' (p. 185). In the proposed model, Stewart further identifies the existence of a chronosystem transecting all the layers within the model. This horizontal 'chronosystem refers to the changes in an environment that occur over the time that the individual lives. These developmental changes are triggered by life events or experiences' (p. 174). Johnson (2010) extended the scope of Bronfenbrenner's (1999) bio-ecological model and recognised the presence of another layer within this model. She named this layer as the ecological techno-subsystem, located between the child and the microsystem (Figure 7.1). Johnson hypothesised this subsystem as the influence of Information and Communications Technology (ICTy), electronic media, innovations, and innovative pedagogies in teaching and learning, which supports student learning and cognition.

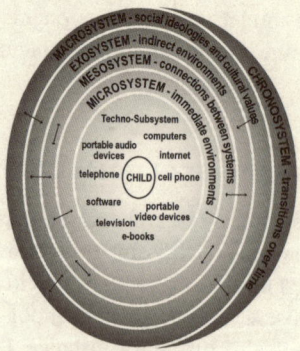

Figure 7.1. Techno-Subsystem in the Bio-ecological Model of Child Development.

The bio-ecological model of child development, as modified by Johnson and Puplumpu (2008: 178).

Birman (2011) also recognises that given increased globalisation, a global perspective should be added to the model using a world lens to highlight the interconnects of countries and emphasise that whatever happens in one country directly or indirectly affects other countries. She argues:

> These factors must be understood not only on the 'Macro' level of Bronfenbrenner's model but from a global perspective that is now an increasingly important, more significant level of analysis. Increasingly we live in a worldwide network where what happens in one country affects what happens in another. (p. 342)

Expanding on the ideal of globalisation and global citizenship, she further proposed a 'community psychology perspective' to facilitate school leaders to understand the cultural complexities of affected students and their families. Applying a community psychology perspective to immigration issues serves as a conceptual antidote to an over-individualistic perspective of traditional cross-cultural research. The diversity and complexity of immigration in the context of diverse sending and receiving countries helps push theories articulated within community of psychology to extend to increasingly varied situations.

Hirani (2014) conducted a study in Pakistan to examine the vulnerability of internally displaced children in disaster relief camps. The author proposed changes in the original bio-ecological model to support vulnerable children living in relief camps during the events of disaster and humanitarian emergencies. They include the homeless, having missing family members, and those experiencing severe trauma. In her proposed model, Hirani used a microsystem as comprising healthcare professionals and educators, a mesosystem representing the community workers, and an exosystem of government and non-government agencies. Hirani (2014) created a link between all these stakeholders within the model and suggested a child-care programme in the microsystem to support these vulnerable children to recover from trauma.

Methodology

This study is based on a systematic policy and literature review on the role of school leadership in supporting students affected by war and terrorism in Pakistan. The policy documents reviewed for this chapter include Pakistan's educational policies as well as various policy documents and frameworks outlined by the UN and its partner organisations, whereas, the literature review consists of literature on the role of school leaders in Pakistan supporting students affected by war and terrorism, as well as on Bronfenbrenner's model which is used by researchers to understand the child development and its relationship with the surroundings and people.

Policy Documents Review

Between January and March 2018, I used online databases namely ERIC, JSTOR, and Brock University Library's Super Search. The policy review included Pakistan's education policies as well as UN's policy papers, documents, and reports pertinent to education and its related initiatives. I reviewed the websites and various internet links of the UN, UNICEF, UNESCO, UNHCR, and the World Bank for the following keywords: children's right to education; universal education; equity and inclusion in education; education for the less privileged; and refugee and asylum seekers' education. I reviewed policy documents on Inclusion in Education, vision 2030, the UN Charter of Human Rights and Freedoms and various other reports, and frameworks related to the following keywords: education; inclusive education; refugee children; education for less privileged or children living in vulnerable situations; and education in developing countries. The rationale behind this research was to understand the global policies and strategies adopted by policy-makers and implemented by school leaders in Pakistan. To sum up, I selected eighteen documents that directly or indirectly discuss education, school, leadership, and children affected by war and terrorism.

National Education Policies

I reviewed Pakistan's educational policies developed by the Federal Ministry of Education (MOE), including the National Action Plan (2009), Achieving Universal Quality Primary Education in Pakistan (MOE, 2013), and the National Educational Policy (MOE, 2009, 2017, 2018). The intention was, first, to ensure that the policymakers recognise refugee and terrorism affected students as a part of student population in the public schools. Secondly, to know if the education policies and frameworks highlight any strategies for school leaders as they support war and terrorism affected students to transit into schools and become resilient. The protocols to conduct this policy review were adopted from Rogers et al. (2005). While reviewing the policy documents, I also looked for policy guidelines that could inform school leaders to implement inclusive leadership practices to support those vulnerable students who encounter marginalisation and stigmatisation in schools. I then developed an annotated bibliography that included all the policy documents I selected.

Online Database Literature Review

Between January to March 2018, I searched three online databases. The purpose of selecting three databases was to ensure the depth and breadth of available literature on the topic. The first database I used was the ERIC database with full terms/tags such as: school leaders supporting refugee students in Pakistan. This search resulted in eight articles, and I selected six articles from this search. These six articles were focused on the challenges of students affected by terrorism in Pakistan. The second database I used for searching was JSTOR. I used key terms, such as 'terrorism-affected students', 'school Principals', and 'Pakistan'. I also used the tag 'school leaders supporting terrorism affected students in Pakistan'. This search did not yield any results. I subsequently changed the key terms from 'school leaders' to 'school Principals' and used 'terrorism' instead of 'terrorism-affected students'. This search generated four results, and I included all the four articles in this review. I further changed key terms and used 'refugee children', 'education', and 'Pakistan'. This search generated six articles and I selected three articles for inclusion in the literature review. Lastly, I used the Brock University Library's Super Search tool to find more articles using the same tags. It returned seven articles, three of which were already mentioned in the earlier searches. I selected two from this search. In total, I selected fifteen articles and a book to develop my literature review. I developed a bibliography of all the selected documents to identify the emerging themes and gaps in the existing literature. Finally, I conducted a systematic literature review on the conceptual framework of Bronfenbrenner. I searched for key terms such as 'Bronfenbrenner bio-ecological model', 'children', 'and refugee students' education'. I reviewed books, journal articles, major research papers, and theses that focus on the role of school leadership in supporting students affected by war and terrorism. I also reviewed articles discussing Bronfenbrenner's (1999) bio-ecological model of child development. Lastly, I examined articles that discuss international and global educational partnerships, specifically those partnerships emphasizing collaboration in education between developed and developing countries, such as Canada and Pakistan. To briefly explain the outcomes of systematic policy and literature review, I use Table 7.1 to demonstrate the number and description of the documents used in this study.

Table 7.1: Reviewed Literature and Policy

Total Literature Reviewed	N = 62
Books reviewed	N = 02
Empirical articles	N = 15
Conceptual framework related articles	N = 15
Newspaper and website articles	N = 08
UN Policy guidelines	N = 02
UN Charter and reports	N = 18
Pakistan educational policies	N = 02

FINDINGS: POLICY RELATED DOCUMENTS

Pakistan is an active member of the United Nations and its partnering organisations such as the United Nations Educational, Scientific and Cultural Organisation (UNESCO), the United Nations International Children's Emergency Fund (UNICEF), and United Nations High Commissioner for Refugees (UNHCR). Pakistan is also a signatory to the UN's Sustainable Development Goals (SDG 4.2). Pakistan's education policies were developed by adopting Sustainable Development Goals (SDG) objectives, incorporating the overdue Education for All (EFA) and Millennium Development Goals (MDGs). The NEP vows to fulfil states' 'International Commitments', which refers to the enactment of the Convention on the Rights of the Child (CRC) and to 'child development including their education and health' (p. 28). The NEP (2017, 2018) also aims to achieve SDG 4.2 by 2030, which primarily focuses on providing an inclusive and equitable education to everyone and 'ensure inclusive and equitable quality education and promote lifelong learning opportunities for all' (UNESCO, 2015b: 7).

Moreover, UNESCO's (2015b) vision for 2030 includes education policy guidance, which is equally useful for developed and developing countries. These guidelines also accentuate the importance of developing equitable and inclusive schools and closing the out of school ratio, stating, 'By 2030, ensure that all girls and boys have access to quality early childhood development, care, and pre-primary education so that they are ready for primary education' (p. 28). Following the lead, the NEP promises to provide equal opportunities of education to every child and embraces these guidelines by stating that 'the main idea behind inclusive education is to offer equal opportunities of learning to all children in an inclusive environment and eliminate discrimination based on gender, economic status of parents, and diversity in physical features and mental aptitudes' (p. 117).

The NEP (2017) recognises that Pakistan is 'currently facing formidable internal security and acts of terrorism…and war-like emergency prevails' (p. 157). Consequently, the policy suggests the reinforcement of the National Cadet Corps (NCC) scheme and aims to provide civil defence training to the youth as well as improvements in its curriculum. These objectives are highlighted as under:

1. Civil defence training
2. Rescue & relief in disaster situations (p. 159)
3. Elementary serving and surveillance duties
4. Assisting in traffic management during emergency situations
5. Basic life-skills related to health rehabilitation
6. Skill in rowing during floods/torrential rain-fall (p. 158)

Apart from this initiative, there is, as such, no mention of any strategies or guidance as to how war and terrorism affected students can be supported in schools. In the context of policy-making and implementation, little has been accomplished and minimal guidance is provided to school leaders. Although Pakistan's existing National Education Policy (2009, 2017) aims to make schools inclusive and equitable, it doesn't provide much guidance to school leaders as to how equity and inclusion could be enacted in schools (Ali, 2014).

FINDINGS: FROM LITERATURE ABOUT SCHOOL LEADERSHIP

The findings of the study respond to the inquiry posed by the research questions. The results suggest that although the role of school leaders is documented as the heads of schools, their role in supporting students affected by war and terrorism is not fully explored. Findings from the policy and literature review are further discussed in this section. It is pertinent to mention that only those findings are included in this section which have been cited by at least three different authors.

SCHOOL PRINCIPALS' SUPPORT TO THEIR TEACHERS

The role of school principals is perceived as support to the school teachers. Nooruddin and Baig (2014) emphasise that school leaders are seen as critical support for teachers. Rizvi (2008) states that teachers respect and trust the authority vested in the role of school leadership; teachers anticipate school principals to help them improve their professional skills through professional training programmes and workshops. Teachers also agree that the teaching and learning culture within the school is cultivated by school leaders, which eventually influences the behaviour of staff, teachers, and students. Solangi (2016) highlights that teachers value the feedback provided by the school principals. It contributes towards their job satisfaction and motivates them towards improving instructional and teaching pedagogies. Finally, Bilal, Inamullah, and Irshadullah (2016) note that teachers highly value school principals' frequent visits to their classroom, which enables them to discipline students' behaviour.

LITERATURE REVIEW: ROLE OF SCHOOL LEADERSHIP IN SUPPORTING STUDENTS AFFECTED BY WAR AND TERRORISM

Contemporary literature can be inspirational to school leaders and could guide them to enact leadership praxis in Pakistan's public schools. However, the present findings reveal a visible gap within the existing body of literature on the role of school leadership in supporting students affected by war and terrorism (Ahmed, 2018). While the current research delves into the challenges of students affected by conflict and terrorism, there is less attention paid to the role of school leadership as to how they support these students to overcome their post-traumatic challenges and achieve high academics. For instance, Bilal et al. (2016) claim that the perennial incidences of terrorism psychologically affect the cognition of students. Another study conducted at the Army Public School in Khyber Pakhtunkhwa after the unfortunate terrorist attack on 16 December 2014 suggests that the students and children in the entire province of KPK suffered from socio-psychological challenges (Durrani et al., 2017). Waheed and Ahmad (2012) conducted a study to identify the impact of terrorism on the socio-economic status of affected families and observe that there is a possibility that children exposed to terrorism experience PTSD. The available literature, however, does not highlight the role of school leadership in supporting students affected by war and terrorism.

School Leadership Challenges

It is essential to study the challenges which limit the potential of school leaders in practicing leadership praxis. Memon (2010) informs us that, in terms of policy and practice, there is not much attention paid to the capacity building of public school leaders (p. 284). Mansoor and Akhtar (2015) and Rizvi (2008) highlight that school leaders are provided with limited financial funding and human resource. Lack of robust infrastructure and school facilities escalate the school leaderships' challenges. Bahadur et al. (2017) highlight that, due to limited financial funding, school leaders hesitate to introduce innovative and creative activities in schools, such as holding extracurricular activities to improve students' engagement. The findings also reveal that public school leadership is challenged by excessive workloads and lack of resources and infrastructure. They further iterate that, due to lack of human resources, school leaders are overburdened with workload and management responsibilities.

Lack of Professional Training Opportunities

The findings of this study suggest that there are limited training and professional development and learning opportunities available to school leaders (Memon, 2010). Drawing on the findings of a comparative study, Khan et al. (2015) observe a 'top-down bureaucratic model' prevalent in public schools in Pakistan. They also note that the selection of 'headteachers' is based on seniority, instead of qualifications or leadership potential. Shafa (2010) mentions that the adoption of headteachers' roles without any formal training obstructs their leadership practices, which eventually leads to inadequate school management skills. He further asserts that most school leadership challenges emerge due to a lack of 'knowledge, skills, and motivation to work as school developers' (p. 83). Mansoor and Akhtar (2015) highlight that there are very few principal preparation programmes available for newly appointed school principals, as their roles change from teachers to headteachers or principals. Bahadur, Bano, Waheed, and Wahab (2017) also observe that the NEP proposes training and professional development programmes for the teacher, while only a few suggestions are made to provide professional training to the school principals, which reveals the level of policy-makers interest in the capacity building and professional development of school leaders.

Lack of Focus on Parental Engagement

It is also evident from the review that there is minimal scholarly attention paid to parental engagement in Pakistan's public schools—more specifically, to families from terrorism or other marginalised groups. According to the NEP (2017), ignorance and illiteracy are more prevalent 'among peasants, labourers, ethnic, linguistic and religious minorities, nomads, persons with disabilities, and prisoners' (p. 34). Moreover, the policy does not recognise that for terrorism affected students to integrate smoothly in schools, their parents must get engaged in their schools. Siddiqui and Gorard (2017) note that in Pakistan, the social and financial status of parents plays an influential role in parental engagement. They note that, due to ignorance, parents from low social income backgrounds do not consider education as a necessity and hesitate to enrol their children, especially girls, in schools. Such parents are hardly participative in schools. They also observe that parents' active participation in schools help their children to thrive academically. Besides, parental disengagement in their children's schooling demotivates teachers. Shafa (2010) observes that teachers also become frustrated due to 'a lack of support from the parents' (p. 91).

Lack of Cross-cultural and International Collaborations

Finally, the findings of this study suggest that the prospects of international collaboration between developed and developing countries are not given much attention. The literature review highlight various successful international projects that are run in Pakistan, in conjunction with partners and international organisations. For instance, the study suggests that, in Pakistan, Canada has assisted with projects such as *Internally Displaced* or *Conflict-Affected Persons*. There have been a few projects which are in progress with the support of the World Bank, such as, *Pakistan: Increasing Access and Quality through Education Reforms in Punjab* (The World Bank, 2016). However, the literature on Pakistan's collaborations with other countries and international organisations is rare.

The findings from the policy and literature suggest that although the NEP (2017) recognises the state (of Pakistan) to be affected by terrorism, there is, as such, no policy guidance provided to the school leaders to support these students as they transit into schools.

Implications for Policy

The NEP promises to make schools inclusive and equitable. There is a visible gap in the policy formulation and implementation concerning supporting students affected by war and terrorism. In such a context, the strategic policy guidelines outlined by UNESCO's (2015b) for Vision 2030 offer key directions that are relevant to the meaning of learning in Pakistan. These guidelines imply that the ideology of educational policies should be grounded in providing social justice, inclusion, and equity in schools. That said, policy-makers, as they frame policies, should consider students' parents as one of the key stakeholders whose engagement could greatly benefit their children in the classroom. Additionally, cross-sectoral and intercultural policies should be implemented to promote inclusion and equity in schools. The educational policies should reflect the voices and expectations of all the stakeholders in education, including school leaders, teachers, students, and their families. To make schools more enabling places for teachers, students, and their parents, school leaders should foster parent engagement in the academic, physical, and mental well-being of their children. Hands (2013) argues that the commitment of parents plays a vital role in the academic, physical, and mental well-being of students; however, poverty and diversity prevent parents from participating actively in schools for their children. In one of the studies, Hands (2013) sets out strategies that promoted parental involvement in schools in Ontario, Canada. Although the recommendations were contextual to Ontario, some of these strategies apply to public schools in Pakistan. For instance, Hands suggests that parents should be provided free of charge training, workshops, and speaker sessions to initiate a relationship between parents and teachers, and to establish a home-school collaboration. School leaders can take initiatives to develop such activities in their schools. Such strategies have the potential to make schools more welcoming for parents from disadvantaged families and at the same time, will help to improve gender disparity, decreasing enrolment, and the drop-out ratio in public schools.

The United Nations (2009) policy guidelines emphasise inclusion with a special reference to the role of school leaders in developing inclusive policies and initiatives. Khan (2010) suggests that a school leader is the 'most influential person' who inspires the students (p. 147). Whereas, Khaki (2010) argues that school leadership plays a vital role in making 'schools better places for learning and teaching' (p. 105). The results of this study also reveal that the role of school leaders is vital in bringing together all educational stakeholders, including policy-makers, teachers, students, their families, and their communities. Learning opportunities should be provided to school leaders to reflect on the existing practices in groups with peers. School leaders' capacity building should be enhanced by offering them professional development training and by encouraging them to participate in local, national, and international forums. There should be a transparent mechanism to reward competent and qualified school leaders. Moreover, school leaders should be held accountable for the performance of their schools, staff, and students. To that end, indicators to judge school performance should be adopted using a mechanism that does not overly stress the mental well-being of the school principals.

IMPLICATIONS FOR THEORY

So far, the study has not come across any theoretical framework for studying war and terrorism affected students from the local context or even from developing countries. But developing a framework to approach this issue is a strong imperative. In my study of the issue, however, I have found a significant and comprehensive conceptual framework which may be followed in future studies; policymakers can use it to give training to leaders and teachers, and school leaders can use it as a framework for their schools to work with all stakeholders concerned. This conceptual framework is Bronfenbrenner's (1999) bio-ecological model of child development. This model has the potential to provide a framework for school leaders to support students affected by war and terrorism as they transit into their schools. It divulges the role school leaders could play in bringing together different stakeholders from each layer. I conceptualise Bronfenbrenner's bio-ecological model as hypothesised by other researchers and maintain the variations of the nanosystem, chronosystem, and techno-subsystem as advocated by Stewart (2012), Johnson (2010), and Birman (2011).

However, I identify the existence of a globosystem within this model (Figure 7.2). Expanding on what Birman (2011) refers to as an 'increasingly global world' (p. 342), this globosystem is a representation of the global changes which have a direct or indirect social, political, economic, and environmental influence across the globe. Captured in the globosystem, the other systems or layers of the bio-ecological systems work within as well as connect through the technosystem. In this proposed model the nanosystem represents the network of those close people who support students affected by war and terrorism. The functioning of the rest of the bio-ecological systems remains the same, except that the chronosystem and the technosystem are parallel systems that intersect through each layer of the bio-ecological model (see Figure 7.2). It is significant to note here that the chronosystem, as described by Stewart (2012), epitomises the constant changes within and outside of the bio-ecological system. The technosystem conceptualised by Johnson (2010), symbolises the ICTy and electronic media that provide a connection between different bio-ecological models. School leaders can connect with other stakeholders in education, nationally and internationally, by using the technosystem, which in this model runs parallel to the chronosytem, and embodies the ongoing changes in our inner and outer worlds. In this proposed model, the technosystem offers a virtual platform based on information and computer technology that could connect the educational stakeholders within and outside of the bio-ecological models inside the globosystem.

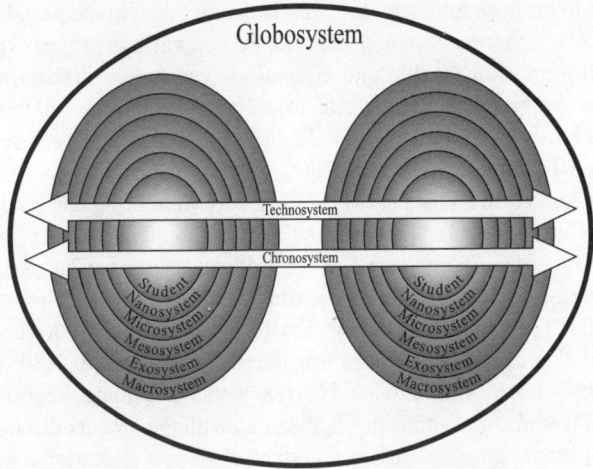

Figure 7.2. Proposed Changes in the Bronfenbrenner's (1999) Bio-ecological Model of Child Development.

IMPLICATIONS FOR PRACTICE

As the findings reveal, there are minimal guidance and learning opportunities available to Pakistani public school leaders to improve on their existing leadership practices. In such circumstances, collaborative partnerships in education can be instrumental in strengthening the capacity building of local school leaders. Sider (2014) studied the outcomes of the Digital Mentoring Project (DMP), which was aimed to develop an educational partnership between the school principals of Canada and Haiti. This project has helped to strengthen the capacity building of the two countries' school principals. Sider (2014) reports that the DMP helped the twenty participants from both countries to develop a professional learning environment, which enabled them to exchange their local knowledge and enhance their existing skills and build capacities.

Given cross-cultural partnerships, such as Canada and Haiti, intercultural cooperation could also be developed between Canada and Pakistan, as Canadian schools are multicultural, diverse, and consist of students who, in their past lives, have suffered traumas due to the events of either war or terrorism. The school leaders' challenges are, therefore, similar as they strive to make these students resilient. The rationale to propose such a partnership is the fact that, in the past, Canada and Pakistan have successfully collaborated on various projects relating to global migration, health, and education. The policy-makers in both countries are familiar and willing to collaborate. These collaborative projects between Canada and Pakistan are Assistance to Internally Displaced People in Pakistan (2009, 2010); Assistance to Conflict-Affected Persons in Pakistan (2011, 2012); and Monitoring and Evaluation of Debt Conversion for Education (2004-2018). The Monitoring and Evaluation of Debt Conversation for Education project, in particular, is a bilateral collaborative project run by the Global Affairs Agency in Canada. The goal of this project is to improve education quality in Pakistan. The initiative involves transferring Pakistan's official debt to Canada ($449.6 million) into local currency, thus providing the provincial and federal education authorities in Pakistan with the proceeds to improve skills of primary and elementary school teachers and education managers (Government of Canada, 2017).

A cross-cultural partnership in education, with particular reference to war and terrorism affected children, between Canada and Pakistan can be beneficial for the two countries and could generate enormous opportunities and prospects for educational stakeholders in both countries. Sider (2014) notes that these partnerships serve as a learning community to exchange professional and personal experiences and ideas. A cross-cultural collaboration can also raise people's awareness of similar situations or challenges. It can serve as a platform for participants to share their local knowledge and personal experiences, generating more perspectives and expertise. The participants can learn from the experience, contexts, challenges, and successes of each other. Contextual to this study, global partnerships like these could generate more excellent knowledge and resources for school leaders working with war and terrorism-affected students worldwide, including school leaders in both developed and developing countries.

Conclusion

Although the literature shows few references to the study of war and terrorism affected education and the role of school leaders in it, whatever the study found suggests that school leaders can support students affected by conflict and terrorism by making their schools inclusive. Schools can successfully create safe spaces where children can express their concerns and feelings and discuss shared experiences in a respectful environment.

The education authorities need to take cognizance of the policy guidelines of the UN on inclusion and equity as a model for multicultural schools and to inspire school leaders who seek to make their schools equitable and inclusive. As global dynamics are changing, schools and classrooms are becoming more and more multicultural and diverse, demanding a more holistic approach to teaching and learning; schools need to make a paradigm shift from an exclusive to a more inclusive environment. School leaders and teachers can adopt such holistic approaches by considering Bronfenbrenner's Bio-ecological Theory of Child Development (1999), which provides a broader framework to make the educational offering more inclusive and comprehensive.

This chapter has examined the complexities around the role of school leadership in Pakistan in supporting students affected by war and terrorism. While most of the available literature on the topic focuses on the experiences of war and terrorism affected students, this chapter sheds light on the emerging role of school leaders, their challenges, and the ways their capacity building could be further enriched. The study goes a step still further. It suggests bilateral collaborations between and among countries affected by war and terrorism and recommends sharing with and benefitting from lessons learned in this regard, such as those between Pakistan and Canada and beyond. This chapter, in short, flags a highly relevant subject and concern of our times as it affects millions of children and their families that have been unfortunately affected by the messy problem of war and terrorism.

8

School Improvement Leadership: Lessons Learnt in the Mountainous Region of Gilgit-Baltistan

MOLA DAD SHAFA AND SHARIFULLAH BAIG

INTRODUCTION

This chapter reports the development and progression of teacher leadership through a comprehensive, integrated, and consortium-based school improvement project known as Educational Development and Improvement Programme (EDIP). It specifically highlights the role of teachers as the leaders to drive and navigate the dynamics of EDIP school improvement model in the targeted public sector schools of Gilgit-Baltistan (GB), Pakistan. In fact, the EDIP school improvement model benefited from the research work and school improvement interventions across the globe (e.g. Datnow & Castelano, 2001; Ertesvag, 2014; Hannay, Ross & Seller, 2005; Sarason, 2002; Shachar, Gavin & Shlomo, 2009), gaining key insights on instructional methods, community involvement, organisational structures of schools, management and governance, and the physical and educational environment of schools. More specifically EDIP intervention focused on improving teacher capacities and practices (Fullan, 2007), enhancing teacher collaboration and a collaborative culture (Waldron & McLeskey, 2010), developing the school as a learning organisation (Senge, 2006), strengthening professional learning communities (Stoll, 2009; Wahlstrom & Louis, 2008), and developing a sense of shared purpose and collective responsibility for student learning (Lomos et al., 2011). However, what repeatedly emanated from the intervention was that teacher leadership was the key driving force influencing and determining what goes on in schools; it was, in fact, a prerequisite for enhancing students' learning achievements (Harris, 2002).

Teachers were the engine to drive the EDIP school improvement initiatives in and outside the classroom by meaningfully contributing to the learning of other teachers and influencing others to adopt improved practices (Katzenmeyer & Moller, 2001). Before embarking upon the study's findings about teacher leadership, it is pertinent to give a comprehensive background and nature of the EDIP intervention around which this study was carried out. The subsequent section gives a detailed account of the aim, nature, and modalities of the EDIP intervention.

Educational Development and Improvement Programme (EDIP) Project

The Australian-Aid (AusAID)-sponsored EDIP considered a cluster-based school improvement approach to facilitate teachers, school community, and students to help and learn from each other in the clusters. The EDIP school improvement cluster includes 4–5 schools, working in close proximity, with a centrally located secondary school as the learning resource school (LRS) and the remaining working as the feeding schools for the cluster. Collectively, the entire cluster is considered as a unit of change and development. The education related component of the EDIP project was implemented by a school-based change facilitator (i.e. a PDCN Faculty), also called a professional development teacher (PDT), who facilitated and worked with the headteachers, teachers, the local level institutions (LLIs), e.g. school management committees (SMCs), mother support groups (MSGs), and the school communities in identifying school improvement needs, developing the school development plans (SDPs), and implementing the SDPs to achieve the school improvement goals. In addition to PDCN, there were several other AKDN specialist organisations working as auxiliary partners to contribute to the cause of EDIP schools. For instance, the Aga Khan Planning and Building Services (AKPBS) identified and addressed the infrastructure related issues of retrofitting and repair and maintenance, the FOCUS Humanitarian Assistance contributed to raising school communities awareness of disaster reduction and management; the Network of Organisations Working with People with Disability in Pakistan (NOWPDP) helped teachers and parents understand the need and approaches to mainstream the education of children with mild to moderate disability; while the Civil Society Resource Center (CSRC) formed and reformed the local level institutions and, through the LLIs, mobilised parents and the wider community to garner their support for schools.

The EDIP Project aimed at 'enhancing access, equity and quality of education with increased gender parity, participation and sustainability of community involvement', so that the overall socioeconomic development in the region is supported. The EDIP objectives were:

- Enhancing gender parity and access to and quality of education in schools;
- Improving quality and relevance of education in schools; and
- Strengthening governance and management of the Department of Education of Gilgit-Baltistan (DoE GB) in targeted districts.

Based on the integrated and holistic nature of the EDIP model, comprehensive planning was done to work with various stakeholders, including teachers, parents, and SMCs/MSGs to achieve the programme goals. School communities' motivation, their viewpoints and attitudes, therefore, determined the degree of success in achieving the objective of enroling the out-of-school children in the project schools and in seeking their ongoing support to the cause of school improvement. In this exciting EDIP journey, teachers, amongst the other stakeholders, emerged as the key players as they acted as linchpins connecting schools, their social environments, and the project intervention team. Therefore, a research study was planned and conducted to explore the perceptions and perspectives of the teachers at the initial stages as well as towards the conclusion of the EDIP project to gain insights on:

1. Change of teachers' perceptions and perspectives on their role as the leaders in educational processes between the initial and culminating stages of the EDIP Project;
2. EDIP's success in influencing the community perceptions related to teachers on their role as the leaders in education of the children;
3. The efficacy of approaches employed by various change facilitators in the project; and
4. The nature of forming and reforming of teachers' perceptions and perspectives by the EDIP project.

Hence, the study was guided by the major question: To what extent and how did the AusAID-sponsored EDIP project influence teacher perceptions and perspectives about their role as the leaders in children's education in the targeted schools of Gilgit-Baltistan of Pakistan? However, this chapter reports only the 'to what extent' part of the question.

Perceptions

Perception is commonly referred to as the ability to see, hear, or become aware through the application of human senses. In other words, perception implies the process of acquiring, interpreting, selecting, and analysing sensory information. According to Schunk (2000), perception is the process of attaching personal meanings to internal and environmental inputs received through the senses and neural impulses. This means that individuals evaluate people with whom they are familiar in their everyday life. Eggen and Kauchak (2001) explicate the cognitive dimension of perception, which is considered as the process by which people attach meaning to their experiences. They note that, when human beings attend to certain stimuli in their sensory memories, they start processing with perception. Their analysis shows that perception is critical because it influences the information that enters the working memory. While exploring the factors, Vygotsky (1978) argues, certain factors such as customs, habits, education, and motivation influence the perceptions of people. Moreover, in his view, perceptions are influenced by cultural and historical factors. Hence, perception is a person's internal understanding of situations based on his or her personal experiences, which get influenced and shaped by several factors including the specific context. Therefore, perception can be considered as a driving force of one's action and a strong source shaping beliefs and attitudes.

Teacher Leadership

Due to the pivotal roles teachers enact in the processes of teaching and learning, a collection of research studies has identified and discussed the notion of 'teacher leadership'. According to Katzenmeyer and Moller (2001), teacher leaders are willing to lead improvement endeavours in and outside the classroom; they meaningfully contribute to the learning of other teachers and always remain ready to influence others for improved practices. In this connection, Katzenmeyer and Moller (2001) forwarded three distinctive facets of teacher leadership, including (i) leadership of students or other teachers, (ii) leadership in operational tasks, and (iii) leadership through decision-making or partnership. Leadership of students or other teachers refers to the role of teacher as the facilitator, coach, mentor, trainer, and curriculum specialist. Leadership in operational tasks is concerned with the role of the teacher as a goal achiever, action researcher, and a member of task forces. Finally, leadership through decision-making or partnership points towards the role of the teacher as a member of school improvement teams, member of committees, and a member of parent-teacher associations.

Harris (2002) suggests four visible dimensions of the teacher leadership role. The first dimension is the teachers' perceptions and the ways in which they translate principles of school improvement in the classroom context and their role in ensuring the opportunities of meaningful development for all teachers. The second dimension focuses on the role of teachers in ensuring a school culture where all teachers feel part of the change process. The third dimension refers to the role of the teacher as a source of expertise and information. Finally, the fourth dimension focuses on the role of the teacher as a cooperative member of the mutual learning team with other fellow teachers. Therefore, exploring teacher perceptions and perspectives particularly related to their multiple leadership roles is an increasingly important area in a school improvement journey. In line with the three distinctive facets of Katzenmeyer and Moller (2001) and the four visible dimensions of Harris (2002), this study sought to explore the change of perceptions of teachers about their role as leaders in the EDIP intervention. The change of perceptions was explored in the areas of their role in ensuring a collaborative school culture, acting as the source of expertise and information, their role as a cooperative member of the mutual learning team, and their leadership in operational tasks and decision-making.

Teachers' Perceptions about Education

Teachers have a significant impact on student achievement. They directly affect how students learn, what they learn, how much they learn, and the ways they interact with one another and with the world around them. Student learning is directly affected by teacher perceptions of their students' subject matter (Helwig, Anderson & Tindal, 2001) and social proficiencies; hence, the leadership role of the teachers can have a manifold effect on student achievements. However, in some of the contexts, the lack of pre-service and in-service professional development and lack of resources hinder the leadership role of teachers for student learning. For example, Joongi, Xiong, Li, and Pan (2009) in China investigated the perceptions of parents, teachers, and students in China's Education Reform in Grades 7 and 8. The findings revealed that most teachers lacked in-service professional development and resources, especially in the rural areas. Therefore, they experienced difficulties in resolving the conflict between activity-based learning and exam-oriented systems. Similarly, in Norway, Hatlevik (2017) reported a longitudinal study to examine the connections between teachers' perceived professional competence acquired during professional preparation and later perceptions as school teachers. The results indicate that theoretical understanding plays an important role in school teachers' professional development. The prospective and practicing school teachers do not tend to perceive themselves as either good theorists or good practitioners. This perception of the teachers about themselves, lack of professional development, and lack of resources pose challenges for the teachers as leaders.

Moreover, the teacher's role in developing a safe and inviting learning environment in the school and the cultivation of a strong home-school relationship for student learning and achievement are the essential elements of teacher leadership. In many societies, teachers struggle to create an inviting and safe environment for students for various reasons. For example, in Spain, Hungary, and the Czech Republic, Linares, Díaz, Fuentes, and Acién (2009) studied and presented valuable insights on teacher perceptions about different problematic aspects including tolerance and coexistence, as well as their impact, in the school environment. The results reveal a high and frequent occurrence of fights and insults which result in demotivation in pupils. According to the teachers in these three countries, demotivation of students is seriously affecting the teachers. Similarly, in the context of Serbia, Jovanovic, Simic, and Rajovi (2014) explored teacher perceptions about students at risk, their relationships with peers, and the teachers' own roles as sources of support. The findings indicate that the students at risk from the ethnic Roma population and poor backgrounds are found to be perceived positively by their teachers. However, most teachers failed to perceive their influence on the improvement of academic performance and peer relationships. These challenges negatively influence the motivation and job satisfaction of teacher leaders. For instance, Mertler (2002) explored teacher perceptions about their overall level of job satisfaction and the extent of teacher motivation. The finding of this study indicated that male teachers reported to be more satisfied with their jobs as compared to their female counterparts.

Teachers in the early stages of their careers, as well as those nearing the ends of their careers, showed greater satisfaction as compared to mid-career teachers. The reason is that the leadership practices of teachers have a correlation with their level of job motivation. In Bangladesh, Mullick, Sharma, and Deppeler (2013) explored teacher perceptions about distributed leadership practices for inclusive education in primary schools. Their findings indicated that teacher perceptions about distributed leadership practices for inclusive education have a significant positive correlation with their satisfaction about the implementation of inclusive education policy. Therefore, teacher leadership roles are critically important and their perceptions and perspectives shape and determine the effectiveness of what and how they perform in their schools and classrooms.

In a nutshell, different researchers have explored teacher perceptions in different dimensions of teaching and learning. Hence, within the above research landscape, this study explored how and to what extent the AusAID-sponsored EDIP project influenced teacher perceptions and perspectives about their role as leaders in children's education in the targeted schools of GB. Hence, the perceptions and perspectives of teachers were focused on in the key areas of school management and administration, teacher capacity building and professional development, physical and social environment of schools, the professional goals of teachers, the notion of teacher job satisfaction, the most challenging aspects for teachers in their profession, and the teacher's classroom practices. This study employed a longitudinal research approach in data collection, before and after the EDIP intervention, to document and report changed teacher perceptions in the above key domains of teacher leadership.

RESEARCH DESIGN

Originally, this study employed a mixed method of quantitative survey and qualitative interviews. The quantitative portion of the study focused on exploring the extent to which EDIP intervention has changed the perceptions and perspectives of teachers about their leadership roles in and outside of the school environment. This survey was followed by qualitative interviews to explore how these perceptions and perspectives were reshaped. Due to the extended nature of the study, it was impossible to include both quantitative and qualitative results in one chapter. Therefore, this chapter reports only the quantitative survey results which focus only on the extent to which the perceptions and perspectives were changed.

This survey was employed to gauge the change of teacher perceptions and perspectives about their leadership roles before and after the EDIP intervention. The first round of data collection took place at the initial stages of the project (October 2011–March 2012) and the second round took place towards the end of the project (January–June 2014). It is important to note that the field-based intervention of the EDIP project had already started before the first round of data collection. This research was conceptualised at the very beginning of this EDIP project but unavoidable circumstances, such as uncertainty and anxiety on the part of the seven partners at the planning and initial intervention stage, and the different steps that the research proposal has to go through before its completion, consumed some very critical months. Consequently, the study started six months after the launch of the project. Hence, the connotation 'pre-intervention' in this study refers to the first round of data collection in which EDIP had already completed six months of its implementation and was already well known to the teachers of the targeted schools.

Therefore, the items in the survey questionnaires for both first and second rounds of data collection began with the EDIP intervention, as even at the first round of the data collection EDIP was already familiar and known to teachers for the previous six months. Secondly, the donors and the implementing partners were keen on seeing the study results, to know the performance of the EDIP project in changing the perceptions and perspectives about their role as teacher leaders, both at the initial and concluding stages of the project. Therefore, this study primarily focused on exploring the performance of EDIP in the targeted public sector schools rather than extending it to other schools for generalisation purposes.

The survey questionnaires were administered in the forty-eight schools organised in twelve clusters of the EDIP Project in GB. Each cluster consisted of four schools, i.e. one learning resource school (LRS) and three feeding schools. Altogether, there were 12 LRSs and 36 feeding schools in the EDIP Project. As all of the LRSs were high schools with a higher number of teachers and the feeding schools were primary schools with less teachers, therefore, three teachers from each LRS and two teachers from each feeding school were randomly selected for this research. Hence, a sample of 108 out of the 456 total targeted teacher population of 48 EDIP target schools in GB was selected for the research.

A specifically designed questionnaire was used for data collection. The questionnaire focused on the change of perceptions and perspectives of teachers about their leadership roles in teaching-learning processes, developing conducive learning environments in schools, teacher collaboration and team work, and relationships with students, parents, SMC members, and with the other colleague teachers. Moreover, the items were related to the content knowledge and their personal perspectives for teaching in future in relation to the objectives of the EDIP Project. Prior to piloting, the instrument was shared with experts in the field of education for content validity assessment. These experts included practitioners and scholars from AKU-IED and the participating schools. Subsequently, the questionnaire was piloted with a group of teachers in public sector schools having similar kind of learning environment to that of the targeted schools. After the final comments and feedback from experts from AKU-IED and the piloting participants, the instrument was improved and used for data collection in the field. A T-Test was employed to indicate the change of perceptions and perspectives of the teachers before and after the EDIP intervention.

Data Analysis

The initial sample size was of 108 teachers but, owing to 6 sample attritions, the data used in this analysis was from 102 teachers working in 12 government high schools and 36 middle and primary schools of Gilgit-Baltistan. In terms of their qualifications, the largest number of respondents (44.8 per cent) comprised graduates, followed by post graduates (29.5 per cent). Twenty per cent of the respondent sample was intermediate, and the lowest number (5.7 per cent) had matric/secondary level qualification.

Table 8.1: District-wise Status of Education Qualification of Sample Teachers

District	Matric/ Secondary (%)	Intermediate (%)	Graduate (%)	Post-Graduate (%)
Gilgit	33.3	19.0	14.9	12.9
Ghizar	16.7	14.3	21.3	12.9
Astore	0.0	23.8	6.4	29.0
Hunza-Nagar	0.0	9.5	23.4	16.1
Skardu	16.7	19.0	17.0	16.1
Ghanche	33.3	14.3	17.0	12.9

In terms of professional experience, 23 per cent teachers possessed 0 to 04-year experience and 26 per cent teachers had 05 to 09-year teaching experience. Likewise, 26 per cent teachers had 10 to 14-year experience, whereas 25 per cent teachers came from the experience category of 15-year and above.

Table 8.2: Experience-wise Status of the Sample Teachers

Years of Experience	Frequency	%
0–4	24	23
5–9	27	26
10–14	26	26
15–above	25	25
Total	102	100

SCHOOL MANAGEMENT AND ADMINISTRATION

Table 8.3 shows the pre- and post-intervention responses of teachers about the six statements for the school management and administration in the EDIP targeted schools. A T-Test between the responses of the pre- and post-intervention phases indicate a significant difference for re-enroling the dropped-out students ($p < 0.007$), for controlling the dropout ratios in schools ($p < 0.001$), and improving the internal monitoring and management of the project schools through teachers ($p < 0.000$).

Table 8.3: The School Management and Administration related Pre- and Post-EDIP Responses

Statements	Disagree (%)		To Some Extent Agree (%)		Fully Agree (%)		Strongly Agree (%)	
	Pre	Post	Pre	Post	Pre	Post	Pre	Post
EDIP did a lot to bring dropped-out children to school	13	5	36	31	37	39	14	25
EDIP controlled the dropout trend in the school to a visible extent	10	3	40	33	41	38	9	25

EDIP has taken effective steps to improve the quality of education in the project schools	3	0	11	17	52	45	34	38
EDIP has satisfied teachers and parents through its educational initiatives in the project schools	4	2	21	18	50	47	25	33
EDIP enabled teachers to bring visible improvements in the effective management of the project schools	4	0	29	15	50	54	17	31
EDIP has devised a fruitful mechanism of professional guidance in the project schools	1	0	15	15	46	44	38	41
Average percentage	6	1	25	21	46	45	23	33

In the categories of 'strongly agree' and 'fully agree', the average percentage responses of teachers in the post-intervention phase are higher than the responses in the pre-intervention phase. Similarly, in the categories of 'to some extent agree' and 'disagree', the average percentage responses of teachers in the post-intervention phase are lower than the responses in the pre-intervention phase.

The Social and Physical Environment of Schools

Table 8.4 shows the pre- and post-intervention teacher responses about the five areas in which the EDIP project strove to improve the social and physical environment of the targeted schools. The T-Test between the responses of pre- and post-intervention phases indicates a significant difference for providing awareness to the school management committees (SMCs), mother support groups (MSGs), and parents through teachers for school development ($p < 0.034$), in providing students, parents, and teachers awareness on natural disasters ($p < 0.004$), and the teacher-led initiatives for providing friendly environment to the children with disabilities ($p < 0.014$).

Table 8.4: The Pre- and Post-EDIP Intervention Responses Related to the Social and Physical Environment of the Schools

Aspect	Don't Know (%)		Satisfactory (%)		Good (%)		Excellent (%)	
	Pre	Post	Pre	Post	Pre	Post	Pre	Post
EDIP contributions to the professional development of teachers for whole school development	0	2	4	4	51	46	45	49
EDIP contributions to the improvement of school building including physical environment	7	4	37	32	37	42	19	23
EDIP contributions in enabling teachers to provide awareness to SMCs, MSGs, and parents for school development	3	0	24	25	50	36	23	40
EDIP contributions in providing awareness to students, parents, and teachers on natural disasters	9	4	18	10	42	42	31	45
EDIP contributions through teacher-led initiatives to provide friendly environment to children with disabilities	26	16	28	22	33	42	13	21
Average percentages	9	5.2	22.2	18.6	42.6	40.6	26.2	35.6

Capacity Building and Professional Development of Teachers

Table 8.5 shows the pre- and post-intervention teacher responses about the thirteen statements for the capacity building and professional development of teachers in the EDIP schools.

Table 8.5: The Pre- and Post-EDIP responses related to Professional Development

Statements/Objectives	Disagree (%)		To some extent Agree (%)		Fully agree (%)		Strongly agree (%)	
	Pre	Post	Pre	Post	Pre	Post	Pre	Post
EDIP played a crucial role in improving my content knowledge	6	1	24	13	45	63	25	24
EDIP enhanced my teaching skills	2	1	23	23	42	40	34	36
EDIP helped me develop better professional relationships with students	3	1	23	18	50	49	25	32
EDIP significantly enhanced my confidence to teach	2	1	22	15	37	42	40	42
EDIP augmented my professional curiosity	3	1	16	13	36	44	45	42
EDIP facilitated me in becoming a better teacher and a good human being	1	2	14	14	38	36	47	48
EDIP helped me to realise my duties and develop a sense of responsibility	1	2	16	7	41	46	42	45
EDIP helped improve my relationships with teachers, headteacher, and the school community	2	1	30	25	43	43	25	31
EDIP helped me to challenge my own thinking and ideas	5	1	24	21	52	49	20	29
EDIP increased my intrinsic motivation to seek knowledge	5	0	13	13	45	52	37	35
EDIP strengthened my feelings of human dignity and respect for humanity	3	0	22	13	41	48	35	39

EDIP enhanced my realisation of other people's importance for children's success	4	2	26	23	51	48	19	27
EDIP increased my realisation of the need to become a better teacher on an ongoing basis	3	1	16	10	37	48	44	41
Average Percentages	3	1	21	16	43	47	33	36

A T-Test between the responses of these pre- and post-intervention phases indicates a significant difference for challenging the personal thinking and ideas of teachers ($p < 0.036$). Also, the T-Test indicates a slightly insignificant difference in improving the content knowledge of teachers ($p < 0.076$), developing better professional relationship of teachers with students ($p < 0.066$), and developing a feeling of human greatness and respect for teachers in the monitoring and management of the project schools ($p < 0.098$). The average percentage responses of teachers in the categories of 'strongly agree' and 'fully agree' in the post-intervention phase are higher than the responses in the pre-intervention phase. Similarly, in the categories of 'to some extent agree' and 'disagree', the average percentage responses of teachers in the post-intervention phase are lower than the responses in the pre-intervention phase.

FUTURE AIM OF TEACHERS IN THEIR PROFESSION

The T-Test indicates a significant difference ($p < 0.041$) between the pre- and post-intervention responses of teachers related to their future aims in the profession. As compared to the responses from the pre-intervention phase, more teachers opted for the choices of becoming headteachers and becoming Assistant Education Officers (AEOs) or District Inspectors of Schools (DISs) in their post-intervention phase. In the pre-intervention phase, 21 per cent of the respondents wanted to become a headteacher in future, whereas in in the post-intervention phase this aspiration increased to 32 per cent. This indicates an enhanced motivation to remain in the profession and to aim for advancement in their professional career of teaching and learning. Hence, motivation to remain in the profession and progress in the career indirectly leads to the willingness of teachers to exercise their leadership roles.

Table 8.6: The Future Aim in the Profession Related Pre- and Post-Intervention Responses of Teachers

Aspect	0–4 (%)		5–9 (%)		10–14 (%)		15< (%)		Total (%)	
	Pre	Post	Pre	Post	Pre	Post	Pre	Post	Pre	Post
Want to be a headteacher	33	28	23	37	14	36	12	27	20	33
Want to be an AEO or a DIS	17	22	17	11	10	14	4	23	12	17
Want to join a national or an international NGO	22	28	29	34	52	18	50	23	38	27
Want to retire as a teacher	28	22	31	17	24	32	35	27	30	24
Total	100	100	100	100	100	100	100	100	100	100

REASONS FOR SELECTION OF THE PROFESSION

In the pre-intervention phase, 77 per cent of the respondents considered 'love for teaching' and 'dignity of the profession' as their key reasons for choosing this occupation; however, their perception related to this particular rationale further strengthened (84 per cent) in the post-intervention phase.

Table 8.7: The Educational Qualification-wise Responses of Teachers for Opting Teaching as Profession at Pre- and Post-EDIP Phases

Aspects	Matric/Secondary (%)		Intermediate (%)		Graduate (%)		Post-Graduate (%)		Total (%)	
	Pre	Post	Pre	Post	Pre	Post	Pre	Post	Pre	Post
Love teaching and teacher dignity	75.0	100.0	76.9	84.6	73.6	81.1	83.9	90.3	77.2	85.1
To get an employment	0.0	0.0	15.4	7.7	13.2	7.5	9.7	6.5	11.9	6.9
It is an easy job in terms of time and exertion	0.0	0.0	0.0	7.7	1.9	1.9	3.2	0.0	2.0	2.0
Government security of job	25.0	0.0	7.7	0.0	11.3	9.4	3.2	3.2	8.9	5.9
Total	100.0	100.0	100.0	100.0	100.0	100.0	100.0	100.0	100.0	100.0

EXTENT OF SATISFACTION IN THE TEACHING PROFESSION

A majority of the respondents (83 per cent) felt highly satisfied at the pre-intervention stage, however, their satisfaction levels ascended much higher (89 per cent) in the post-intervention phase.

Table 8.8: The Pre- and Post-EDIP Intervention Educational Qualification-Wise Responses Reflecting Satisfaction with Teaching Profession

Aspects	Matric/ Secondary (%)		Inter- mediate (%)		Graduate (%)		Post- Graduate (%)		Total (%)	
	Pre	Post	Pre	Post	Pre	Post	Pre	Post	Pre	Post
To what extent are you satisfied with opting for teaching as a profession										
I regret it	0.0	0.0	0.0	7.7	5.7	0.0	9.7	0.0	5.9	1.0
Very much satisfied	100.0	100.0	76.9	92.3	86.8	84.9	77.4	93.5	83.2	89.1
No regrets, no happiness	0.0	0.0	23.1	0.0	7.5	15.1	12.9	6.5	10.9	9.9
Total	100.0	100.0	100.0	100.0	100.0	100.0	100.0	100.0	100.0	100.0

In their open comments, a majority of teachers in the pre- and post-intervention phases maintained that they are satisfied in the profession because they love this profession; it gives them the opportunity to play a positive role in society, they are valued by others, and their job is to help children become better human beings. Some of the respondents maintained that they are satisfied because this is a prophetic profession and it is like engaging in meditation. The T-Test for this theme did not indicate a significant difference between the pre- and post-intervention responses, yet the trends of the percentages reflect that the respondents gradually shifted to the option of feeling very much satisfied in the profession of teaching and learning.

THE MOST ATTRACTIVE ASPECT IN TEACHING PROFESSION

In the pre-intervention phase, a majority of the respondents (77 per cent) considered dignity of the profession and opportunity to make a difference in the lives of children as the most attractive aspect in the profession. Most of the teachers in the pre- and post-intervention phases maintained that the most attractive aspect in the profession is the dignity of teaching, positive role of teachers in society, developing children for the society, developing the nation, contributing to the future of the child, and getting an opportunity to know yourself and God. Some of the respondents considered the good financial earning opportunities and ability to spare time for family and personal development opportunities as the attractive aspects in this profession. The T-Test did not indicate a significant difference between the pre- and post-intervention responses; however, the trends of the percentages reflect that the respondents are considering the dignity of the profession and making a difference in the lives of children as the most attractive aspects of this occupation.

Table 8.9: The Pre- and Post-EDIP Intervention District-wise Responses Related to the Most Attractive Aspects in Teaching Profession

District	Good salaries and benefits (%)		Relatively independent and less accountability (%)		Near to home and in village employment (%)		Dignity of the profession and contributing to children's lives (%)		Personal career development and learning (%)	
	Pre	Post	Pre	Post	Pre	Post	Pre	Post	Pre	Post
Gilgit	0	0	0	0	11	25	72	75	17	0
Ghizar	0	0	0	0	6	11	83	89	11	0
Astore	0	0	0	0	17	0	83	93	0	7
Hunza-Nagar	6	0	0	0	17	12	67	82	11	6
Skardu	0	6	0	0	6	0	94	83	0	11
Ghanche	12	0	0	6	29	22	59	67	0	6
Total	3	1	0	1	14	12	77	81	7	5

The Most Challenging Aspect in Teaching Profession

In the pre-intervention phase, 62 per cent respondents considered lack of cooperation by the parents as the most challenging aspect of the profession.

Table 8.10: The Pre- and Post-EDIP Intervention Experience-wise Responses Related to the Most Challenging Aspect in Teaching

Aspect	0–4 (%)		5–9 (%)		10–14 (%)		15 above (%)		Total (%)	
	Pre	Post	Pre	Post	Pre	Post	Pre	Post	Pre	Post
The injustices by the authorities	0	11	17	14	18	32	4	19	11	19
The individual differences of the children	22	6	17	17	18	5	15	8	18	10
Lack of interest in teaching and learning	0	0	3	0	5	5	0	0	2	1
Lack of cooperation by the parents	61	83	63	69	50	59	69	73	61	70
Any other	17	0	0	0	9	0	12	0	8	0
Total	100	100	100	100	100	100	100	100	100	100

In the pre- and post-intervention phases, a majority of them maintained that the most challenging aspects of their profession are: lack of attention by parents to the education of their children, lack of parental appreciation of the importance of education, and parents' reluctance to visit schools to know the progress of their children. Some of the respondents considered injustice from authorities, social and cultural differences between the children, lack of children's attention in education, lack of facilities in schools, and huge student headcounts as challenging aspects of this profession. The T-Test did not indicate a significant difference between the pre- and post-intervention responses; however, the trends of the percentages reflect that the respondents are considering the lack of cooperation by the parents and injustices by the authorities as the most challenging aspects of this occupation.

Classroom Practices

Table 8.11 shows fifteen statements about classroom practices before and after the EDIP intervention in the targeted schools. In the post-intervention phase, the respondents were asked to rate and compare the practical implementation of these classroom practices in their schools. A T-Test between the responses before and after the EDIP intervention indicates a significant difference for following the lesson plan in their classes ($p < 0.000$), getting help in their teaching ($p < 0.000$), avoiding physical punishment to children ($p < 0.000$), and involving students in their teaching ($p < 0.000$).

Table 8.11: The Responses of Before and After EDIP Intervention about Classroom Practices

Aspects	Before EDIP Intervention				After EDIP Intervention			
	Never	Occasionally	Often	Regularly	Never	Occasionally	Often	Regularly
Following lesson plan	36	43	20	3	0	10	55	37
Getting help in their teaching	9	66	21	6	0	14	57	31
Avoiding physical punishment to children	2	34	42	24	3	1	21	78
Involving students in their teaching	4	38	36	24	0	0	33	69
Ensuring individual attention to students	10	36	40	16	0	7	34	61
Reflecting on own teaching	14	40	35	13	0	5	36	61
Checking homework on regular basis	5	30	38	29	0	2	35	65
Informing parents about student performance	12	53	23	14	1	12	47	42
Maintaining children's performance records	22	35	27	18	1	9	42	50
Getting help from other teachers to improve her/his teaching	8	56	25	13	1	14	49	38
Avoiding domestic problems and concentrate on teaching	8	22	39	33	1	2	34	65

Reaching schools in time	3	14	33	52	0	0	21	81
Taking interest in workshops and training for professional development	16	31	32	23	0	6	33	63
Making efforts to improve the quality of student's learning	3	27	42	30	0	1	29	72
Making the physical school environment attractive for students	9	39	32	22	0	3	35	64
Averages	10	37	32	21	0	5	37	.58

Similarly, the T-Test between the responses before and after the EDIP intervention also indicates a significant difference for providing individual attention to students ($p < 0.000$), reflecting on their own teaching ($p < 0.000$), checking homework on regular basis ($p < 0.000$), and informing parents about student performance ($p < 0.000$). The T-Test between the responses before and after the EDIP intervention also indicates a significant difference for managing performance record of children ($p < 0.000$), getting help from other teachers to improve teaching ($p < 0.000$), avoiding domestic problems and concentrate on teaching ($p < 0.000$), and reaching punctually at the school ($p < 0.000$).

The T-Test between the responses for before and after the EDIP intervention also indicates a significant difference for taking interest in workshops and trainings for professional development ($p < 0.000$), always making efforts to improve the quality of student's education ($p < 0.000$), and trying to make the physical environment of schools attractive for the children ($p < 0.000$). In their open comments, a majority of teachers in the pre- and post-intervention phases maintained that the role of EDIP had been effective in teacher capacity building, improved classroom practices, teacher confidence, enhanced team work, school management and administration, improving social and physical environment of schools, and the overall school development. Some of the respondents considered that EDIP has contributed to child happiness in schools and has brought a positive change in the perceptions of the parents and the wider school community.

DISCUSSION

The insights emanating from this study highlight EDIP's significant contributions in changing teacher perceptions and perspectives and in improving their role as teacher leaders. Crowther, Kaagan, Ferguson, and Hann (2002) argued that teacher leaders are the teachers who are aspiring to lead school improvement whereas, according to Katzenmeyer and Moller (2001) teacher leaders lead in and outside the classroom, contribute to the development of colleague teachers, and influence others to adopt improved educational practices in their institutions. The data indicates a significant difference in teacher perceptions and perspectives between the pre- and post-project situations. The change of perceptions was particularly noted in teachers' personal career development and commitments, instructional practices, community involvement, organisational structures of schools, management and governance, and the physical and educational environment of schools. These parameters are directly linked to teacher leadership. Hence, it can be safely concluded that the project intervention has visibly contributed to the development of teachers as leaders.

The findings indicate that the EDIP has significantly influenced teacher perspectives and thinking about their future aims related to the teaching profession in the targeted schools. Their responses reflected a paradigmatic shift in the manner in which they viewed their profession. The post-EDIP data indicates a significant impact of the professional development opportunities provided to them during the project life. For instance, a majority of teachers believed that due to the insights gained from the capacity building courses they have shown remarkable improvements in the subjects they teach in schools.

In the pre-intervention phase, a majority of respondents considered love for teaching and dignity of the profession as the key reasons for choosing this occupation; however, their perspectives in this category further strengthened in the post-intervention phase. It is noteworthy that teachers' pre- and post-project descriptions of how they saw and understood the teaching profession were more or less the same in terms of viewing teaching as a respectable and desirable occupation. However, at the post-intervention stage, a marked shift took place in terms of how the profession contributed to the development of the younger generation of the community.

In the pre-intervention phase, the majority of respondents felt highly satisfied with the profession; however, this level of satisfaction further shot up in the post-intervention phase. The responses to the question on their memorable moments in the profession were somehow diversified in terms of their quality and understanding. In the pre-intervention phase, their responses were mostly focused on school level celebrations and school trips as the most precious events, while at the post-intervention stage the focus related to memorable events shifted to their school level achievements and career development. Furthermore, in the pre-intervention phase the memorable moments were mostly based on physical appearance, while at the post-intervention stage their focus diverted towards more analytical and quality-related aspects. Hence, the significant positive shift regarding teacher thinking and understanding on their memorable moments after the intervention could be safely attributed to the EDIP project interventions.

Teacher responses also indicate that the EDIP project made a significant difference in improving teacher leadership in the internal monitoring and management of the project schools. Improving the quality of education, satisfying teachers' and parents' expectations, and providing professional guidance to teachers were also highly rated by the respondents as the key contributions of the EDIP project. In the area of teacher professional development, the data reflected that the EDIP project made a significant difference in enabling teachers to challenge their personal thinking and ideas. Additionally, the teacher responses show that EDIP had made a positive contribution to improving their content knowledge, developing professional relationships of teachers with students, developing teachers' sense of human dignity and respect, and enhancing their teaching skills. Also, the data indicated that the EDIP played a very positive role in improving teacher confidence, augmenting their interest and motivation for knowledge, enhancing teachers' sense of responsibility, and further strengthening school-community relationships.

In the post-intervention phase, the respondents were asked to rate and compare the practical implementation of these classroom practices in their schools, on a 15-statement scale, for before and after the EDIP intervention. Teachers' pre- and post-project perspectives regarding their school experiences were to some extent different. In the post-project responses, the respondents have a greater emphasis on their achievements as compared to their pre-project views. The responses clearly portray their success which happened as a result of different capacity building initiatives, and the learning-conducive environment promoted in schools.

The data indicate that the EDIP intervention made a significant difference in terms of teachers following the lesson plans, getting help in their teaching, avoiding physical punishment to children, and involving students in their teaching. The data also indicated a significant difference in providing individual attention to students, reflecting on their own teaching, checking homework on regular basis, and informing parents about student performance. The data also indicated that EDIP intervention made a significant difference to maintaining children's performance records, getting help from other teachers to improve their teaching, avoiding domestic problems to concentrate on teaching, reaching schools in time, taking interest in workshops and training for professional development, always making efforts to improve the quality of student learning, and trying to make the school physical environment attractive and learning-conducive for students.

Teachers' pre- and post-project perspectives regarding their school experiences were to some extent different. In the post-project views, they emphasised on their achievements as compared to their pre-project views. They specifically mentioned their success which they attributed to different trainings as well as to the encouraging environment in schools. The findings also showed that teachers demonstrated their greatest productivity during their experiences on the job. Teachers' pre- and post-project perspectives on the institutional policies which stifle the spirit of professional development and school improvement in schools were comparatively different and analytical. At the pre-project stage, a majority of teachers shared their concerns and issues facing them in schools; for instance, they shared that shortage of teachers, lack of resources, and untrained teachers in schools as the major issues which stifled the spirit of professional development and school improvement. However, at the post-intervention stage, a good number of teachers referred to the Early Childhood Education Development (ECED) initiatives and the school- and PDCN-based professional development opportunities as the most motivating initiatives of the EDIP project.

The EDIP made a significant difference in providing awareness to the school management committees (SMCs); mother support groups (MSGs), parents and teachers on the issues of natural disasters and making the school environment friendly for children with disabilities. The professional development of teachers for whole-school development and the improvement of school building and physical environment of schools have also been highly rated by the respondents as the contributions of the EDIP project. However, it is also noteworthy that the respondents still feel the lack of cooperation by the parents as the most challenging aspect of the profession. In the pre-intervention phase, a majority of respondents considered lack of cooperation by the parents as the most challenging aspect in the profession. This perception of the respondents further strengthened in the post-intervention phase. The overall scenario reflects that the teachers appreciated the efforts made by the EDIP in bridging the gaps between the parents and the teachers for the education of children. However, the respondents still feel that it is the most challenging aspect of their professional life which indicates that this aspect of school improvement needs more attention in future. The government authorities and other relevant development partners need to come up with creative ideas and projects in future to enhance parent cooperation and support in the education of the children.

Injustices by the authorities emerged as the second key area of concern for the respondents. The increasing dissatisfaction among teachers is indicative of the governance and supervision issues in the system. One of the prime objectives of the EDIP was to improve governance and supervision; however, this study indicates no improvement in this regard. The data shows that since the inception of the EDIP, teacher concerns in the area of governance and supervision modalities employed by the department are gradually increasing. Therefore, this study suggests that the government authorities as well as the development partners may want to come up with alternative ways to improve governance and supervision in the system to address teacher concerns related to the issue of the institutional injustices facing them.

Conclusion

This study identifies and highlights various aspects of teacher leadership, both in the implementation and sustainability of school improvement initiatives. Teachers' pivotal roles in linking the development partners with students and their parents emerged as the most significant aspect of the EDIP. Therefore, improving teacher competence and their leadership was considered as an overarching theme of the project and resources were invested to sharpen and augment their leadership roles. The study provided the insight that teachers do possess massive potential in terms of their ingenuity and accomplishments; hence, the need to unleash and give direction to their creative impulses to accelerate the process of school improvement.

The tangible evidence related to the difference of perceptions and perspectives between the pre- and post-intervention responses challenges and contradicts the popular stereotypical notions and generic thinking that the public sector schools merely provide children an access to education but cannot deliver quality due to the manifold and complex systems characterizing the system. The paradigmatic shift in the perceptions and perspectives among the public sector school stakeholders reflected by this research study provides and supports the understanding that these schools in GB are capable of successfully focusing on both the access to as well as quality of education provided to children in these schools. These schools can be turned around as 'schools of choice' for parents and their children, provided that carefully planned school improvement interventions, such as the EDIP, are launched and sustained by the authorities managing these schools. Hence, the institutional capacity to support, monitor, and evaluate the project initiatives by the school and district leadership will be the key determinants in sustaining the school improvement interventions.

In GB, a number of school improvement initiatives were taken over the last couple of decades by the government and the other development partners to improve education in schools. These initiatives achieved their goals to a great extent during the implementation phase of the interventions. However, many of these interventions faced difficulties in sustaining the positive changes after the projects concluded. Therefore, it can be concluded that a well-thought-out sustainability plan and a carefully engineered gradual phase-out strategy must be included in the design of future educational projects. This could be a challenging task for the government education department, donor community, and the implementing partners, as all of them have their own priorities and limitations. However, in the educational milieu of GB, the time has come to address this vital need, if we are to achieve sustainable educational development in this part of the world.

The second key aspect is the monitoring and evaluation mechanism of the educational development initiatives. Monitoring and evaluation of the educational interventions in public sector schools has two dimensions: first, the internal monitoring contrivance of the projects and, second, the monitoring and evaluation mechanism of the government education department. At the project level, the monitoring and evaluation appliances must dig down to the sustainable impact of the interventions rather than confining them to outputs and immediate outcomes. At the government level, the monitoring and evaluation mechanism needs to have the resources, professional capacities, and attitudes to embed and synchronise the development project interventions in order to achieve maximum benefits from the development projects. However, in treading this key path to ensure sustainability of project impacts, it would be imperative to have the wholehearted and unwavering sense of ownership of the educational projects by the government education department and the local communities.

9

Transformative Leadership as/for Emancipation: A Journey towards Exploring Self and Beyond in the Field of Educational Leadership

SADRUDDIN BAHADUR QUTOSHI AND BAL CHANDRA LUITEL

The purpose of this chapter is to explore how transformative leadership as/for[1] empowerment contributes towards developing knowledgeable leaders, not only as lifelong learners and agents of change, but also as learners with inclusive behaviour, essential skills, and wisdom. This we believe is important in order to create a better world to live in 'with embodied values of intention of doing good for others, humility for humanity, and care for self and others. To address this question, we embraced an innovative yet inclusive research paradigm, within new social sciences, called Multi-paradigmatic Research Design (MRD) (Taylor, 2008; Taylor & Luitel, 2012; Luitel, 2009). This design offers post-post modern researchers to take on board multiple lenses, inclusive logics and genres as multi-epistemic approaches to knowing self and beyond in the field of transformative educational leadership.[2] To this end, we embraced auto/ethnography as a method of inquiry that enabled us to employ reflexivity as a transformative lens. Auto/ethnography as a transporter facilitated us to delve into the ocean of a complex undetached-fluid-self (Qutoshi, 2015: 1) in order to explore approaches to knowing transformative leadership in practice from within two-country contexts. With this inquiry, we used critical reflections on technical, practical, and emancipatory views of education (Habermas, 1972) from the standpoint of transformative educational leadership, which enabled us to experience a journey towards leadership as praxis. We came to know that employing this approach would raise wisdom and develop positive attitudes, skills, and knowledge that could liberate both researchers and readers.

This critical reflection-driven approach to meaning-making of our roles as learners, teachers, teacher educators, and researchers facilitated us to gain some insights into how a transformative view of leadership can empower self to think about an emancipatory view of educational leadership. Why is such a transformative leadership necessary for organisations in the context of developing countries, including Pakistan and Nepal? It appears that engaging with the questions at the deep level of consciousness, challenging self/beyond and developing new perspectives in order to bring continuous improvements in self/others, are the signs of transformative leadership engaged in a lifelong learning process. On the contrary, conventional leaders always appear to resist bringing changes in self and beyond because they believe, see, and act within the domain of positivism. This study highly recommends educational leaders to think beyond the borders of conventional ways of knowing self/others to experience a transformative leadership that is embedded within an emancipatory interest of education, not a reformative one.

Contextualizing Self/others within the Research Agenda

It was on a fine sunny day of September 2015 that Bal and I sat to chat, sipping coffee, in the Kathmandu University School of Education (KUSOED) canteen. For a short while, I (henceforth it refers to the first writer) was lost in thinking that having a supervisor as a critical yet caring, creative, and enabling friend was one of the best gifts of God for PhD scholars. That feeling reminded me of a proverb 'a friend in need is a friend indeed'. At Kathmandu University (KU), we used the term 'cup-shop',[3] flexi time for some purpose-oriented discussions. One can ask us a host of questions about such engagement: What was the purpose of that cup-shop? How can such a flexi time with a friend create ways to critical engagement? How can a supervisee claim to be a friend of his/her own supervisor? Is it possible for a supervisee to make friendship with his/her mentor? How can a supervisor remove limits between a teacher/supervisor and a student/supervisee?

Probably, it would be something strange for us, who are living in a post-colonial regime and/or affected by colonisation,[4] to think about such practices and relationships between a supervisor and a supervisee. Yes, we agree with the view that leaders, such as heads, directors, deans, vice-chancellors, or others in managerial posts in both public and private educational institutions, in the context of developing countries, including Nepal and Pakistan, are rarely seen as critical friends of their subordinates. They appear to believe in themselves as superior beings, as they have the opportunity to exercise authoritative power over others while they are in administrative positions. Post-colonial culture is replete with such barriers and borders. In such a situation, it would be impossible to expect them to behave fairly and provide you with guidance to enable you to be their next leader.

There, we began to reflect that leaders with such a limited view of leadership as dictating, controlling, and commanding in institutions are guided by a technical interest in leadership (Habermas, 1972) that focuses mostly on administrative control to promote an unquestioning mindset among learners in relation to their heads/teachers. The learners and their teachers/heads who are inculcated with such a narrow view of education (i.e. guided by the notion of education as/for technical control) may not believe in unconditional support to others. Moreover, it makes no sense for leaders as position holders[5] to create an enabling environment for their followers. Such leaders do not believe in an environment where both the leaders and the followers can sit together to discuss the issues related to empowerment of the latter. Rather, they believe in an authoritative-hindrance[6] in the everyday life of their followers.

We argue that educational leaders working in post-colonial contexts and/or influenced by colonisation un/wittingly believe in, and practice, the notion of leadership as position holders. However, leadership as transforming self/others is strongly embedded within the philosophical underpinning of education for emancipation (Habermas, 1972; Taylor, 2008; Taylor, Taylor & Luitel, 2012). The Habermasian view of education demands the creation of conditions for the highest level of freedom to the learners, thereby helping them to think, reflect, and create new knowledge. Educational leaders with such a transformative view of education—a view that leadership is fair in using diverse approaches to facilitation, empowerment, and liberation—work for a greater freedom to live with peace, love, care, and ecological consciousness (Qutoshi, 2016). Such transformative leaders challenge the taken-for-granted ways of knowledge generation and look for un/conventional[7] ways of knowing (Taylor, Taylor & Luitel, 2012). To engage the readership about how transformative educational leadership contributes towards liberation of learners/followers for a sustainable future, we structured this chapter around four key thematic areas: un/conventional paradigms as transformative; multiple lenses as/for exploring; transformative leadership as praxis; reflexivity as wisdom raising approach.

Un/Conventional Paradigms as Transformative

Our use of MRD space as a research approach is an integrative and holistic way of looking at the phenomenon under discussion. We believe that researchers using the un/conventional paradigms can open different windows to see the world around self and beyond. With such a view in mind, we employed MRD to embrace inclusive logics in our narratives and multiple genres to create opportunities for writing in different ways. In exploring the answer of what it means to be a transformative leader, we used different theoretical perspectives on board and employed diverse philological views and innovative ways to data generation.

In MRD space, the paradigm of interpretivism enabled us to embrace new perspectives during the meaning-making process. The paradigm of criticalism as an inquiry process helped us critique our own practices of leadership in the context of educational institutions and those of socio-cultural and socio-pedagogical others. It served as a basis to work as change agents. Moreover, the paradigm of post-modernism empowered us to make sense of different voices in the changing world. The paradigm of integralism helped us develop a logical flow of our view of traditional ways of leading as informing, an improved version of leadership as reforming, and a liberating view of leadership as transformative (Qutoshi, 2015, 2016, 2019; Taylor, 2008; Taylor, Taylor & Luitel, 2012).

At this stage, we would like to share snippets of our conversations that were carried on largely through emails as a way to promote conversational knowing. Conversational knowing is considered to be the beginning of transformative learning aimed at developing educational leadership that works for creating empowering educational processes. Such engagements open multiple windows to see the world of self and others to raise consciousness/awakening.

In a conversation, I asked Bal, 'Bal, would you recall the moments when we used to be engaged in critical discourse on how multiple paradigms serve as data referents? In what ways do multiple logics and genres within these paradigms enable us to generate a diverse range of data sets to make meaning of our being and becoming as transformative learners?'

In response, Bal recollected, 'Of course, I remember those ... moments, Sadruddin Ji. Such discourses are the ways and means of transforming self and others. So, keep in contact to discuss beliefs, perceptions, and practices of our professional lifeworlds. In so doing, we will be able to develop new perspectives by critically examining and challenging our old views with a critical lens'.

Here, we share one of our letters as a genre of research that explains how critical engagement generates possibilities for transformative learning (Mezirow, 2000, 2003).

August 10, 2016

Dear Bal,

I hope this letter will bring many smiles on you and will generate a hope for an emancipatory interest of education in the context of Pakistan.

You remember we used to discuss most of the times about un/conventional paradigms especially, criticalism embedded within the philosophy of critical theory perspective, postmodernism rooted within the notions of possibility of anything and everything, and integralism as for synergy etc. Bal, you know these multi-epistemic research paradigms which we used in our writings especially in doctoral studies, perhaps, enabled us to embrace the risk of challenging taken-for-granted ways of being and becoming leaders in our own context(s).

Believe me or not, now I feel more confident in myself while expressing self as a change agent and sometimes feel proud of self while contributing towards the field of transformative leadership domain in my own context. Perhaps, you will recall our discussions during 'advanced qualitative' class and our cup-shop flexi time on these powerful paradigms as data referents (which enable us to generate data as per our need) rather than considering them as frameworks (the strict rules which bound us to rely on whatever data that comes from chosen sources).

By reflecting on those views, now I can realise how empowering and liberating these philosophical standpoints were and the need for us to take them on board as data referents to generate data sets coming out of our lived experiences. You know, such kind of engagement with un/conventional paradigms as transformative is rooted within imaginative powers of thinking. Perhaps such kind of creative ways of knowing can enable researchers to make better sense of their beliefs, perspectives and perceptions in the light of their leadership practices.

Now let me seek your views on how I came up with reconceptualisation of these un/conventional paradigms as liberating. Probably, you could reiterate the views that thinking beyond the borders of conventional mindsets and

> challenging taken-for-granted ways of looking at research problems could raise consciousness in a manner that may lead towards transformation.
>
> Bal, you know I have been very appreciative towards your loving and caring yet very critical stand to develop deeper level of thinking on and about our ways of being and becoming transformative leaders. I remember your critical engagement with unconventional paradigms at that time was very challenging for scholars like me, who came with very conventional research practices like simple qualitative, quantitative or mixed method approach, but that was perhaps the most enabling discourse.
>
> Arriving at this point of my reflections, I came to realise the importance of transformative leadership. I experienced myself as a mentee during my transformative journey. Writing the chapters on leadership from the standpoint of technical, practical, and emancipatory interest (Habermas, 1972) of teacher education, I came up with leadership as dictating, to communicating, and then envisioning a transformative one.
>
> Bal, my purpose of writing this letter to you, at this stage of our collective being and becoming, is to seek your intellectual input on un/conventional paradigms as transformative. So, with this note I would like to close my letter here and hope to receive your comments that would further make clear to me how multiple lenses as awakening would serve our agenda of research as empowering self/others.
>
> With Best Regards and Love.
Sadruddin

Multiple Lenses as Exploring/Awakening

To us, the concept of using multiple lenses as sources of exploration appears to be an enabling way of looking at our beliefs and practices within teacher education in the context of both countries. We focus on multiple and/or inclusive logics and a perspectival language rather than the word/s of certainty used in such an unconventional approach to research. To us, inclusive means the logics and genres that are not conventional yet have the power of generating multiple forms of data sets with ample opportunities for meaning-making at a subjective level (readers/researchers). We believe that taking a diverse range of data generating sources (e.g. reflective notes, conversations, memoirs, historical documents), which are not common in practice, would be an inclusive approach to making the meaning of how we as educational leaders operate within our domains.

These inclusive logics and genres generate new knowledge in a unique manner regarding transformative leadership. For example, we used various logics and genres—dialogic, poetic, metaphoric, letter writing, dialectical, etc.—throughout this chapter. In so doing, the multi-epistemic lenses enabled us to capture unheard voices and unthinkable ideas of self/others to make better sense of transformative leadership. Moreover, we used a perspectival language, also known as language of doubt, such as 'possibly', 'probably', 'likely', 'seems to be', and 'appears to be' while exploring transformative leadership concepts and practices. We avoided the use of claiming words or the words of certainty that appear in conventional writings. To us, the purpose of using perspectival language was to create a wider space for readers to think about their own positionality.

With these lines of thought, we started exploring the possibilities and got engaged in making the meaning of our personal-professional lives as leaders. We used to discuss how things would be if we thought something un/conventional whenever we had a little chance to make a better sense of supervisor-supervisee educational endeavour as/for a meaning-making process. Bal was fond of using dialectical logics 't/here' un/intentionally to create a space for knowing both sides of the picture of a situation. We realised that discussing the present things means imagining their future. Understanding my curiosity to know more about dialectical logics, Bal said, 'Here I have used a slash (/) so as to demonstrate the dialectical relationship between seemingly opposite constructs, ideas and phenomena'.

That was one of the approaches that gave us the inspiration for not only learning the meaning of this epistemic logic, but also the other logics we used in our daily practice of discussions, dialogues, and emails, while envisioning a transformative teacher education programme for countries like Pakistan and Nepal. The complexity associated with the use of these multiple lenses can be understood from the following letter writing genre that serves as a powerful source of awakening. We understand how powerful these logics are in making the meaning of our past and present in a retrospective manner, thereby envisioning a sustainable future in our professional career as transformative leaders.

> September 20, 2017
>
> Dear Sadruddin Ji,
>
> It gives me an immense pleasure to know that you, as a transformative leader, are consciously engaged with writing as knowing and meaning-making. Sadruddin, you would recall the moments where scholars like you at the school of education were given multiple opportunities to use a diverse range of lenses while making meaning of your lived experiences. To me, being in a state of consciousness would lead to knowing the inner and outer world at a deeper level from within the contextual, philosophical and other dimensional ways.
>
> For instance, when you use critical self-reflection as a lens it enables us to explore our own strengths and areas for improvement rather than finger pointing towards others. In such a way, we can engage the self with a professional development endeavour. Now, you can better realise the situation where you are engaged with a discussion, discourse and reading a stuff on a theory and making sense of philosophical stands of a framework, a concept and viewpoint regarding transformative leadership endeavours that would generate an energy flowing within you. There, you create positive rays in yourself, and that energy might attract others (students, colleagues and wider community in your field) about your approach to leadership that transforms others. If your leadership creates such a situation in self and others it means you are a transformative leader.
>
> The moment you feel that you are really contributing without any bias and attachment for a return against your contribution rather just for the sake of empowering self and others and making lives better, you become a transformative leader. I can understand that you also came across the inspiring ideas about the notion of transformative leaders who are committed to enabling others in order to create conditions for co-leading, co-evolving and co-becoming.
>
> Sadruddin Ji, my purpose of writing this letter to you was twofold. On the one hand, the purpose was to appreciate your efforts that you have been contributing in the field of transformative education leadership in your country context that is what our agenda of working as contributors in the field of transformative education and research for sustainable futures. On the other hand, I, as your mentor, would like to share the developments at our end in the context of Nepal and beyond. One of those is the acceptance of your paper in second International Conference on Transformative Teacher Education and Research (TER) for Sustainable Future, and it is coming in the form of a

book chapter soon. Moreover, I would like to share my international travels, including the current visit to South Africa for a keynote address on TER as an approach to work towards exploring the world beyond our practices.

Let me tell you that such a process of engagement has been an illuminating one for me. I get engage with my practices as a critically reflective practitioner by embracing an innovative approach to knowing. I believe that challenging one's own leadership practices and envisioning an empowering and enabling form of leadership that is embedded within the philosophical underpinnings of leadership as/for emancipation is a liberating experience. To me, this could be one of the ways of transformation as praxis that is embedded within the process of bringing the theoretical/conceptual perspectives followed by reflections into actions within a particular socio-cultural and socio-pedagogical lifeworld (van Manen, 1977, 1991, 1992).

Sadruddin Ji, I guess, this letter is becoming very long and I would like to stop here with a hope that this will contribute to your thinking more about how transformative leadership as praxis would be contributing towards creating the conscious citizenry in the world.

With this hope and love see you in the next episode.

Yours loving
Bal

Transformative Leadership as Praxis

Education researchers aiming to cultivate transformative leadership (see Taylor, Taylor & Luitel, 2012; Taylor, 2008) and living-educational theorists (see Whitehead, 1989; Whitehead & Huxtable, 2015) claim that by looking into barriers and borders, it is possible to develop transformative leaders and living theorists who can play a key role in transforming individuals, organisations, and societies for the sustainable future. Transformative researchers as leaders serve as critical-creative friends who do not care about the positions/offices, but create opportunities to solve the problems of their followers and encourage them to prepare themselves as change agents. Perhaps, with such a view of education for emancipation (Habermas, 1972), Bal (as a mentor) sat with me (as a mentee) even during the tea break with a cup of tea/coffee and engaged me in discussions. The mentor presented himself as a critical-creative friend before the mentee.

At the KU canteen, the purpose of the cup-shop between the mentor and the mentee was to build a basis of a research design (within a contemporary transformative educational-research paradigm). The more meetings between us, the stronger the belief—that writing the stories of our professional life and reflections could lead us to make sense of the research as/for transformation. Making sense of the aims of research, we finally agreed to focus on three thematic areas: curriculum, pedagogy, and assessment.

One may ask as to why the three broader areas were selected for a doctoral study purpose and what the rationale behind it was. Both of us used to discuss the nature of the traditional teacher education and the prospects of reforms, both in the context of Pakistan and Nepal. We came to realise that exploring retrospectively on an informing and reforming state of teacher education,[8] thereby envisioning a transformative state of education[9] in the context of Pakistan, would be a contribution for the county in future. Initially, with this view in mind, we worked on curriculum, pedagogy, and assessment with: (1) *informing*, a very narrow view of education that falls within post/positivism; (2) *reforming*, changes in existing practices that represent a 'metaphor of an old house being repaired outwardly—quick fix' (Luitel, 2018); and (3) *transformative*, a liberating view of teacher education.

While narrating and re/constructing stories of our personal-professional life, the mentee came to know that the mentor was very much aware of the interest and skills of the former in technology. The latter was constantly encouraging the former to integrate technology in all key thematic areas of being and becoming of a lifelong learner in the field of teacher education. However, with the passage of time, this journey led us to think about teacher education leadership and research practices in order to explore teacher education with a *holistic lens*.[10] Thus, the mentor's encouragement and guidance spurred the intrinsic motivation of the mentee to do something meaningful in teacher education in Pakistan that could address the culturally embedded problems and issues and find contextually responsive solutions.

However, in this chapter, our focus is to discuss one of the five themes—teacher education leadership—with a specific lens of a transformative educational leadership in teacher education in the context of Pakistan. Let me tell you how important it is to create the relationship between a mentor and a mentee in a co-transformative environment. When I was at KUSOED, working on the transformative teacher education programme for my doctoral study, I came to realise how lucky I was to have such a learning opportunity with my supervisor as a transformative leader in that he made me think about transformative leadership.

Now, I can recall those moments of our professional engagement and cherish the productive moments. I can say that my mentor not only inspired, encouraged, or empowered me, but also created a conducive environment for conducting research within the field of educational leadership. To us, the idea of a co-leader is deeply rooted in the notion of working together towards a joint mission to becoming and being as transformative educational leaders. Unfortunately, in our context, the idea of co-leading seems missing and such a powerful view of leadership is fundamentally required for liberating self/others. The question arises here as to how transformative leadership liberates self and others. To us, one of the answers to this critical question is to engage with working together (co-leading) to improve self/others that may lead to improving organisations and societies. To this end, it is imperative to remove the gap between being leaders (as superior beings) and followers (as an uncritical work force).

Why is a transformative leader necessary for an organisation in general and educational institutions in particular? To us, it is necessary because transformative leaders can create conditions for the empowerment of their followers and facilitation beyond the traditional and organisational cultural settings, norms, and rules. Transformative leaders know every individual in their organisations at a deeper level and accordingly, they create opportunities for them to grow and enable them to strive for the highest level of efficiency in their performance. In so doing, the followers begin to liberate themselves from socio-cultural and socio-pedagogical taken-for-granted ways of doing things. They start thinking out of the box to improve their performance. In such a situation, both the leader (mentor) and the follower (mentee) become friendly and informal towards achieving a common goal and they start thinking un/conventionally. Thus, this *informal yet very critical aspect of liberation of self/others is embedded in the philosophical underpinnings of transformative leadership.* One of the things we can do is to explore how we can raise awareness among educational leaders basically serving as organisational 'big-guns'.[11]

We believe that this liberating leadership enabled us to make up our minds about research as transformative in its nature. Reaching to such a point of understanding led us towards a departure from an informing to a reforming approach, thereby envisioning a contemporary view of transformative tool. Here, it makes better sense to me to confess that such an empowering way of mentorship enabled me to choose a path to being an innovative, creative, and critically reflective practitioner (Schon, 1983). In such an interactive and engaging environment, I came to make sense of employing auto/ethnography as an approach to knowing cultural self/others. It was the research as transformative leadership that triggered my curiosity and interest in pursuing a doctorate.

I came to realise that such a research approach was selfless and for a common good with the highest level of liberation (of colleagues, students, and beyond) from the darkness (*jahalat*, unknowingness) and canonical ways of (taken-for-granted traditional approaches) knowing, to envisioning alternative and inclusive yet innovative ways of knowing self. So, autoethnography (Adams, Jones & Ellis, 2015; Qutoshi, 2019) is a powerful research genre to explore how our leadership practices and beliefs have been empowering self/others for common good.

Arriving at this point of exploration, we begin to ask the question: Who is a leader? A leader is one who exposes his/her followers as co-leaders to employ such complex yet liberating epistemic techniques. A leader is one who empowers and liberates self as well as others. In this case 'leadership as co-evolving, co-leading and co-becoming' (Qutoshi, 2016: 368) seems a joint venture of both leader and follower. To us, transformative leadership involves a joint action-oriented leadership and the leader is constantly evolving self and followers, working as a practical change agent, empowering self/others, creating conditions for continuous professional development with practical activities.

We argue that the leader, in transformational leadership, believes in theoretical and philosophical views of leadership that may and may not transform into actions. For example, in our lives, we personally experienced some so-called and self-proclaimed transformational leaders who talked about the theories and tried to inspire others with their words only. Such leaders tend to deprive their followers from professional development opportunities and do not want their followers to hold positions similar to their own. Perhaps this type of leadership conceals a professional jealousy that keeps co-workers away from opportunities leading to leadership positions and beyond. Now one can simply take an example of leaders in their institutions, especially in educational institutions and reflect what they are actually doing. Are they joint-action-oriented leaders who work for the empowerment of self/others for co-evolving and co-becoming or are they just theory-driven-leaders who believe only in theoretical and philosophical underpinnings?

Seeking answers to such questions and critically reflecting on self/others, using multiple logics and genres, helped us develop imaginative power as a way of unearthing our deeper insights. Perhaps, it is an empowering approach for us to get engaged in an evolving process of being and becoming. Let me share one of the pieces of such a dialogic logics[12] so as to create an opportunity for my readers to think about how transformative leadership as a process of imaginative engagement develops the sixth sense at different levels.

Bal: Look Sadruddin Ji, you have been working as a school principal for almost a decade, and you have a wealth of lived experiences of how you came across with your decisions in dealing with and leading people at school and university level. What about the idea of writing a story about those experiences?

Me: Yes, it's an interesting idea Sir Ji! Let me think about how story writing genre, as you know is one of the powerful ways of knowing, as you were discussing in the Advanced Qualitative Research classroom, will help me to come up with my lived experiences of leading a school as a vice/principal in my past and that would contribute towards reflecting my past leadership practices. In so doing, it will give me a chance to think about how my knowledge, skills, and most importantly, my attitude at that time could be facilitating or hindering the process of empowering my fellow staff members and learners.

Bal: Oh yes, go ahead and get engaged in writing those nodal moments of your professional life in the form of narratives, and as soon as you finish it, just let me know. But Sadruddin Ji, do remember you are writing stories of and about all those events and eventualities from the vantage point of that time. Though you are not carrying all those key memory chips in your head, and you really don't need a memory chip in your head…. (laughing). But you use them as sources of making sense of (semi)non/fictive stories.[13] In so doing, keep one thing in your mind that creating the pedagogical thoughtfulness in the mind of your reader is a must.

Me: Yes, that is fine with me. Just one thing I want to make clear: Do you mean creating a pedagogical thoughtfulness in the audience is one of the quality standards of this sort of writing?

Bal: Oh yes, it is. Though there are different quality standards of this sort of inquiry and you know it is one of the most important ones. However, we will discuss other quality standards in coming days while engaging with different stories. Now just start with writing narratives of and about

	your 'principalship' and let's see how those practices make sense of your leadership that emerges from those narratives.
Me:	I guess, my stories will expose my inner leader/principal. Perhaps, what we believe/perceive and practice in a situation that itself informs the readership to make meaning of those perceptions and practices and to me that would open new ways of thinking about one's own perceptions and practices. However, telling others about our practices in our own words in the form of stories of lifeworld increases vulnerability that writers, probably, have to face. I guess, for a common good it can be done!
Bal:	I guess, Sadruddin Ji, you are making better sense of the power of narratives that carry powerful meaning and insights, and attract the readership not only to just think about their own perceptions and practices of leadership but also would enable them to critique their own for the sake of changing those taken-for-granted ways of thinking and doing in a conventional manner. Yes, I do agree with you that embracing such a critical-creative genre makes one vulnerable (yet another quality standard) that the writers have to face in order to devote self for improving self and others.
Me:	Sir Ji, do you think challenging taken-for-granted ways of being and becoming is one of the paths/ways to transformative leadership? And, to this end, in what ways these critical-creative genera would contribute towards transformative self and others?
Bal:	Probably, you are making a very good point here. To me, transformative leadership is not something that is one directional travel to reach at a destination for a leader, rather it appears to be a deeper level of consciousness raising activity/approach that changes our way of believing, thinking, making sense, and then doing in a certain way. Perhaps, it is a rigorous process of challenging our own mind and guide our actions to empower self and others in order to provide better facilitation, care and love for self and others, create enabling environment, and most importantly generate love for wisdom that embraces both un/conventional approaches to knowing the wider cosmos with an emancipatory interest of education.
Me:	That's great Sir Ji, from this what I understand if I am not wrong... and just give me your critical feedback, is that for

a transformating or a transformative leadership one needs to delve into deep root level of consciousness and start critically-self reflecting on beliefs, perceptions, and practices. Probably, in so doing, the practitioner/transformative leaders could embrace self-knowing as philosophical basis for empowering self and beyond (other colleagues). I guess, this very aspect of empowering self and beyond is embedded within the notions of learning organisations where individuals as leaders exhibit an organisational citizenship behavior (OCB). To me, educational leaders with OCB appear to be inspiring leaders who are committed to transform self and others.

Bal: Probably, such a view of leadership, a leader with a very positive attitude, excellent skills, and powerful knowledge can inspire others to follow the leader with their own willingness.

Me: Yes Sir Ji, to me, helping others, thinking for not only self but others' development and betterment in order to create a better place for living appears to be a positive attitude that is embedded within OCB. Perhaps, that could be one of the examples of how theories of learning, empowering, and emancipation are applied in the forms of critical reflections, the basis to raise reflexivity, to make better sense of transformation.

CRITICAL REFLEXIVITY AS A WISDOM RAISING APPROACH

The dialogical logics as an epistemic approach to knowing enabled us to make sense of our being and becoming educational transformative leaders. Employing critical self-reflection and meaning-making of our being and becoming served as a way of helping us to develop wisdom. For instance, I (the first writer) came up with critical reflections on self/others within a culturally disempowering and disconnected nature of teacher education. It generated in me new ways of looking at teacher education in Pakistan.

On the other hand, Luitel (the second writer and my supervisor) used his embodied values of practice, such as 'intention of doing good to others, humility for humanity, care of self and others with ecological consciousness, love and peace' (Qutoshi, 2016: 3). These embodied values served as explanatory principles to critique his own ways of looking at teacher education and research practices. Employing critical self-reflection as a lens, he came across living contradictions, the contradictions that existed in his practices. This is one of the examples of reflexivity that explains how practitioners come up with their own critique to improve their practice. In this journey of reflexivity as praxis, he could come up with his own transformation of his professional lifeworld.

The question is: What is reflexivity and how does it develop human wisdom? We found the answer in one of the poetic expressions of Qutoshi (2019: 155) in a book chapter 'Cultural-self knowing: An Epistemic Approach to Transformative Education and Research for Sustainable Future'. He writes:

Critical Reflexivity

It is the bell that awakens sleeping fellows
Enabling critique of self and others
It is the philosophy of action, not just words
Helping together self and others
It is the epistemology of lived identity construction
Raising creativity, reducing rigidity
It is the rider of past to engage in present
Opening windows, both in past and present
It is the mirror of one's inside-out to envision the future
Infusing thrust for explorative adventure
It is the driller to create cracks in frozen rocks
Enabling light to pass through to the other side
It changes those who are loyal to self and beyond
Enlightening one's heart and mind
It is the agent of change, not traditional inquiry
Empowering self and others for emancipation
It is the discourse for a sustainable future
Bringing transformation to the lives of self and others

I remember that, in one of the sessions, I talked about the importance of productive engagement that fosters critical thinking. Sofia, one of my students, asked me, 'Would you further explain this productive engagement? How does it foster critical thinking?' I explained, 'When a teacher and students become conscious about learning and reflect on their roles, it possibly fosters critical thinking'. To us, critical thinking is an epistemic approach that enables the knower to develop wisdom where self becomes an instrument of exploration with a lens of insider-out. In other words, the knower becomes a critical self-reflective practitioner (Schon, 1983). Thus, reflexivity comes through critical self-reflective practice (van Manen, 1995).

Reflexivity is a powerful lens that demands vulnerability of both the researcher and the researched where the practitioners highlight their weaknesses in order to bring about transformation. We believe that developing a liberating view of education seems difficult without such a lens because wisdom does not come with a superficial level of thinking (Dewey, 1933). It needs deep root-level conscious thinking and reflections in order to improve one's own practices and develop new perspectives (Mezirow, 1978).

Conclusion

Building on our personal-professional experiences rooted in different traditional identities, we argue that the metaphor of *leaders as position holders* has been a great threat to a sustainable future for educational institutions. To us, such a metaphoric expression of leadership represents a mindset that reflects the practices of the people who merely hold positions as leaders, but do not exhibit the transformative behaviour that makes a difference in the lives of their followers. They work as theory-oriented leaders, who believe in a narrow concept of education through control with suppressive forms of administration. Metaphorically, this form of leadership, to us, is leadership as controlling, commanding, and/or imposing. Leaders with such a view of leadership believe in positions rather than in roles. Our decade-long experiences reveal that, in developing countries, including Pakistan and Nepal, departmental/institutional heads as leaders, inspired from and/or affected by our colonial past, believe in an informing state of education and appear to be struggling towards *reforming* one or the other form of education. On the contrary, another brand of *leadership as transforming* believes in facilitation and empowerment of the followers with care, love, and ecological consciousness. However, this appears to be missing in most situations.

We argue that bringing reforms in today's educational institutions is necessary to bring some changes in a very conventional structure of education. However, it is not a sufficient condition to liberate learners/followers from the taken-for-granted ways of being and becoming. In such a situation, these leaders *as* merely new colonial masters who simply rely on Newtonian Physics and follow the canonical ways of doing research, need to change their practices. This change could be a serious challenge for institutions and societies to bring meaningful reforms. To us, a meaningful reform means a deep conscious-level change in beliefs and practices that challenge the old perceptions and develop new views of being and becoming. Such a deeper level change in thoughts, beliefs, and practices of leaders is embedded within the philosophical underpinnings of transformative education and research as/for empowerment of followers. To this end, working towards education with an emancipatory interest, a liberating and empowering view of education, appears to be the need of the time where transformative leaders can employ innovative approaches to being and becoming.

Embracing the transformative research paradigm, having multiple identities as contemporary social science researchers, we believe that transformative leadership as/for liberation and empowerment appears to be embedded within praxis, reflexivity and multi-epistemic approaches to knowing self/others. Under such enabling paradigms, educational leaders as transformative researchers and living-educational theorists can empower followers through the highest level of facilitation. It also makes it possible to develop transformative leaders and living theorists who can work effectively for a sustainable future. Such transformative researchers as leaders serve as critical-creative friends who do not care about the positions they hold, but believe in creating opportunities to solve the problems of their followers. Such leaders engage in a selfless struggle with dedication and a shared vision for empowerment of followers in order to bring changes in their thinking, actions/performance, and attitudes. Such leaders can serve as change agents with the notion of lifelong learning for empowering self and others with embodied values of practice such as care, love, peace, and ecological consciousness.

Notes

1. We have used the slash to refer to dialectical relationships between seemingly opposing constructs, categories, or phenomena.
2. To us, transformative leadership, especially transformative educational leadership, means leadership that believes in empowering the followers. Transformative leaders believe in co-leading, co-evolving, and co-becoming. Leadership becomes the process of a joint venture. Such leaders go beyond theoretical views and engage practically to test concepts and ideas that support a liberating view of education. With this belief, they create equal opportunities for self and others to enable self and others to achieve the goal of becoming lifelong learners.
3. A time for having a cup of tea or coffee at the Kathmandu University canteen to entertain out of office but still use that free time in a very friendly chat to discuss research activities. We call that meeting a 'cup-shop'.
4. Even after the demise of colonisation, people living in post-colonial regimes (the countries who have been under the rule of colonial powers) and/or are affected by the influence of colonisation, un/consciously think with a particular mindset that the

western modern world views are always right. Un/wittingly they begin to neglect their own local wisdom and traditions of knowledge generation. Resultantly, education and research as ways of knowing has been under the domain of taken-for-granted ways of knowledge production.

5. The metaphor of leaders as position holders means those people who are heads, supervisors, directors, deans, vice-chancellors, etc. with a particular mindset of being superior to others. The feeling of superiority reflects from their everyday actions un/consciously. These leaders work as theory-oriented leaders who believe in a very narrow view of education through control with suppressive forms of administration rather than facilitation and empowerment of followers. This is what Habermas (1972) calls a technical interest of education that does not provide freedom to learners/subordinates, but it focuses on control and dictation.

6. Administrative personnel, who have authority to deal with everyday activities of people (especially the people working in educational institutions), believe that since they have the authority, so they must create obstacles in the form of unnecessary delays, procrastination, and avoidance. Such leaders as controllers have a negative mindset to harm, rather than to support, people because they are products of the lowest interest of education that does not believe in common good.

7. Transformative learners as leaders focus on unconventional ways to research as/for knowing, yet they do not reject conventional approaches. They hold an inclusive lens that enables them to think beyond the limits of conventional ways.

8. An 'informing' state of teacher education would be a technical interest in education that is a highly controlled form of providing education. Whereas, a 'reforming' state of teacher education appears to be somewhat practical interest of education that the Habermasian view provides, a limited freedom, but not enough freedom, to learners.

9. A transformative state of education is deeply rooted within the philosophy of empowerment, support, and facilitation that create conditions for liberating minds from a narrow view of education. Such a view enables learners to become more innovative and creative by challenging conventional ways of looking at the world around self and others.

10. A holistic lens means a view of teacher education that is inclusive in nature and covers almost all key areas of teacher education as a whole. For instance, a holistic lens looks at teacher education with: Leadership; curriculum; pedagogy; assessment and teacher education research. Moreover, all these five key areas are viewed with these three levels of informing, reforming, and transformative. Therefore, to us a holistic lens is an approach to exploring teacher education in such a broader way.

11. To us, *organisational big-guns* are the leaders who believe in formal, traditional, top-down approaches to leading and holding positions in organisations especially in educational institutions. The leaders as position holders appear to serve as organisational big-guns. To bring such leaders out of their mindsets, institutions as learning organisations (Qutoshi & Rajbhandari, 2016) need to engage both leaders and followers with innovative research as a transformative practice. Thus, this is the transformative educational leadership that converts traditional institutions into learning organisation where both leader and followers join hands for co-becoming, co-leading, and co-evolving.

12. Dialogic logics as a genre of research powerfully engages researcher(s) as knowledge creators. It provides a platform to engage in a critical yet creative dialogue that fosters ways of reflecting in innovative ways of knowing.

13. The use of '/' as a dialectical logic enables the writers to make sense of both fictional and nonfictional ways of writing stories in addition to semi fictional approaches so as to create multiple possibilities for creating pedagogical thoughtfulness.

10

Culture and Organisational Knowledge Creation Processes: A Case Study in Afghanistan

OMIDULLAH KHAWARY

Culture has a profound influence over organisational learning, knowledge creation, and sharing processes of any organisation. It can either function as a facilitating or hindering factor towards knowledge creation and sharing. In today's knowledge economy, knowledge upgradation and capacity expansion are no more a choice. They are a prerequisite to enabling organisations to be responsive to both internal and external environmental changes (Dierkes et al., 2003). Culture to an organisation is like water to a fish. This means that organisations cannot survive without having an appropriate culture that enhances and supports learning. It is up to the organisational management and leadership to foster an environment and create a culture where everyone continuously upgrades and expands their capacities to deliver the desired results. This chapter is based on an empirical investigation using qualitative design and is conducted in a non-profit organisation that works in the areas of agriculture, economic inclusion, education, health, and civil society. The focus of this chapter is on the influences of cultural dimensions identified by Hofstede (2001) such as individualism-collectivism, uncertainty avoidance, and power distance on organisational knowledge creation and sharing processes in the context of Afghanistan.

This chapter suggests that collective culture, employee diversity, and face-to-face communication and interactions can contribute towards knowledge creation processes. However, knowledge protection, presence of a strong in-group and out-group phenomenon, language barriers, shyness, inadequate sharing of one's ideas, low risk taking, high power distance, absence of job security and trade unions, and a conformity syndrome are major hindering factors/barriers in the context of a least developed country like Afghanistan. The chapter will have a contextual analysis of the cultural facilitators and hindrances following recommendations on how leadership and management should dispense with their functions.

INTRODUCTION

The concept of organisational culture characterises leaders and managers as key variables in the success or failure of organisational knowledge creation processes. As Schein (1985) states, 'A deeper understanding of cultural issues in organisations is necessary not only to decipher what goes on in them but, even more importantly, to identify what may be the priority issues for leaders and leadership' (p. 2). Despite a strong linkage between the organisational culture and the creation and sharing of new knowledge and implementation of new behaviours and practices, the relationship between the two is not adequately researched (Detert & Schroeder, 2000). Investigation on how culture affects knowledge creation capability has a distinct contribution towards knowledge creation and sharing processes.

This linkage is minimally researched and there is a serious gap to be filled (Wang, et al., 2011). Therefore, the aim of this chapter is to address this gap by exploring the influences of organisational cultural dimensions such as individualism-collectivism, power distance, and uncertainty avoidance on the organisational knowledge creation processes in the context of Afghanistan. This will help the organisational leadership to understand which dimensions of organisational culture are supportive of knowledge creation that ultimately will help them to align their culture with knowledge management processes. Learning organisations create an environment where everyone is continuously engaged in upgrading their knowledge and expanding their capacity to reach the results they truly desire (Senge, 1990b). Hence, knowledge up-gradation and capacity expansion are no more a choice. Rather, they are the prerequisites for enabling organisations to be responsive to internal and external environmental changes (Dierkes et al., 2003). Therefore, the capacity of an organisation to learn, acquire, apply, and spread new insights is considered as the fundamental strategic capability (Fiol & Lyles, 1985) and a leading source of competitive advantage (de Geus, 1988).

Advocates of the knowledge-based view of the firms emphasise that the dominant role of an organisation's leadership is generation and application of knowledge (Spender, 1996; Nonaka & Takeuchi, 1995; Nonaka, 2007). The resource-based view (RBV) of the firms also suggests that organisations can remain competitive if they possess valuable resources, including the rare, non-imitable, and non-transferable resources (Barney, 1991). Organisational knowledge is one of the intangible resources of organisations which is hard to imitate or transfer. Thus, if knowledge is considered as a unique and rare resource of the organisation then its leadership becomes vital (Heinrichs & Lim, 2005). Knowledge management has gone through three distinct phases: (i) a before 1990s phase, (ii) an early 1990s phase, and (iii) a late 1990s phase. In the first phase of knowledge management, the focus was on collection of data and information and how it was stored in databases like any other organisational asset. In this phase, knowledge was assumed to be objective, absolute, and context-free. In the second phase, the focus shifted towards exchange of organisational knowledge.

Today, learning theorists (Lave & Wenger, 1991) reject the traditional concept of transfer models that keep knowledge objective, absolute, and isolated from its context. New theories suggest that in a learning organisation, knowledge is created in a specific context where it has meaning (Brown & Duguid, 1991). Thus, it is not enough to only have an efficient information processing system. The organisation itself should become a hub for further knowledge creation. Therefore, today, knowledge is not considered as a free-standing phenomenon. It is considered to be context-dependent and is therefore influenced by the organisational culture that is part of the context. This chapter is based on the assumption that knowledge is created, given meaning, utilised, and re-shaped in a specific context. As Czarniawska (2007) writes, knowledge is created as an outcome of human action that is deeply reflected through its cultural roots. It is generated in a specific context where it has its relevant and contextual meaning (Jakubik, 2008).

There are essentially two types of knowledge, categorised as tacit and explicit (Nonaka, 1991). As Polyani (1958) states, 'We know more than we can tell' (p. 4).

This statement highlights the fact that people know more than they share, which is called tacit knowledge. Tacit knowledge is possessed by individuals and is highly rooted in individual actions and experiences (Nonaka, 1994). This is the type of knowledge that separates a master from an ordinary person (Lawson & Lorenzi, 1999). Therefore, tacit knowledge is the means through which 'know-how' is converted into 'know what' and is practiced throughout the organisation (Brown &

Duguid, 1998). Explicit knowledge, on the other hand, is the codified type of knowledge which is easily transmittable into formal and systematic language. Organisational knowledge is created through a delicate dance between the tacit and explicit knowledge through a four-stage process espoused by Nonaka and Takeuchi (1995) explained below.

Stage One, Socialisation: This is a tacit-to-tacit process where individuals get together and share their experiences, mental models, worldviews, and mutual trust, face-to-face with each other. To be effective, socialisation should go beyond the very superficial everyday neutral dialogues to the deeper layers of one's experiences and stored knowledge.

Stage Two, Externalisation: This is a tacit-to-explicit process, where individuals articulate the shared tacit knowledge and convert it into explicit concepts. Externalisation lies at the heart of the knowledge creation processes because in this process new concepts take shape and are shared with others through analogies.

Stage Three, Combination: This is an explicit-to-explicit process where newly externalised pieces of explicit knowledge are integrated into new integral structures.

Stage Four, Internalisation: This is an explicit-to-tacit process taken up by individuals to embody the explicit knowledge into tacit knowledge. Through internalisation, the combined explicit knowledge is shared throughout the organisation and is practiced by individuals to broaden, extend, and reframe their tacit knowledge.

The foundation for the above mentioned four-stage processes is called *ba* (roughly meaning 'place'). The *ba* concept was initially introduced by Japanese philosopher Kitaro Nishida and is considered the context where knowledge is shared, created, and utilised. The concept implies that knowledge creation needs a context to exist. *Ba* can be a physical space or a virtual/mental space where individuals interact, create, share, and amplify their knowledge. As noted above, an individual's interaction within an organisation is the major source for knowledge creation, sharing, and application. Therefore, it can act as enabler or constraint on the way organisations learn (Biloslavo & Zornada, 2004). This implies that organisational culture has a significant influence over the organisational knowledge creation processes (Park et al., 2004).

Geert Hofstede conducted a worldwide survey of IBM employees between 1967 and 1973. He proposed a theory of four cultural dimensions: individualism-collectivism, uncertainty avoidance, power distance, masculinity-femininity. After continuous researches he added two more dimensions, which are long-term orientation and indulgence versus self-restraint to the previous dimensions. This study will only focus on the three main cultural dimensions, namely individualism-collectivism, uncertainty avoidance, and power distance, to explore how these cultural dimensions facilitate or hinder the four-stage process of knowledge creation. The three cultural dimensions under study not only have more relevancy to be studied against knowledge creation and sharing processes but also have been largely validated and used in existing researches on organisation culture (Wuyts & Geyskens, 2005).

Research Methodology

The aim of this research is to explore the influence of culture on the organisational knowledge creation processes. Knowledge here is considered to be embodied in individuals who create it in specific context(s) and give meaning to it (Brown & Duguid, 1991). Ontologically speaking, the nature of this study rests upon the relativist argument that there is no single truth to be discovered (Easterby-Smith, Thorpe & Jackson, 2012) rather there are multiple truths varying from context to context and time to time (Collins, 1983: 88). Epistemologically, the research follows the social constructionism argument that reality is not out there, independent of the individual; rather it is constructed socially and given meaning by individuals (Easterby-Smith, Thorpe & Jackson, 2012). This epistemological stance fits well in this study because knowledge creation is a context-specific process which differs from one place to another (Korac-Kakabadze & Kouzmin, 1999) and is constructed and utilised socially. Literature also states that in social constructionism the focus is on how people make sense of the world around them and how they think, feel, and communicate, whether verbally or non-verbally (Easterby-Smith, Thorpe & Jackson, 2012).

Considering the above epistemological stance, this study employed a qualitative design and methodology that enables the researcher to have a thorough interaction with participants, listen to their perspectives, and explore their experiences of knowledge creation and externalisation. In other words, qualitative design becomes the most appropriate approach, when it comes to meaning making out of what people say and do (Gillham, 2000).

DATA COLLECTION METHOD AND SELECTION OF THE RESEARCH PARTICIPANTS

The main data collection method for this study was in-depth interviews. Interviewing was a suitable data collection method because it helps the researchers to gather thick and rich data and explore how the participants experience the world around them and make sense of it (Bogdan & Biklen, 1992). This method proved to be effective, as it allowed the researcher to ask for more elaborations, clarify inconsistencies, touch on sensitive issues, and do further probing to get the rich and thick data required. The data analysis was also conducted hand-in-hand with the data collection. A thematic analysis approach was used by coding and segregating the collected data into different themes. The data collected were colour-coded to help in the emergence of different themes, which are discussed in detail as the major findings of the study.

Sampling and selection of the research participants heavily depends upon the research question. Merriam (1998) explains two types of qualitative case study samplings; random and purposive. Purposive sampling is non-random where the researcher locates people who are willing to and have the capacity to share information by virtue of their knowledge or experience (Lewis & Sheppard, 2006). The strength of this method is that it allows the researcher to focus on people who have a sound understanding of what they believe that ultimately helps the researcher to come up with thick and rich data.

Considering the nature of this study, a purposive sampling is employed to get perspectives of various concerned entities, such as the employees who have worked in Learning and Development (L&D) departments, the Director of Human Resources' department, the Monitoring, Evaluation, Research and Learning Unit (MERLU) employees, and the Chief Executive Officer (CEO) who is assumed to be the gatekeeper of the organisation. In the context of the non-government organisations, the CEO is generally the ultimate decision-maker who leads the entire organisation. Presence of the CEO along with the HR director and MERLU director helped a lot in collection of data from a leadership perspective.

The sample size for this study comprised nine participants: The Chief Executive Officer as the gatekeeper of the organisation, three participants from the MERL unit, including its director, because this department has a component of learning attached to it, three participants from the L&D unit who are directly engaged with the organisational knowledge management; and two participants from HR, including the HR Director, who can provide information on how the organisational structure and culture influences the knowledge creation processes.

Table 10.1: Interviewees

Participants Interviewed	Number of Participants
Monitoring, Evaluation, Research, and Learning Unit Team	3 members
Learning and Development Unit	3 members
Chief Executive Officer	1 participant
Human Resources Unit Team	2 members
Total number of participants	9 participants

KEY FINDINGS AND DISCUSSION

Facilitators of Knowledge Creation and Sharing

The analysis of the data shows that the overall organisational culture does not function on the extreme ends of the individual or collective dimensions. However, the data suggests that elements of collective culture are more clearly pronounced and practiced. One of the participants noted, 'Our cultural orientation is more towards the collective culture because people share certain values and goals and it's not possible for the employees to work individually as one person's input is required for another employee's output'.

Collective culture is more facilitative towards knowledge creation and sharing. As one of the participants said, 'Sharing a common goal and cooperation among people contributes towards organisational knowledge creation and sharing – the more collective an organisation, the easier the externalisation and combination of knowledge can take place'. Research also supports that in collective cultures, the overall organisational goals are more valued than the personal objectives; therefore, to realise the organisational goals, employees will put their endless efforts towards knowledge combination and exchange processes (Bates et al., 1995).

Communication mostly occurs face-to-face in collective cultures. The culture of having face-to-face communication is another major facilitating factor. As one of the participants shared: 'As per my experience, face-to-face communication better helps the employees to share their tacit knowledge and probe in cases where they have confusions. The face-to-face communication better facilitates the ground for knowledge sharing'. Evidence suggests that face-to-face communication with people can be superior to those involving only documents exchange (Allen, 1977; Galbraith, 1990). Empirical evidence shows that even poorly articulated knowledge could be better transferred through personal contact (Hakanson & Nobel, 1998). The culture of face-to-face communication in the context of Afghanistan can facilitate knowledge creation because the knowledge transfer gets smoother when various parties are brought together physically (Davenport & Prusak, 1998).

Employees' diversity can also positively influence the organisational knowledge creation and sharing processes. A participant shared, 'The fact that the organisation is so diverse is to be considered as a plus point because people with diverse backgrounds come together, share a diverse type of knowledge that can greatly influence the quality of performance and as well as knowledge sharing'. Studies show that working teams with mixed and diverse abilities are more fruitful (Maham, 2013). Another participant said: 'We can create great things by putting the ideas of different people together'. Employees' diversity provides organisation with access to different ideas and skills that ultimately enhance their knowledge creation and sharing abilities (Elmuti, 2001).

BARRIERS TO CREATION AND SHARING OF KNOWLEDGE

The research findings reveal that organisational culture has a profound effect on the flow of knowledge and information. This part will focus on analysing the themes that emerged as hindering factors such as knowledge protection, presence of a strong in-group and out-group phenomenon, language barriers, feelings of being shy or inadequate, low risk taking, high power distance, absence of job security/trade unions, and conformity syndrome that hinder the flow of knowledge and information sharing.

INDIVIDUALISM–COLLECTIVISM

On the flip side of what was discussed on the collectivism side of the culture earlier, the data also suggests that in the organisation under study, collectivism is practised in silos and within the spheres of each unit.

People tend to share information in smaller groups or in silos. One of the participants shared:

> This collective culture does not appear at the entire organisational level rather each unit works in collective groups. This type of collective culture can create issues because of its trial to function better than other units even at the expense of degrading or harming other units.

This type of culture may encourage the flow of knowledge from individuals to groups but it hinders the knowledge migration across groups. Therefore, it hampers the internalisation of the knowledge creation throughout the organisation. One of the major barriers to the process of knowledge sharing at this organisation is the absence of the knowledge flow across the units. As one of the participants highlighted, 'I see very little information sharing with other team members because people see their work as their work and not as part of the bigger whole'. While the tacit knowledge possessed by individuals lie at the heart of knowledge creation, its practical benefits centre on its externalisation and amplification through sharing the information and knowledge from the individual level to the group and then to the organisational level (Nonaka, 1994). Therefore, the organisation does not benefit if knowledge is only hoarded with the individuals or within the units only unless it widely migrates throughout the organisation.

Moreover, there is a strong presence of in-group and out-group phenomenon that heavily influences the flow of knowledge and information sharing. For instance, one of the research participants shared, 'I do think that there are different units/sections in this organisation and some of them really are very exclusive in sharing their knowledge and information and try to share only within the group'. Such type of groupings can adversely affect the process of knowledge sharing because strong in-group orientations are often accompanied by negative feelings towards out-groups (Ashwin, 1996). Therefore, knowledge sharing at the organisational level can be significantly inhibited by in-group versus out-group orientations (Hutchings & Michailova, 2004).

Unlike what is shared in literature, in-groups can significantly inhibit the knowledge sharing process (Hutchings & Michailova, 2004). However, it should be noted that in-groups do not always adversely affect the knowledge sharing processes. For instance, one of the participants shared:

> One of the groups in this organisation includes smokers and since I smoke I used to stay at the balcony, sitting with the smokers and I would hear things that I never hear in meetings—I call this the cooler culture, you go for water around the cooler and that's where you get information.

This also indicates that when the official environment of the organisation is not conducive enough for the employees to share their knowledge and information, then employees choose to speak out their minds in informal spaces. From a very young age, people in Afghanistan have raised their children not to speak in front of elders because the cultural understanding is that it is not a child's place to speak in front of an elder. One of the participants stated, 'There is a strong correlation between politeness and being expressive—once you are told again and again to be silent and not to speak out particularly among elders then when you grow up, you have a lesser ability to express yourself and to speak your mind'. This type of culture raises silent children and breeds elders who are silent by default and are reluctant to share their views in wider gatherings.

In the context of Afghanistan, saving 'face' is a cultural reality and having a good face is considered a symbol of a person's dignity (Varner & Beamer, 2005). It is because face is considered as the claimed sense of favourable social self-worth and the estimated other-worth in an interpersonal situation (Ting-Toomey & Oetzel, 2002). It has a direct link with the individual's identity, in terms of respect, disrespect, dignity, honour, shame, guilt, status, and competence issues (Ting-Toomey & Oetzel, 2002). In such a culture, where the concept of face is collectively possessed and de-facing of one individual can be attributed to the whole group or family, saving face becomes the most significant attribute. When it comes to sharing ideas, people are conscious of saving their face. People may usually prefer staying silent rather than sharing things that they are not fully confident about. Such cultural orientations create an environment where people are expected to be perfect to share any piece of information and if they feel that they are inadequate and not competent enough to share their tacit knowledge, they choose to remain silent. For instance, one of the participants shared:

> In a formal organisational environment, people often feel threatened; the risk of being seen as not knowing everything which they think is an expectation, or being found out to be wrong is a major barrier to information sharing. Sharing any information which is considered as wrong will lead to losing face in the eyes of colleagues, supervisor, and the overall organisation.

Uncertainty Avoidance

The data suggest that the organisation functions in a high uncertainty avoidance culture. In this type of culture, employees do not feel empowered to innovate, make mistakes, or learn from their experiences. As one of the participants shared, 'I think that this organisation is not a risk-taking organisation at all because we are concentrating on what we know and not on what we don't know. So, we keep on doing what we know'. The literature states that organisations working with high uncertainty avoidance need predictability and uniformity and have a strong preference for codification (Erramilli, 1996). Therefore, they are more keen to maintain the stability of the current knowledge base rather than pursuing new knowledge (Bochner & Hesketh, 1994).

Therefore, to remain predictable, employees in this organisation take the safer side as opposed to experimenting with new ways of working that could be considered risky. For instance, one of the participants shared, 'In general, people who have been in this organisation for a significant amount of time want to stay on the safe side. They will do the same thing and the same practice again and again without questioning if the activity they have embarked on is required and effective'. In such an organisation, where risk taking is not encouraged, employees will continue doing what they have been doing.

These types of organisations are risk-averse and work against sharing and combining knowledge and ideas (Smith et al., 2005). Therefore, organisations with high uncertainty avoidance impede the process of knowledge creation and sharing.

As a result, these types of organisations will remain stuck with single-loop learning where errors are detected and corrected without going towards double-loop learning, which means altering the governing variables and the actions (Argyris, 1999), or triple-loop learning, where the foundational governing principles are questioned (Swieringa & Wierdsma, 1992). For instance, one of the participants stated, 'There is a continuation of practices in the way they have been done unless the practices have failed before (irrespective of whether this was successful or not) but if the practise has not failed or led to a disaster and it seems safe, reliable, and predictable, then it is practiced without being questioned'. In sum, high uncertainty avoiding cultures can decrease the willingness of the employees towards risk taking and experimentation with new ideas and as a result, learning and knowledge creation and sharing is hindered significantly.

Power Distance

The organisation functions in a highly power distance culture which is in itself a barrier towards knowledge creation and sharing. For instance, one of the research participants shared:

> In a mixed group of senior and junior staff, the junior staff is reluctant to share their ideas in front of the senior staff because they think that it's not appropriate to speak when seniors are there. They believe that the proper behaviour for seniors is to speak and juniors to listen.

The literature also supports the view that, in a high power distance culture, equality is not valued and instead people in higher status see themselves as different from others in social status. In fact, such differences are not only accepted but also expected (Hofstede, 2001). Moreover, knowledge flow is significantly hindered in an organisation with a tall hierarchy, since the organisational leadership needs to filter all the information that flows in and outside the organisation. The reason behind information filtration is to ensure that only the information they feel useful is to be shared. One of the participants divulged:

> Sometimes within an organisational structure you have information and knowledge which should really be kept within a certain group of decision makers because they have a different understanding of the work or the problem and if that knowledge gets defused outside it gets interpreted very differently; that can cause problems.

Hofstede (2001) also states that, in high power distance cultures, information flow is usually constrained by hierarchy. This can lead to an exclusion of lower-level employees from access to certain types of information. Furthermore, in a highly-structured organisation, employees can hardly dare to speak out their minds and share ideas. For instance, one of the research participants shared, 'Employees hide or protect information, especially when the information is negative, because they have a fear if the information is leaked then it will negatively affect their performance rating or maybe their career promotion'.

Another participant shared:

> Actually, my experience is such that people refrain from sharing their opinions or impressions if its opposite to that of a senior person specially the person in the hierarchy that they work for—so in that sense I don't think information or knowledge flows within the organisation.

Another critical barrier is the conformity syndrome where employees try to share what their supervisors expect them to share. One of the participants said, 'If one of our managers shares any point where his/her regional director is present then they tend to share what their regional director wants to hear'. Another participant stated: 'When I joined this organisation people were not speaking their minds until they came to know how I reacted to specific information shared and only then they started to share their ideas'. This type of culture creates an environment where tacit and genuine information is not shared and knowledge can neither be created nor shared. Literature also supports the view that organisations with high power distance cultures have a tight control mechanism on governing the inter-individual activities, which inhibits the creativity of the employees such as knowledge sharing (Shane, 1995).

Conclusions

The research findings show that cultural dimensions of individualism-collectivism, uncertainty avoidance, and power distance can significantly hinder or enhance the knowledge creation processes. The study concludes that there is no single barrier but a series of barriers that are highly integrated and intertwined and can either hinder or facilitate the smooth flow of the knowledge creation and sharing processes. Collective culture within different sections of the organisation has positive effects towards knowledge creation and sharing. Face-to-face communication is another cultural dimension that can facilitate employees to work together and share their tacit and explicit knowledge. The literature also supports the idea that collective culture has a positive effect on the knowledge creation capability of an organisation. For instance, collective culture can foster teamwork and cooperation among the employees (Chen et al., 1998) which creates a conducive environment where employees can exchange knowledge (Nahapiet & Ghoshal, 1998). To sum up, collective culture is more conducive to, and has a positive impact on, creation and sharing of organisational knowledge.

Uncertainty avoidance refers to the extent to which an organisation feels threatened and tries to avoid uncertainty and ambiguity (Hofstede, 2001). In a highly uncertainty avoiding culture, more predictability and uniformity is required (Erramilli, 1996). This means that employees are encouraged to do what they have been doing and avoid any initiatives or new ways of working that might put the organisation at risk. Therefore, employees are keener to maintain the stability of a current knowledge base rather than pursue new knowledge (Bochner & Hesketh, 1994). Analysis of the findings reveals that the organisation studied has a very high uncertainty avoiding culture. In such a culture, employees are expected to act error-free; the organisation expects a failure-free culture. This type of culture is harmful to organisational health because employees do not feel free to think innovatively and take new initiatives because of the possibility of making mistakes or being wrong. This type of organisational culture can lead to 'organisational silence'. Organisational employees will not feel encouraged to share their ideas as they believe that sharing new ideas might not carry weight when shared (Sun & Scott, 2005). This type of organisational culture is considered as a hindrance in allowing employees to share their tacit knowledge that ultimately leads the organisation to become dependent on only their explicit knowledge. While explicit knowledge is required for any organisation, it is often the tacit knowledge that separates the master from the common (Lawson & Lorenzi, 1999). Despite its importance, tacit knowledge is difficult to code and share because it is highly based on individual experiences (Polanyi, 1958) and is created through personal practice that makes its diffusion difficult (Augier &Vendelo, 1999).

The case is even true when the context is not conducive enough and the employees do not feel free to speak their minds. Knowledge tacitness, ambiguity, and a high uncertainty avoiding culture can function as a barrier to knowledge creation processes.

In the long run, this type of culture encourages superstitious learning, where the organisational successes are interpreted to be caused by managerial actions (Levitt & March, 1988). Often, leaders and employees view their achievements as a confirmation of their own actions which further enhances their confidence in current practices (Miller et al., 1997). Thus, in such a culture, organisational success is oversampled and failures are under sampled. The organisation will lose the ability to capitalise on its diversity and will remain stuck with its current practices because everyone will try to find out information that can confirm their own actions. Chances are that the organisation has put on blinkers and has fostered a monolithic culture where everyone is there to confirm and abide by the current practices without accepting and building on the diverse range of activities and information (Sitkin, 1996). This type of culture encourages its employees to take the safer side and remain in their comfort zones resulting in a single-loop learning organisation where the ultimate goal is to detect and correct errors without questioning the governing variables (Argyris & Schon, 1974). In sum, a high uncertainty avoiding culture hinders knowledge creation processes because such type of culture detests risk-taking and experimentation and works against sharing and combining knowledge and ideas (Smith et al., 2005).

Power distance refers to the 'practice of inequalities in the distribution of power and authority' (Hofstede, 1980, p. 72). Analysis of the findings reveals that this organisation functions in a high power distance culture. High power distance cultures encourage a tight control over employees and make them more task-oriented. As a result, employees heavily focus on their task completion and do not value knowledge creation and sharing (Bochner & Hesketh, 1994). People in high power distance cultures tend not to value equality and see themselves differently from others. In fact, such status differences are not only accepted but also expected (Hofstede, 2001). In such cultures, social status speaks louder than having innovative ideas. This leads the organisation to appreciate the ineffective ideas of employees with higher status at the expense of overlooking or ignoring the innovative ideas of the lower level employees. As a result, the organisation breeds a culture where lower level staff listen, and higher-level staff speak. In sum, organisations with a high power distance culture have a negative effect on knowledge creation processes.

Recommendations

Below are the major recommendations that may assist the leadership to consider moving the organisation towards a learning organisation where knowledge is continuously created, shared, and re-created throughout the organisation. Currently, this organisation is exploiting the knowledge available by capturing and locating the information. However, the organisation has the potential to capitalise on its resources to minimise the boundaries within its different sectors/units and encourage the flow of information and knowledge throughout the organisation. The organisation should move from a rare capturing and locating of knowledge towards transferring and sharing and then even further towards creating an enabling organisational environment. This movement from capturing and locating to transferring/sharing and to creating and enabling should be done simultaneously within each individual, each group, and overall at organisational level.

Moreover, the findings suggest that the flow of knowledge sharing and creation is restrictive in this organisation. Knowledge is not shared in the first place and if it is shared the focus is only on sharing explicit knowledge, which is limited to sharing books, articles, or any other forms of written knowledge. However, the organisation should focus on developing a platform where tacit knowledge is shared among its employees. To create such an environment, the organisational leadership needs to create a shared *Ba* (roughly means 'place' in Japanese). *Ba* is basically the foundation that advances individuals' interactions and enhances the mentality of realizing the self in all. It is the platform that harbours meanings and interpretations among a diverse range of people. Thus, knowledge is created in an environment where the self is freed to become a larger self and the employees see themselves as one within the group rather than mere individuals. It is only in an effective *Ba* where individuals can socialise, externalise, internalise, and combine their tacit knowledge. For this organisation to become a knowledge creating organisation, it needs to create a *Ba* where individuals transcend their inner and outer boundaries and become one with each other. Such an environment can help the organisation to develop a setting where knowledge is not hoarded in the heads of individuals, but is shared in groups, and ultimately migrates throughout the organisation.

The leadership can create such a *Ba* only when they consciously work to decrease the high level of uncertainty avoidance culture. It is only in a low uncertainty avoiding culture, where employees can make mistakes, learn from mistakes, share their concerns, feelings, intuitions, knowledge, and experiences with each other freely.

The leadership can also work to decrease the high level of power distance. As discussed in the findings of this chapter, it is only in a low power distance culture, where individuals frequently interact with each other, that employees can free themselves from their individual barriers and see themselves as a larger presence within the organisation. In such an environment, employees enjoy the comfort zone to speak their minds and share their tacit knowledge that helps the knowledge creation cycle rolling.

Furthermore, the organisational leadership can also look into upgrading its learning from a mere single-loop learning towards double- or even triple-loop learning. The best way would be to minimise the high level of uncertainty avoidance and let the employees initiate, take risks to do new things, and make mistakes. When mistakes occur, they should be taken as an opportunity, not merely to fix the situation quickly, but rather to question that underlying variable due to which such mistakes happened and try to change the founding variables instead of stopping at quick fixes.

Finally, the leadership should have a clear knowledge vision that has the ability to determine the type of knowledge required to be created and its appropriate means and domains. As the organisation studied has a wide scope of mandate, therefore, the organisation should articulate a knowledge vision that can transcend the boundaries of knowledge creation, its long-term direction, and how it should evolve in the long run (Nonaka & Toyama, 2007). The knowledge vision should highlight the value system of the firm, defining what is considered to be the truth, goodness, and beauty for the whole organisation. In such a situation, employees will be able to contribute towards sharing and creating organisational knowledge.

Limitations and Future Research

Although the present study has revealed some important findings, its design is not without flaws. Several limitations are there to be acknowledged regarding the present study. First of all, the participants selected for this research study were not all of Afghan origin, but a diverse group of people from different countries of the world. The chances that they experience the social interactions within this organisation differently may have affected the findings of this study. Second, this study was conducted with a limited number of participants from a single organisation; therefore, the findings cannot be generalised to all non-government organisations in Afghanistan. Third, this research was conducted employing a qualitative design while future research using a quantitative methodology can shed still further light on broader factors that facilitate or hinder the knowledge creation processes. Finally, all the participants selected were from the national office, thus limiting the findings of the research to national office staff only and may not reflect the views of the employees working in the remote areas and regions.

There are a number of areas that call for further attention in the future. First, the number of female participants were limited compared to male participants. Therefore, the findings of this study have not been analysed using a gender lens. A future study can be conducted to specifically find out how different genders see the hindering and facilitating factors towards knowledge creation and sharing. Research on how organisational structure, hierarchy, control systems, and types of leadership approaches affect the knowledge creation processes in the context of Afghanistan are yet further research areas to be considered.

11

Educational Leadership Policies and Practices: Key Lessons and Way Forward

GULAB KHAN AND JAN-E-ALAM KHAKI

The chapters in this volume looked at a variety of leadership policies, perceptions, and practices of headteachers/principals and District Education Officials in three developing countries. The main aim of putting these chapters together was to help researchers, educators, and practitioners obtain some insights about the way leadership is practiced in LDCs like Pakistan, Afghanistan, and Kyrgyzstan. Through these studies, an attempt was made to bring different voices from various contexts to share with the larger audiences, though mostly focusing on the LDCs.

So, what do we learn from these chapters or voices? What key lessons can the readers learn from them to theorise or to put into practice or to get some insights for future research? This chapter attempts to put together from all preceding chapters the crosscutting themes to respond to these questions and summarises the learnings from the book as a whole.

While we, the editors, understand that the readers will draw their own takeaways, based on their reading and interpretation of each chapter, however, this concluding chapter puts together some key lessons readers might consider as additional learning from this volume. This is not to say that each chapter thus is dispensable and that this chapter is enough for better understanding of the whole volume. Each chapter has an interesting story to tell and, as it is rightly said that the devil lies in the detail, so does each chapter provide the highlights of the entire picture from which we are taking some snaps and calling them 'lessons'.

The chapter identifies five themes drawn from different chapters, followed by an overarching sixth meta-theme that takes the level of analysis to a higher and more comprehensive level. Based on these conclusions, some key recommendations are offered for the consideration of policymakers, researchers, practitioners, and trainers of leadership at different levels.

Lesson 1: LDCs are increasingly acknowledging the critical importance of leadership both at the policy and practice level

The studies in this volume show, directly and indirectly, that LDCs are beginning to acknowledge the critical significance of educational leadership in the developing countries, including the emerging countries of Central Asia, such as Kyrgyzstan. These studies show that the history of the focus on leadership through policy and practice is not a very old one. The chapter by Khan and his colleagues on policy studies amply demonstrates how, since the birth of Pakistan, till the late 1980s, educational policy papers in the realm of higher education do not even mention the word 'leadership', let alone emphasizing its significance (Memon, Nazirali, Simkins, & Garrett, 2000).

From the beginning, Khan and colleagues aptly argue that the higher education policy has placed demands on universities and their leadership to pursue goals that were *heavenly in stature but earthly in practice*. At the same time, while universities were mandated to contribute significantly in the national development, they were also expected to balance the dynamics of internal and external control. With 'leadership' on the sidelines and administrative efficiency as the primary unit of action in policy discourses, the challenges for university leadership appear to abound in steering the university into a highly uncertain future with many promises but with just as many pitfalls.

Interestingly enough, when Quaid-i-Azam, the founding father of Pakistan, saluted henceforward as the Quaid, was addressing the Dacca University Convocation on 24 March 1948, he hardly ever mentioned the role of universities to prepare 'leaders' for the nation.[1] Instead, he focused on developing technical skills and encouraged going more for private than government jobs (Siddiqui, 2016: 293). What this means is exactly what we have been emphasizing, that the leadership notions used in educational governance in Pakistan are relatively a new development (Ali & Babur, 2010). As we can see here, even one of the supposedly most enlightened leaders, the Quaid, could not visualise this role for the university graduates of his time. While summarizing the key reasons for failure of policy implementations, Siddiqui (Ibid, p. 274) counts the reasons as lack of participatory approach, unrealistic goals, lack of political will, ineffective monitoring and accountability systems, political interference, lack of political stability, and poor governance.

From the above discussion, the leadership picture at the apex of the education system is less than promising as it emerges from Khan and colleagues' study. The good news, however, is that at the lower levels there are enough indications to pay attention to the training and development of leadership in various educational organisations. A variety of programmes are being offered in this regard through, for example, the training colleges, professional development centres, and departments of education at the universities. Interestingly enough, new professional development centres, particularly in the private sector, have emerged since the inauguration of the new millennium. The Institute for the Educational Development of the Aga Khan University in Karachi, the School of Education at the Lahore University of Management Sciences, the Ali Institute of Education in Lahore, and the University of Education in Lahore, Pakistan, besides many other educational institutions that have been working for many years are but some examples of this change. These newer developments have been targeting educational leadership in an environment where the larger governance mechanisms centre on tight bureaucratic principles.

In Pakistan, centralised bureaucratic leadership has stifled creativity, innovation, and leadership at all levels (Khaki & Safdar, 2010; Shafa, 2003, 2010). New levels of qualification and accreditation need to be established for the appointment and promotion of leaders at all levels, including the school leadership and District Education Officers. Appointments on and promotions to leadership positions should be based on ideals of engendering a culture of creativity, effective accountability, and collective responsibility and action in schools and organisations (Govinda, 2002: Memon, 2010, 1999: Qutoshi & Khaki, 2014). There is a strong need of such changes at all levels of policy and practice. The contributors mentioned above demonstrate that such a change of policy or even a paradigm shift is imperative if Pakistan and similar LDCs need to leap to more creative ways of leading their educational policies, structures, and practices (Niyozov & Khaki, 2017).

Lesson 2: Leadership models, imported from MDCs must be carefully selected and contextualised to serve local needs

There are numerous models of leadership, to the extent that it has now become a challenge to select from so many competing models, each claiming to be the best one. For example, instructional (Blasé & Blasé,

1998), pedagogical (Sergiovanni, 1998; Shareef, 2010), transformational (Leithwood et al; 1999), trasnforma*tive* (Qutoshi, 2016), distributed (Gronn, 2008), and more recently, the adaptive (Heifetz, Linsky, & Grashow, 2014), have all been promoted as effective models of leadership. Firstly, all these models have been developed and applied in largely the developed and industrialised world, with varying degrees of success. Secondly, it cannot automatically be assumed that if they have worked well in the MDCs, they will work as well in the LDCs. Both contexts are hugely different, considering, for example, the enormously different infrastructure of school organisations, polices and cultural norms of governance. Summing up the conclusions of this strand of argument, Leithwood and his colleagues (2000), as cited in Khaki (2005: 286), argue that:

> History has taught us…that the meaningfulness of each approach to leadership is *significantly context dependent* (emphases added). Truly productive leadership depends not only on engaging in commonly helpful practices, it also depends on recognizing and responding to the unique challenges and features presented by particular types of organisational contexts.

What this argument leads to is that, care must be taken to see which model will better fit in the LDCs, and within them, even in a particular context of a country or nation, or even within a district (Khaki, 2008). Such contextual fitting is important because each context is politically, culturally, and demographically different and, therefore, one model may not fit all. This is obviously easier said than done and, therefore, leadership at all levels must be cognizant to see which model—or even a combination of models—fits their context.

The study by Qutoshi and Luitel suggests a concept similar to, yet different from, the transformatio*nal* leadership model. They call it the 'transforma*tive*' leadership model. The writers argue based on their decade-long experiences that, in developing countries, departmental/institutional heads as leaders, inspired from and/or affected by colonisation, believe in a transforming state of education and appear to be struggling towards reforming in one or the other forms of education. On the contrary, the transformative leadership, they believe, is more facilitative of empowering the followers with care, love, and ecological consciousness. Their study recommends that educational leaders think beyond the borders of conventional ways of what they call 'leading with oppressive management' outlook. Rather, they argue, leaders need to reflect critically on their ways of leading and believing in the taken-for-granted ways of looking at the world. Educational leaders, as critical reflective practitioners, can create conditions for research as knowing self/others with multi-epistemic approaches, which foster transformative learning. Critical reflective practitioners, as transformative leaders, having an emancipatory interest in education, can better serve self/others and institutions for a more sustainable future.

Taking the debate on models of leadership further, Tajik, Shah, and Shamatov in their respective chapters talk about the efficacy of pedagogical leadership models used in many professional enhancement programmes, such as at the AKU-IED. Tajik provides a bird's eye view of the different leadership models and highlights the significance of a pedagogical model of leadership as a more viable model for professional development of the school heads. He provides a template of how he and his colleagues applied this model in their institution (AKU-IED) and how it was found to be viable and effective. Policymakers, practitioners, and trainers are advised to look at the model more closely and see if it can work for them as well. Similarly, Shah provides us a glimpse of a professional development programme at AKU-IED in which he was one of the facilitators as a professional development teacher (PDT) and faculty assistant. Those who are interested in the professional development of leaders may particularly be keen in this model which was based on an episodic and multi-dimensional professional development programme across two provinces of Pakistan. Shah provides very useful insights about the way this programme was conceptualised and implemented.

Shamatov's study situated in a school in Kyrgyzstan reports the way a headteacher mentored a newly inducted teacher and how she (the teacher) perceived the role and the attitude of the headteacher and how she actually experienced it. The study gives us a sense of the leader and follower roles as mentors and mentees and one could also call it a pedagogical leadership model displayed in a mentor's role. The pedagogical leadership is all about the capacity building of all concerned (Sergiovanni, 1998). Thus, this is another facet of the pedagogical role of the headteachers displayed in building teachers' pedagogic capacities. Shamatov brings out the lesson that, if the headteachers nurture the self-efficacy of the teachers, they can build confidence in them, and help them perform better, and in turn, become leaders in their own right. Similar findings have come through in Pakistan's context (e.g. Bashiruddin & Retallick, 2008) as well that show how incumbents become novice teachers with stories similar to the mentee teacher in Shamatov's study. Khan's (2010) study on the way teachers and students relate to the headteacher or principal is also an insightful study that unpacks how these relationships unfold in a school context.

The headteacher in Shamatov's study plays a role that Irwin (2018) refers to as an easy job of 'a pat on the back' to a deep level of appreciating personal worth that he calls 'affirmation'. The author describes it as 'words of life' spoken to us by someone who matters to us. Comparing 'compliment' and 'affirmation', he argues that 'a compliment goes skin deep', as it may convey esteem and appreciation, 'but not a deep affirmation of who we are'. Compliments, by their very nature, Irwin argues, are 'superficial social rituals'. They are perfect for social customs as we might need to be in our lives polite and civil' (p. 21). On the contrary, Irwin thinks, affirmation is 'acknowledging our strength of character'. He believes that one can influence employees, organisations, families, teams, and groups for the good through affirmation. He even brings evidence from the cognitive sciences that affirmation sets in motion huge positive changes in the brain, triggering favourable attitudes and moods towards more positive self-image, productivity, happy feeling, self-worth, and leading to more innovative thoughts. In Shamatov's study, the school leader seems to affirm some of these attributes that helped the teacher, grow so well. If leaders were to adopt these traits or habits in themselves, it is more likely that they may become 'transformational' in Leithwood's term, or 'transform*ative*' in Qutoshi and Luitel's term. School and educational leaders do need to be inspired by these ideals to make a difference in the lives of their followers.

Following the lessons in this volume about school or District Education Officers, another dimension of leadership—an extension of the headteacher or principal leadership—is the teacher leadership. In their chapter on teacher leadership, Shafa and Baig share their insights about the significant role of teacher leadership, in so far as their EDIP project was concerned, both in the implementation and sustainability of school improvement initiatives. The teachers' pivotal roles in linking the development partners with students and their parents emerged as the most significant aspect of the EDIP as the key lesson. Therefore, improving teacher competence and leadership was considered as an overarching theme of the project and resources were invested to sharpen their leadership roles. The study tells us that teachers do possess massive potential in terms of their ingenuity and accomplishments; hence, there is a need to unleash and give direction to their creative impulses to accelerate the process of school improvement.

The tangible evidence related to the difference of perceptions and perspectives between the pre- and post-intervention response challenges and contradicts the popular stereotypical notions that public sector schools merely provide access without care for quality. The paradigmatic shift in the perceptions and perspectives among the public sector school stakeholders reflected in Shafa and Baig's study supports the understanding that these schools in GB are capable of focusing on both. These schools, the study claims, can be turned around as 'schools of choice', provided school improvement interventions are carefully planned and sustained by the concerned authorities. This turnaround is possible, the study argues, provided there is institutional capacity to support, monitor, and evaluate the initiatives undertaken by the school and district leadership under the EDIP project.

The second key lesson the study highlights is the monitoring and evaluation mechanism of the educational development initiatives. At the project level, the monitoring and evaluation must dig down to the sustainable impact of the interventions rather than confining to the outputs and immediate outcomes. At the government level, the monitoring and evaluation mechanism need to have the resources, professional capacities, and attitudes to embed and synchronise the project interventions to achieve maximum benefits from development projects. Thus, in the gloomy picture of the public sector context, these are some silver linings that one could see as has been noted by many other studies (e.g. Benz, 2014; Iqbal, 2016) in the context of GB.

Lesson 3: Disabling organisational and cultural environments can hamper the efficacy of district level leadership in LDCs

In Pakistan, district offices and officers work somewhere in the middle of the hierarchy with largely tribal cultures, socially stratified and politically volatile conditions, and in a top-down, iron-hand bureaucratic leadership environment. This, in combination with personnel and organisational inefficiency, render the District Officers as 'toothless tigers' in metaphorical terms. This is the conclusion by Khaki and colleagues in their study of District Education Officers in Pakistan. Based on their empirical study of and working with the professional enhancement programmes targeted at DEOs for over a decade, the authors conclude that it is difficult, if not impossible, to work diligently, creatively, and effectively, as the DEOs consistently find themselves in a milieu where the tribal chieftains (*sardars*) are far more powerful than any government bureaucrat or education officer. The chapter reflects how the sociocultural factors in the work of the District Officers adversely affect their performance. This could very well be seen in a more recent tragedy (while we were writing this chapter) in which, according to news reports, a DEO was gunned down in his office due to differences over his decision to transfer some of his subordinates, or appoint some teachers, at the instigation of a particular person (*Dawn*, 13 October 2019). Khaki and his colleagues suggest that the DEOs feel helpless and inadequate to deal with a number of factors, including the tribal and political influences that give rise to un-enabling and daunting environments in most of the rural, and to a significant degree, in urban education ecosystems in Pakistan.

The system inevitably becomes crippled in the absence of appropriate mechanisms to support and reward good work and to address systemic inefficiencies. A DEO comments that, if he fires a dishonest employee, before he (the DEO) can reach home, he himself gets fired or transferred to another school, while the errant comes back to school more confident. This speaks volumes of the way educational administration is (mis) managed in the public sector in at least two provinces in Pakistan. In such largely lawless situations, it is indeed daunting to administer education effectively.

Stories abound of schools being used as barns or cattle pens by local chieftains. Stories of ghost schools still haunt educational governance in Sindh and Balochistan. Amid all this, the pertinent question that begs answering is: What kind of leadership theory would work in situations of social apathy for the critically important life and death issue of education?

However, on a more optimistic note, the positive side of human ingenuity *does* give some hope, preventing us from drawing a downright pessimistic conclusion. Many daring DEOs and headteachers do struggle hard to do what they *can*. Often, for example, they pay from their own pockets to buy fuel for their bikes to visit their schools, or literally 'carry a gun' to ward off risks to their lives in the largely still lawless tribal areas in almost all provinces of Pakistan. Unless the educational administration is delinked from negative political or crippling social influences, there is no way to smoothly run an educational organisation.

In contexts such as these, perhaps an unconventional set of leadership skills may be needed. Sergiovanni (1992) calls this the 'moral leadership', while Greenleaf (2003, 1977) calls it 'servant leadership'. In a more contextual phrasing, Khaki (2005) calls it Prophetic Professional

Leadership, committed to and inspired by moral and spiritual values coupled with a sacred mission, such as a saint or a prophet would strive to achieve. This would require a deep and abiding sense of purpose through an unwavering commitment despite severe odds. In such unruly environments it is difficult, if not impossible, to administer the educational governance of a vast population of a developing country. However, what could possibly make a difference is the right kind of nurturing through proper training of both minds and souls. Higgins, McGowan, Murphy, and Trafford (1991) rightly argue, and it makes sense in the context we are talking about, that a heightened moral sense can inspire administrators to make a difference in their context. They suggest:

> The test of moral leadership as in servant leadership is whether the competence, well-being and independence of followers are enhanced and whether the enterprise ultimately benefits. Moral considerations are both beginning and the end of value-added leadership. Morality and leadership are inextricably intertwined. (p. 261)

Greenleaf (2003), who has championed the concept of servant leadership, believes that the principles of servant leadership are:

> [M]ore likely to emerge in practice in those segments of the society where the concern is most intensely felt for justice (rather than order), for the performance (rather than the form) of our institutions, and for the appropriateness (rather than the result) of power and authority [all brackets in the original]. (p. 33)

This is similar to what Hargreaves, Boyle, and Harris (2014) call 'uplifting leadership'. They explain that 'emotional and spiritual uplift is the beating heart of effective leadership. It raises people's hopes, stirs up their passions, and stimulates their intellect and imagination' (p. 3). In faith-based societies such as Pakistan and Afghanistan, these lofty values and ideals may be employed to inspire the headteachers and principals to enhance their resilience to the culturally, ethnically, and politically difficult situations in which they work.

Coming back to the central role of DEOs, although the chapter may reflect overall the DEOs' role as less than heroic, it is equally revealing about the way they describe their exceptional roles. Although they appear as *toothless tigers* to their subordinates, they work selflessly as much as possible to make sure to carry out at least the minimum administration that is required of them. This dimension reflects courage, confidence, sacrifice, and steadfastness inspired by their faith, in times of intimidation, coercion, and threatening situations even to their lives. Doing one's best even in the worst situations is the lesson they leave us with. Khaki and colleagues find a glimmer of hope in these leaders who operate at the middle levels of their hierarchies, thus offering stimulus to such ideas as Leadership from the Middle (LftM) proposed by Hargreaves and Braun (2012). The DEOs and AEOs are at a position in the hierarchy in Pakistan's public education edifice where they can act as the ameliorating and amalgamating factor up and down the hierarchy. This is only possible when they are developed and supported to deliver on their daring duties in the heterogeneous and highly differentiated mix of Pakistan's education ecosystem. Thus, LftM appears to be a more viable option for leadership development and school improvement on a significant scale in Pakistan. As Fullan (2016) explains:

> The top (state or provincial government) cannot adequately lead the whole system from the centre. Bottom-up strategies don't work either because movement is desultory. Therefore, perhaps the glue of coherence lies in the middle. In this case the middle consists of districts...The idea is to indicate to districts that (1) they need to build their internal capacity..., and (2) they need to work laterally with other districts in focused, purposeful networks... (p. 203).

Given the scale of the problems in Pakistan and other similar LDCs, LftM is an idea holding potential. It is only through a motivated, uplifted mass of middle leaders who can act as glues and guides that the educational change process can take place.

In a similar vein, Takbir Ali's chapter reflects a pessimistic picture about the roles played by the monitoring and evaluation teams. These two roles—roles of the district offices and the supervision and follow up roles—do intersect. Ali argues that what is done in the name of monitoring and evaluation (M&E) is a 'sheer waste of time and resources'. Although the M&E functions are indeed carried out and quite frequently, they seldom lead to any efficiency and improvement in the functioning of the organisation. Both studies, by Ali and Khaki and colleagues, show that the role of the supervisors through district office or M&E of school performance are not productive, owing to numerous hindering factors. These factors include:

- Safety and security, as one of the major concerns for supervisors, particularly women working in these positions;

- Almost non-existent job descriptions or terms of references (ToRs) for supervisory staff; and even if there exist rudimentary job descriptions, they need revisions to make them compatible with the contemporary needs of school improvement;
- Too much time spent by supervisors in administrative activities, neglecting the importance of reorienting them towards academic support;
- Attention to the training needs of supervisors, ADOs, and other administrative officers in the areas of supervision, monitoring, and leadership skills, so that they can become effective and efficient along modern lines, especially when appointments are largely made without any training in school supervision and monitoring;
- Political interference in school affairs and nepotism on the part of influential persons making the supervisors' work even more complex.

This analysis and suggestions for improvement are consistent with the study of DEOs as Khaki and colleagues show.

Lesson 4: Schools catering for war and terrorism affected children in LDCs need holistic and broadly informed leadership

War and terrorism devastate all sections of the society, especially the vulnerable ones, chief among those being children. The agony and pain of war and terrorism deeply affect children physically, mentally, and emotionally. They often become refugees within their own or that of neighbouring countries, having sometimes lost their parents or caregivers or close relatives. If they are lucky, in some cases, they might get access to schooling in the host country or if they happen to come back to their own country, they might again go to their schools. In either case, these are not the same children; they are traumatised, intimidated, and frightened to the core and may by then develop many mental health problems, even if they are physically safe. Few countries or societies are ready to face these situations, much less headteachers and teachers. From Neelofar Ahmad's study, we learn how the leadership of schools, such as that in Pakistan, beset as they are with so many chronic problems, are stretched to their limits when they are confronted with children who have been affected by war and terrorism. They are neither equipped with nor do they have any resources to meet the needs of such children, thus becoming the proverbial last straw on their fragile backs.

While informing us through literature review on the ground realities in the Pakistani schools, Ahmad suggests a holistic model for school leadership that has, the writer hopes, the potential of meeting the needs of children affected by war and terrorism. If adopted, the model can address a wide range of such issues, and if the heads are equipped with the author's recommendations, it is more likely that they will be able to meet their needs to a great extent. The policymakers, district management, and training colleges and institutions, both in the public and private sectors, can adopt and benefit from the comprehensive and viable model that the author proposes. Also, Ahmad suggests cross-cultural or cross-national collaborations for sharing resources, knowledge, and expertise on such issues.

Lesson 5: Organisational learning is an important dimension of institutional learning

Organisational learning is an important dimension of today's institutional cultures (Hofstede, 2001). Situated in an organisational context in Afghanistan, Khawary explores the intricacies in and dynamics of organisational learning and the key players involved in it. Using the four-fold scheme of cultural study by Hofstede, Khawary tells us how these four schemas apply to the organisations in his context, the Afghan cultural milieu. From his study, we quite understandably learn that culture has a profound influence over organisational learning, knowledge creation, and sharing processes of any organisation. It can function either as a facilitating or hindering factor towards knowledge creation and its sharing. He emphasises that, 'in today's knowledge economy, knowledge upgradation and capacity expansion are no more a choice, rather a prerequisite to enabling organisations to be responsive to both internal and external environmental changes'. Analysis of the findings reveals that the organisation studied has a very high uncertainty avoidance culture. In such a culture, employees are expected to act in an error-free manner, assuming a failure-less culture. This type of culture is harmful to organisational health because employees hesitate to take risks and do not feel free to think innovatively or take new initiatives because of the fear of making mistakes. This type of organisational culture can lead to what Khawary calls 'organisational silence'.

Sharing his insights, Khawary tells us that in such a culture, (organisational) successes are over- and failures are under-sampled. The organisation will lose the ability to capitalise on its diversity and will remain stuck with its current practices because everyone will seek information that can confirm their own actions. It is likely that such organisations have put on blinkers and have fostered a monolithic culture where everyone is there to confirm and abide by the current practices without accepting and building on the diverse range of activities and information. This type of culture encourages its employees to remain in their comfort zones resulting in a single-loop learning organisation where the ultimate goal is to detect and correct the errors without questioning the governing variables. Thus, the key learning Khawary shares is that a high uncertainty avoiding culture may hinder the knowledge creation processes because such type of culture detests risk-taking—a conclusion that is worth reflecting on for schools as learning organisations.

School leaders have a lot to learn in this case study. The leadership can create, to use Khawary's term, *Ba* only when they consciously work to decrease the level of uncertainty avoidance culture. It is only in low uncertainty avoidance culture that employees make mistakes, learn from them, share freely their concerns, feelings, intuitions, knowledge, and experiences with each other. The leadership can also work to decrease the high level of power distance. Findings in Khawary's chapter lead us to conclude that low power distance cultures help individuals to frequently interact with each other and see themselves as parts of the larger tapestry within the organisation. In such an environment, employees enjoy a certain degree of psychological safety (Edmondson, 1999) to let loose on their vulnerabilities, leading to speaking their minds and sharing their tacit knowledge that helps augment knowledge creation in the organisation. According to Edmondson (1999), when members feel that their team is safe for taking risks, their learning behaviour changes and, hence, organisational learning. More recent research study (Rozovsky, 2015), suggests the key dynamics associated with successful team work include psychological safety. The organisational leadership can also look into upgrading its learning from a mere single-loop learning towards a double or even triple-loop learning. Building on increasing psychological safety, organisational members would initiate, take risks, and make mistakes such that underlying variables are explored to address the issues at the root cause rather than resorting to any quick fixes.

Finally, Khawary suggests, leadership should have a clear vision that has the ability to determine the type of knowledge required to be created as well as its appropriate means and domains. The knowledge vision should highlight the value system of the organisation, defining what is considered to be truth, goodness, and beauty for the whole organisation.

Lesson 6: Overall Lesson is that LDCs are experimenting with new ideas about leadership

The above mentioned five lessons or sets of lessons lead us to yet another overall lesson. Educational leadership is an emerging concept in the developing countries and is gradually and steadily being welcomed by schools and educational institutions. The traditional and age-old governance of schools and educational institutions is giving way to more participatory and distributed leadership (Bolden, 2011; Gronn, 2000, 2008; Tajik, 2010, 2014). The research studies in LDCs tend to demonstrate, though on a local and limited scale, that the age-old ways of governing schools may not yield optimal learnings for ALL learners if they continue with the bureaucratic top-down approach with high power distance and conflict avoidance attitudes and cultures. The national policies of many developing and emerging countries, such as Pakistan and Central Asia, tend to be in 'controlling phase' due to ideological and national aspirations, often taking precedence over what is right to do.

Participatory decision making, a more horizontal than vertical management system, is making inroads. However, traditional inertia is prevalent overall in many educational institutions within the overarching bureaucratic culture of the public education systems in these countries. Understandably, it will take time to change this frozen culture before policies are geared towards innovative governance, guided by evidence-based knowledge of management and leadership. However, the air of change is blowing. This is the optimistic spirit that has inspired us, the editors, to show through a keyhole some of these trends found in many places. Grown and Lee (2019) rightly argue:

> The need for leadership in education is unprecedented. Research studies show that talented leadership plays a pivotal role in improving student achievement. Clearly, it is incumbent on the profession of education to pay close attention to developing leaders by making sure they get the proper training. (p. 2)

This will not happen automatically. Public and private organisations will have to make concerted efforts to develop and train managers as leaders.

The emergence of new training colleges or leadership development institutions and programmes, for example, in Pakistan, can help do this task, provided the government policy frameworks and financial commitments are in place. Organisations, including of course schools and school systems in the 21st century have to be enlightened ones at all levels of governance to deliver cutting edge leadership to help develop learners who can thrive in a global village. Rather than keeping the age-old educational institutions' culture that focus more on discipline and maintaining the status quo (Ashraf, Tajik & Niyozov, 2017), they need to do what Kirtman and Fullan (2016) suggest:

> Leaders believe that educational environments should be exciting, creative, and vibrant places for everyone involved. What is more, these leaders realise that they do not have to wait for permission. Far from being reprimanded for showing initiative, they instead gain professional and political power. (p. xii)

Though this statement may not be true everywhere, as many societies in developing countries still follow tight bureaucratic governance systems, and showing initiatives may not always be admired due to many issues of legal and political implications. However, what is said by the learned authors makes sense for those societies that wish to change their governance cultures. Kirtrman and Fullan believe that these are opportune times to be an educational leader, to identify kindred spirits, and to cultivate and mobilise real leaders. Despite this, 'high performing leaders may feel alone'. The scholars further add:

> [H]igh performing leaders have to forget a path to success that is against the grain and counter to the practices of their colleagues. They have felt the need to keep quiet about what they believe is needed to improve the education process. Such leaders feel they are destined to be alone because the majority of regulators and political leaders will be critical of their practices or, even worse, try to stop them. However, these pioneers [can be found] ... everywhere ... (Ibid., p. 1)

These valuable suggestions do make sense when we think of the LDCs as contexts for developing innovative leadership concepts (Bana, 2010). The studies contained in this volume do suggest a silver lining in the clouds and further suggest that the LDCs will move forward in terms of fostering educational leadership, although it may take time to catch up with those who are accelerating their pace on this path. There are also interesting concepts for leadership that we believe are useful to adopt. For example, leaders building vision and mission for their organisations, and rigorously following them (Colwell, 2018) could be yet another way to strengthen leadership practices. Similarly, many emphasise on what they call transforming school culture through mindfulness and compassion in an increasingly volatile world (Jennings, McMauro & Mischenko, 2019). Not only this, there is an insistence to even 'rewiring education' in view of the technological advances both in teaching and learning (Couch, 2018). This is now a whole new area that needs attention if our future schools are to provide innovative teaching and learning opportunities. We are alive to the fact that these ideas may be ambitious for the LDCs at the moment, but leaders at all levels need to reflect on these powerful ideas and see how incrementally they could be made use of...the sooner, the better. We agree with Collwell (2018) who rightly claims that 'from the first-year assistant principal to the veteran district superintendent of schools, leaders matter' (p. 1). Leaders can benefit from the enormous brain research which is so helpful in bringing out the best in others, not so much with an iron hand, but with inspirational leadership that uses a strategy of affirmation, creating enormous brain triggers for positive action rather than just harsh criticism (Irwin, 2018).

IMPLICATIONS FOR POLICY, RESEARCH, AND PRACTICE

Whereas we understand that changing the leadership scenarios in schools in LDCs is undoubtedly a daunting task, this volume synthesises its key lessons into the following implications for policy, research, theory and practice:

- Educational policy development is a dynamic process ever responding to the emerging needs and situations. These policies need to be responsive to the changing socio-political and global dynamics guided by market needs (Ashraf, Tajik, & Niyozov, 2017; Couch, 2018). In that spirit, policy on educational leadership will need to be geared towards developing contextual models that suit the socio-political realities of LDCs. The models from the MDCs can undoubtedly play a lighthouse role in exploration for models with contextual fit.
- Schools and school systems need to be converted into learning and engaging communities, rather than places that perhaps serve the purposes of the past rather than the present or the future.

- Curriculum development as a dynamic process needs to respond to the current and emerging needs of the learners and the societies around rather than turning into a frozen document of the ideological and political ends indoctrinated by manifestos on the wide spectrum of political divide in LDCs. Pakistan is a pertinent example in this case where education policy development has remained a turf war between parties on the left and the right and anything that goes in between.
- Educational leaders need to be encouraged to become transformative, mindful, compassionate, and competent leaders, who lead schools both from the mind and the heart and who strive to develop schools as meaningful learning places, where learners become analytical, critical, and reflective thinkers helping to build a better world for themselves and their future generations.

These ideas may appear far away from the current realm of possibilities for many schools, especially the public schools in the LDCs, but they are the ideals that need to be vehemently pursued to make schools viable places for learning for ALL. If we are to provide a meaningful education to the youth of the 21st century in the LDCs, schools in these countries will have to double their efforts with pragmatic ideas such as the improvement of governance through effective leadership policy development, implementation, and meaningful monitoring and evaluation, thus nudging the schools and school systems into becoming learning organisations and communities of practice. This volume is a small attempt to provide some insights towards achieving the vision of making educational leadership an effective agent of meaningful change in the overall cultures of schools and educational administration in LDCs. We hope that it has achieved some, if not all, of that purpose.

Note

1. Jinnah, M.A. (1948). Students role in nation-building. Speech at the Dhaka University Convocation on 24th March, 1948 (recorded by Radio Pakistan, Dhaka). http://www.jinnahofPakistan.com/2010/04/students-role-in-nation-building-24th.html.

References

Abbasi, K. (2017, October 5). *QAU students protest against admin, VC*. Dawn. https://www.dawn.com/news/1361759

Aga Khan University, Institute for Educational Development (2008). ED-LINKS Program Handbook.

Ahmed, H. (2018, January 23). *Students involved in Punjab University clashes charged with terrorism*. Pakistan Today. https://www.pakistantoday.com.pk/2018/01/23/police-book-students-under-terrorism-act-after-punjab-university-clashes/

Ahmed, N. (2018, August 30). *Supporting students affected by war and terrorism: A Comparative study of school leadership in Canada and Pakistan*. Brock University. http://dr.library.brocku.ca/handle/10464/13629

Alameen, L., Male, T., & Palaiologou, I. (2015). Exploring pedagogical leadership in early years education in Saudi Arabia, *School Leadership & Management*, *35*(2), 7–28. https://doi.org/10.1080/13632434.2014.992773

Ali, S. (2014). Education policy and social justice: Exploring possibilities within education policy context of Pakistan. *Pakistan Perspectives*, *19*(1), 77–86. https://doi.org/10.2139/ssrn.2576033

Ali, S., & Babur, M. (2010). Educational governance in Pakistan: A historical policy perspective. In J. Khaki and Q. Safdar (Eds.), *Educational Leadership in Pakistan: Ideals and Realities* (pp. 3–21). Karachi: Oxford University Press.

Ali, S. M., & Sāqib, M. A. (eds.). (2008). *Devolution and Governance: Reforms in Pakistan*. LUMS-McGill Social Enterprise. Karachi: Oxford University Press.

Ali, T. & Niyozov, S. (2018). *Lessons from Implementation of Educational Reforms in Pakistan: Implications for Policy and Practice*. Karachi: Oxford University Press.

Allen, T.J. (1977). *Managing the flow of technology: Technology transfer and the dissemination of technological information within the R&D organization* (1st ed.). Cambridge, MA: MIT Press.

Aly, J. (2007). Education in Pakistan: A white paper revised document to debate and finalize the national education policy. http://planipolis.iiep.unesco.org/en/2007/education-pakistan-white-paper-revised-document-debate-and-finalize-national-education-policy

Amnesty International. (2019). Pakistan: End crackdown on student protests. 1 December 2019. https://www.amnesty.org/en/latest/news/2019/12/pakistan-end-crackdown-on-student-protests/

Argyris, C. (1999). *On Organizational Learning* (2nd ed.). Oxford: Blackwell.

Argyris, C., & Schön, D. (1974). *Theory in practice: Increasing professional effectiveness*. San Francisco: Jossey-Bass.

ASER (2014). Annual Status of Education Report, Pakistan. Idara-e-Taleem-o-Agahi, Pakistan.

Ashraf, D. Tajik, M.A. & Niyozov, S. (2017). *Educational Policies in Pakistan, Afghanistan and Tajikistan: Contested Terrain in twenty-first century*. Lanham: MD: Lexington Books.

Ashwin, S. (1996). Forms of collectivity in a non-monetary society. *Sociology, 30*(1), 21–39.

Aspfors, J. & Fransson, G. (2015). Research on mentor education for mentors of newly qualified teachers: A qualitative meta-synthesis. *Teaching and Teacher Education, 48*, 75–86.

Augier, M., & Vendelo, M. T. (1999). Networks, cognition and management of tacit knowledge. *Journal of Knowledge Management, 3*(4), 252–261.

Ayoub, M. N. (2014). *An investigation of the challenges experienced by Somali refugee students in Canadian elementary schools* (Master's thesis). http://scholar.uwindsor.ca/cgi/viewcontent.cgi?article=6119&context=etd

Bahadur, W. Z., Bano, A. A., Waheed, Z. Z. & Wahab, A. A. (2017). Leadership behaviour in high-performing government boys secondary schools in Quetta: A grounded theory analysis. *Journal of Education and Educational Development, 4*(2), 153–176.

Ball, S. J. (1987). *The micro-politics of the school: Towards a theory of school organization*. London: Methuen.

Bana, Z. (2010). Katha of leadership: Reimagining educational leadership. In J. Khaki & Q. Safdar (eds.), *Educational leadership in Pakistan: Ideals and realities* (pp. 22–38). Karachi: Oxford University Press.

Barney, J.B. (1986). Organizational culture: can it be a source of sustained competitive advantage? *Academy of Management Review, 11*(3), 656–665. https://doi.org/10.5465/amr.1986.4306261

Barney, J.B. (1991). Firm resources and sustained competitive advantage. *Journal of Management, 17*(1), 99–120.

Bashiruddin, A. & Retallick, J. (2008). *Becoming a teacher in the Developing World*. Karachi: The Aga Khan University Institute for Educational Development.

Bass, B.M. (1985). *Leadership and performance beyond expectation*. New York: Free Press.

Bass, B. M. (2008). *Concepts of Leadership. The Bass Handbook of Leadership* (4th ed.). New York, USA.

Bass, B. M., & Avolio, B. J. (1997). *Full rang leadership development: Manual for the multifactor leadership questionnaire*. Mindgarden, Palo Alto, Calif.

Bates, K. A., Amundson, S. D., Schroeder, R. G., & Morris, W. T. (1995). The crucial interrelationship between manufacturing strategy and organizational culture. *Management Science, 41*(10), 1565–80. https://doi.org/10.1287/mnsc.41.10.1565

BBC News. (2014). Pakistan School Massacre. Who are the dead? *BBC News: Asia*. 22 December 2014. https://www.bbc.com/news/world-asia-30508689

Bell, J. (2005). *Doing your research project*. Buckingham, Oxford University Press.

Benz, A. (2014). *Education for Development in the Northern Pakistan*. Karachi: Oxford University Press.

Bertocci, D. I. (2009). *Leadership in organizations: There is a difference between leaders and managers*. Lanham, MD: University Press of America®, Inc.

Bilal, M., Inamullah, H. M., & Irshadullah, H. M. (2016). Effects of terrorism on secondary school students in Khyber Pakhtunkhwa. *Dialogue (Pakistan), 11*(3), 258–269.

Biloslavo, R., & Zornada, M. (2004). Development of a knowledge management framework within the systems context. Proceedings of the 5th European Conference on Organizational Knowledge, Learning and Capabilities, Innsbruck, Austria, 2–3 April.

Birman, D. (2011). Migration and well-being: Beyond the macrosystem / Migración y bienestar: más allá del macrosistema. *Psychosocial Intervention, 20*(3), 339–342. doi:10.5093/in2011v20n3a11

REFERENCES

Blasé, J. & Blasé, J. (1998). *Handbook of instructional leadership: How really good principals promote teaching and learning.* Thousand Oaks, CA: Corwin Press, Inc.

Blase, J. (1997). The micropolitics of teaching. In B. J. Biddle, T. L. Good, & I. F. Goodson (Eds.), *International Handbook of Teachers and Teaching* (pp. 939–970). The Netherlands: Kluwer Academic Publishers.

Blase, J., & Anderson, G. (1995). *The micropolitics of leadership: From control to empowerment.* London: Cassell Teachers College Press.

Bochner, S., & Hesketh, B. (1994). Power distance, individualism/collectivism, and job-related attitudes in a culturally diverse work group. *Journal of Cross-Cultural Psychology*, 25, 233–257. https://doi.org/10.1177/0022022194252005

Bogdan, R. C., & Biklen, S. K. (1998). *Qualitative research in education: An introduction to theory and methods* (3rd ed.). Boston: Allyn and Bacon.

Bogotch, I. (2011). A History of Public School Leadership. In F. W. English (Ed.), *The Sage Handbook of Educational Leadership* (2nd ed.), (pp. 3–26). London, UK.

Bok, D. (2003). *Universities in the Market Place: The Commercialisation of Higher Education.* Princeton, NJ: Princeton University Press.

Bolden, R. (2011). Distributed leadership in organizations: A review of theory and research. *International Journal of Management Reviews*, *13*(3), 251–269. https://doi.org/10.1111/j.1468-2370.2011.00306.x

Borich, G. (1995). *Becoming a teacher: An inquiring dialogue for the beginning teacher.* Bristol, London: The Falmer Press.

Borman, G. D., & Dowling, N. M. (2008). Teacher Attrition and Retention: A Meta-analytic and Narrative Review of the Research. *Review of Educational Research*, *78*(3), 367–409. https://doi.org/10.3102/0034654308321455

Brock, B. L. & Grady, M. (2001). *From first-year to first-rate: Principals guiding beginning teachers.* (2nd ed.). Thousand Oaks: A Sage Publication Company.

Bronfenbrenner, U. (1999). Environments in developmental perspective: Theoretical and operational models. In S. Friedman & T. Wachs (Eds.), *Measuring environment across the life span: Emerging methods and concepts* (pp. 3–28). Washington, DC: American Psychological Association.

Bronfenbrenner, U., & Morris, P. (1999). The ecology of the developmental process. In W. Damon & R. Lerner (Eds.), *Handbook of child psychology* (5th ed.) (pp. 793–828). New York, NY: Wiley.

Brown, J., & Duguid, P. (1998). Organizing knowledge. *California Management Review*, *40*(3), 90–111.

Brown, J. S., & Duguid, P. (1991). Organizational learning and communities of practice: Toward a unified view of working, learning, and innovation', *Organization Science*, *2*(1), 40–57.

Brown, K. M., & Wynn, S. R. (2009). Finding, supporting, and keeping: The role of the principal in teacher retention issues. *Leadership and Policy in Schools*, *8*(1), 37–63. http://dx.doi.org/10.1080/15700760701817371

Browne-Ferrigno, T. (2007). Developing school leaders: Practitioner growth during an advanced leadership development programme for principals and administrator-trained teachers. *Journal of Research on Leadership Education*, *2*(3), 1–30.

Bruce, R. E. & Grimsley, E. E. (1987). *Readings in educational supervision (Vol. 2). History, nature, and purposes of educational supervision.* Association for Supervision and Curriculum Development.

REFERENCES

Bryan, L. K., & Wilson, C. A. (2015). *Shaping work-life culture in higher education: A guide for academic leaders.* New York, NY: Routledge.

Bullough, R. (1997). *'First-year teacher' eight years later: An inquiry into teacher development.* New York: Teacher College Press.

Bullough, R., Knowles, J., & Crow, N. (1992). *Emerging as a teacher.* London: Routledge.

Bullough, R. V. (1989). *First-year teacher: A case study.* New York: Teacher College, Columbia University.

Burns, J. M. (1978). *Leadership.* New York. Harper & Row.

Bush, T. (2015). Understanding instructional leadership. *Educational Management, Administration and Leadership, 43*(4), 487–489.

Bush, T., & Glover, D. (2014). School leadership models: what do we know?' *School Leadership and Management 34*(5), 553–571.

Campbell, D.T. (1976). *Assessing the impact of planned social change.* Hanover, NH: The Public Affairs Center, Dartmouth College.

Chapman, D.W. (2000). Trends in educational administration in developing Asia. *Educational Administration Quarterly, 36*(2), 283–308

Chen, C. C., Chen, X., & Meindl, J. R. (1998). How can cooperation be fostered? The cultural effects of individualism-collectivism. *Academy of Management Review, 23*(1), 285–304.

Cohen, L. & Manion, L. (1997). *Research methods in education.* (4th edition). London: Routledge.

Cole, A. (1996). Teacher development in the workplace: Rethinking the appropriation of professional relationships. In M. Beattie, H. Grunau & D. Thiessen (eds.), *Interpersonal sources of development for beginning and experienced teachers* (pp. 215–237). Proceedings of the Stoney Lake Invitational Conference, 10–11 May 1998, Toronto.

Collins, H. M. (1983). An empirical relativist programme in the sociology of scientific knowledge. In K. D Knorr-Cetina., & M. Mulkay (Eds.), *Science Observed: Perspectives on the Social Study of Science* (pp. 3–10). London: Sage.

Colwell. C. (2018). *Mission-driven leadership: Understanding the challenges facing schools of today.* Lanham: Rowan and Littlefield.

Couch, J. D. & Towne, J. (2018). *Rewiring education: How technology can unlock every student's potential.* Dallas: BenBella Books, Inc.

Couzin, I. D., Krause, J., Franks, N. R., & Levin, S. A. (2005). Effective leadership and decision-making in animal groups on the move. *Nature, 433*(7025), 513–516. https://doi.org/10.1038/nature03236

Covey, S. R. (1992). Principle-centered leadership. University of Michigan, USA.

Crawford, N. (November 2018). Costs of war: 17 Years After 9/11, Nnearly half a million people have died in global 'War on Terror.' *Democracy Now.* https://www.democracynow.org/2018/11/21/costs_of_war_17_years_after

Crawford, N., Davidson, J., Evangelista, M., Saleh, Z., Stern, J. (2020) *Costs of war: Human costs.* Boston University. https://watson.brown.edu/costsofwar/costs/human

Crawford, N. C. (2016) *Costs of war: Update on the human costs of war for Afghanistan and Pakistan, 2001 to mid-2016.* Boston University. http://watson.brown.edu/costsofwar/files/cow/imce/papers/2016/War%20in%20Afghanistan%20and%20Pakistan%20UPDATE_FINAL_corrected%20date.pdf

Creswell, J. W. (1998). *Qualitative inquiry and research design: Choosing among five traditions.* London: Sage Publications.

Creswell, J. W. (2014). *Research design qualitative, quantitative and mixed methods approaches* (4th ed.). Thousand Oaks, CA Sage.

Crowther, F., Kaagan, S., Ferguson, M., & Hann, L. (2002). *Developing teacher leaders: How teacher leadership enhances school success.* California: Sage Publications.

Czarniawska, B. (2007). *Shadowing, and other techniques for doing fieldwork in modern societies.* Malmö/Copenhagen: Liber/CBS Press.

Darling-Hammond, L., Meyerson, D. La Pointe, M., & Orr, M. T. (2010). *Preparing principals for a changing world: Lessons from effective school leadership programme.* San Francisco, CA: Jossey-Bass.

Datnow, A., & Castelano, M. (2001). Managing and guiding school reform: Leadership in success for all schools. *Educational Administration Quarterly, 37*(2), 219–249.

Davenport, T.H. (1998). *Information ecology: Mastering the information and knowledge environment.* NY: Oxford University Press.

Davies, B., & Davies, B. J. (2011). Strategic leadership. In B. Davies (Ed.), *The Essentials of School Leadership* (2nd ed.) (pp. 13–36). London, UK: Sage.

Davis, B. & Higdon, K. (2008). The effects of mentoring/induction support in beginning teachers' practices in early elementary classrooms (K-3). *Journal of Research in Childhood Education, 22*(3), 261–274.

Dawn, (2009, September 26). DEO's complaint against higher-ups. https://www.dawn.com/news/949108/deos-complaint-against-higher-ups

Dawn, (2009, May 8). 20 arrested as official manhandled. https://www.dawn.com/news/953910/20-arrested-as-official-manhandled

Dawn, (2010, December 14). Fourth education secretary in two years. https://www.dawn.com/news/590845/fourth-education-secretary-in-two-years-2

Dawn, (2019, October 13). Murder of district education officer. http://www.dawn.com/news/1510816/protests-staged-across-kp-against-murer-of-district-education-officer

Dawn, (2019, February 02). Pakistani educator Ahmed Saya has won the prestigious Cambridge University's Dedicated Teacher Award for 2019.

De Geus, A. (1988). Planning as learning. *Harvard Business Review, 66*(2), 70–74.

Detert, J., Schroeder, R., & Mauriel, J. (2000). A Framework for Linking culture and Improvement Initiatives in Organizations. *The Academy of Management Review, 25*(4), 850–863. https://doi.org/10.5465/amr.2000.3707740

Dewey, J. (1929). *The sources of a science of education.* New York: H. Liveright.

Dewey, J. (1933). *How we think.* New York: Heath and Co.

Dewey, J. (1938). *Experience and education.* New York: Macmillan Publishing Company.

Dierkes, M., Berthoin A., Child, J., & Nonaka, I. (Eds.) (2003). *Handbook of organizational learning and knowledge.* Oxford: Oxford University Press.

Duckworth, K., & Carnine, D. (1987). The quality of teacher-principal relationships. In V. Richardson-Koelher, D.Berliner, U.Casanova, C.Clark, R.Hersh, & L. Shulman (Eds.), *Educators' handbook: A research perspective* (pp. 457–471). New York: Longman.

Durrani, A., Mahsood, N., Ali, I., Kibria, Z., & Imtiaz, A. (2017). Psycho-social impact of Army Public School terrorist attack on high school children in District Peshawar, Khyber Pakhtunkhwa, Pakistan. *Khyber Medical University Journal, 9*(3), 130–134.

Easterby-Smith, M., Thorpe, R., & Jackson, P. (2012) *Management research.* (4th edition). London: SAGE Publications.

Edmondson, A. (1999). Psychological safety and learning behavior in work teams. *Administrative Science Quarterly, 44*(2), 350–383.

REFERENCES

Eggen, P., & Kauchak, D. (2001). *Educational psychology: Windows on classrooms.* New Jersey: Prentice Hall, Inc.

Eisner, E. W. (1998). *The enlightened eye: Qualitative enquiry and the enhancement of educational practice.* Upper Middle River, NJ: Merrill.

Elizebeth, W. M., & Milliken, F. J. (2000). Organizational silence: A barrier to change and development in a pluralistic world. *Academy of Management Review, 25,* 706–725.

Elmuti, D. (2001). Preliminary analysis of the relationship between cultural diversity and technology in corporate America. *Equal Opportunities International, 20*(8), pp. 1–16.

Erramilli, M. K. (1996). Nationality and subsidiary ownership patterns in multinational corporations. *Journal of International Business Studies, 27*(2), p225–248.

Ertesvag, S. K. (2014). Teachers' collaborative activity in school-wide interventions *Social Psychology Education, 17,* 565–588.

Everton, C. M. & Green, J. (1986). Observation as inquiry and method. In M. C. Wittrock (Ed.), *Handbook of research and teaching* (pp. 161–213). New York: Macmillan Publishing Company.

Feiman-Nemser, S. & Remillard, J. (1996). Perspectives on learning to teach. In F. Murray (ed.). *The Teacher Educator's Handbook: Building a knowledge base for the preparation of teachers* (pp. 63–91). San Francisco: Jossey-Bass. Final report submitted to Teacher Education Council, Ontario.

Feiman-Nemser, S., & Floden, R. E. (1986). The cultures of teaching. M.C. Wittrock (ed.), *Handbook of research and teaching* (3rd ed.) (pp. 505–525). New York: Simon & Schuster Masmillan.

Ferguson, N. & Earley, P. (1999). Improvement through inspection: A better system? *Management in Education, 3*(3), 22–28.

Feuerverger, G. (2011). Re-bordering spaces of trauma: Auto-ethnographic reflections on the immigrant and refugee experience in an inner-city high school in Toronto. *International Review of Education, 57*(3), 357–375.

Fiol, C. M., & Lyles, M. A. (1985). Organizational learning. *Academy of Management Review, 10*(4), 803–813.

Fontana, A., & Frey, H. J. (2000). The interview: from structured to negotiated text. In N. K. Denzin, & Y. S. Lincoln (Eds.), *Handbook of qualitative research* (2nd edition), (pp. 645–673). Thousand Oaks: Sage Publications Inc.

Fullan, M. (1998). Reshaping school leadership: Leadership for the 21st Century: Breaking the Bonds of Dependency. *Educational Leadership, 55*(7), 6–10.

Fullan, M. (2007). *The new meaning of educational change* (4th ed.). New York, NY: Teachers College Press.

Fullan, M. (2007). *The new meaning of educational change (*4th ed.). New York, Routledge: Teacher College Press.

Fullan, M. (2016). *The new meaning of educational change* (5th ed.). New York, NY: Teachers College Press.

Galbraith, C. S. (1990). Transferring core manufacturing technologies in high technology firms' *California Management Review, 32*(4), 56–70

Gillham, B. (2000). *Case study research methods.* London: Continuum.

Glatter, R., & Kydd, L. (2003). Best practice in educational leadership and management, *Educational Management Administration & Leadership, 31*(3), 231–243.

Gold, Y. (1996). Beginning teacher support. Attrition, mentoring, and induction. In J. Sikula (Ed.), *Handbook of research on teacher education* (pp. 548–594). New York, London: Macmillan.

REFERENCES

Goodlad, J.I. (1984). *A place called school: Prospects for the future.* New York: McGraw-Hill.

Government of Canada. (2017). *Project profile: Monitoring and Evaluation of Debt Conversion for Education.* http://w05.international.gc.ca/projectbrowser-banqueprojets/project-projet/details/a032274001

Government of Pakistan [GoP], (n.d.). *Proceedings of the Pakistan Educational Conference held at Karachi from 27th November to 1st December 1947.* Ministry of Education [MoE] (Education Division).

Government of Pakistan. (1969). *Proposals for a new Educational Policy.* Ministry of Education and Scientific Research [MoE & SR].

Government of Pakistan. (1970). *The New Education Policy of the Government of Pakistan.* Ministry of Education and Scientific Research, Islamabad.

Government of Pakistan. (1972). *The Education Policy 1972–80.* Ministry of Education, Islamabad.

Government of Pakistan. (1979). *National Education Policy and Implementation Programme.* Ministry of Education, Islamabad.

Government of Pakistan. (1992). *National Education Policy 1992.* Ministry of Education, Islamabad.

Government of Pakistan. (1998). *National Education Policy 1998–2010.* Ministry of Education, Islamabad.

Government of Pakistan. (2009). *National Education Policy 2009.* http://www.aserpakistan.org/document/learning_resources/2014/National%20Education%20Policy%202009.pdf

Government of Pakistan. (2009). *The National Education Policy.* http://www.infopak.gov.pk/National_Education_Policy_2009.pdf. Ministry of Education, Islamabad.

Government of Pakistan. (2017). *National Education Policy 2017.* Ministry of Federal Education and Professional Training. http://www.moent.gov.pk

Government of Pakistan. (2017). *National Education Policy 2017–2025.* http://moent.gov.pk/userfiles1/file/National%20Educaiton%20Policy%202017.pdf

Government of Pakistan. (2018). *National Education Policy Framework 2018.* http://planipolis.iiep.unesco.org/en/2018/national-education-policy-framework–2018–6524

Govinda, R. (2002). *Role of headteacher in school management in India: Case studies from six states.* India: Asian network of Training & Research Institutes in Educational Planning (ANTRIEP) in collaboration with European Commission.

Greenleaf, R. K. (1977). *Servant leadership.* New York: Paulist Press.

Greenleaf, R. K. (2003). *The servant leadership within: A transformative Path.* Mahwah, NJ: Paulist Press.

Gronn, P. (2000). Distributed properties: A new architecture for leadership. *Educational Management Administration & Leadership*, *28*(3), 317–338. https://doi.org/10.1177/0263211x000283006

Gronn, P. (2008). The future of distributed leadership', *Journal of Educational Administration*, *46*(2), 141–158; https:// doi.org/10.1108/09578230810863235

Gronn, P. (2010). Leadership: Its genealogy, configuration, trajectory. *Journal of Educational Administration and History*, *42*(4), 405–435.

Grown, P. & Lee, N. M. (2019). *Leadership case studies in education.* Los Angeles: Sage Publishing.

Habermas, J. (1972). *Knowledge and human interest* (2nd ed.). London, England: Heinemann.

REFERENCES

Hahs-Vaughn, D. L., & Scherff, L. (2008). Beginning English teacher attrition, mobility, and retention. *Journal of Experimental Education*, 77(1), 21–53. https://doi.org/10.3200/jexe.77.1.21-54

Haider, M. (2014). *Pakistan world's largest host of refugees: UNHCR. Dawn*. 20 June 2014. https://www.dawn.com/news/1114057

Hakanson, L., & Nobel, R. (1998). Technology characteristics and reverse technology transfer. Paper presented at the Annual Meeting of the Academy of International Business, Vienna, Austria.

Hallinger, P. (1992). The evolving role of American principals: From managerial to instructional to transformational leaders, *Journal of Educational administration*, 30(3), 35–48. https://doi.org/10.1108/09578239210014306

Hallinger, P. (2009). *Leadership for 21st Century Schools: From Instructional Leadership to Leadership for Learning*. Hong Kong: Hong Kong Institute of Education.

Hambrick D. C., & Brandon, G. L. (1988). Executive values. In D.C. Hambrick and G.L. Brandon (Eds.), *The Executive Effect: Concepts and methods for studying top managers* (pp. 3–34). Greenwich, CT: JAI Press.

Hambrick, D. C. & Mason, P. A. (1984). Upper echelons: The organization as a reflection of its top managers. *The Academy of Management Review*, 9(2), 193–206. https://doi.org/10.5465/amr.1984.4277628

Hands, C. (2013). Including all families in education: School district-level efforts to promote parent engagement in Ontario, Canada. *Teaching Education*, 24(2), 134–149. https://doi.org/10.1080/10476210.2013.786893

Hannam, C., Smyth, P., & Stephenson, N. (1984). *The first year of teaching*. Chippenham: Bristol Classical Press.

Hannay, L. M., Ross, J. A., & Seller, W. (2005). Clashing cultures, clashing paradigms: Lessons from district research on secondary school restructuring. *Journal of Educational Change*, 6(1), 7–27. https://doi.org/10.1007/s10833-004-7778-0

Hargreaves, A., & Braun, H. (2012). Leading for all: Final report of the review of the development of essential for some, good for all—Ontario's strategy for special education reform devised by the council of directors of education. Toronto: Council of Directors of Education.

Hargreaves, A., Boyle, A., & Harris, A. (2014). *Uplifting leadership: How organizations, teams, and communities raise performance*. San Francisco, CA: Jossey-Bass.

Harris, A. (2002). *School Improvement: What's in it for schools?* London: Falmer Press.

Harris, A. (2004). Distributed leadership and school improvement: Leading or misleading. *Educational Management Administration & Leadership*, 32(1), 11–24.

Hatlevik, I. K. R. (2017). The impact of prospective teachers' perceived competence on subsequent perceptions as schoolteachers *Teachers and Teaching: Theory and practice*, 23(7), 810–828.

Heifetz, R. A., Linsky, M., & Grashow, A. (2014). *The practice of Adaptive Leadership: Tools and tactics for changing your organization and the world*. Harvard, MA: Harvard Business Press.

Heinrichs, J. H., & Lim, J. S. (2005). Model for organizational knowledge creation and strategic use of information. *Journal of the American Society for Information Science and Technology*, 56(6), 620–629.

Helwig, R., Anderson, L., & Tindal, G. (2001). Influence of elementary student gender on teachers' perceptions of mathematics achievement. *Journal of Educational Research*, 95(2), 93–102.

REFERENCES

Hendrickson, M. H., Lane, J. E., Harris, J. T., & Dorman, R. H. (2013). *Academic leadership and governance of higher education: A guide for trustees, leaders, and aspiring leaders of two- and four-year institutions.* Sterling, VA: Stylus Publishing.

Higgins, M., McGowan, B. Murphy., & Trafford, L. (1991). *Catholic transforming our world: A Canadian perspective.* Quebec, Canada: Novalis

Higher Education Commission [HEC], (n.d.). University-wise enrollment of year 2014–15. http://www.hec.gov.pk

Hirani, S. A. (2014). Vulnerability of internally displaced children in disaster relief camps of Pakistan: Issues, challenges, and way forward. *Early Child Development and Care, 184*(9), 1499–1506.

Hitchcock, G., & Hughes, D. (1995). *Research and the teacher: A qualitative introduction to school-based research.* London: Routledge.

Hofstede, G. (1980). *Culture's consequences: International differences in work related values.* Beverly Hills, CA: Sage.

Hofstede, G. (1984). The cultural relativity of the quality of life concept. *Academy of Management Review, 9*(3), 389–397.

Hofstede, G. (1991). *Cultures and organizations: Software of the Mind.* London: McGraw-Hill.

Hofstede, G. (1993). Cultural constraints in management theories. *Academy of Management Executive, 7,* 81–94.

Hofstede, G. (1997). *Cultures and organizations: Software of the Mind.* New York: McGraw Hill.

Hofstede, G. (2001). *Culture's consequences.* Beverly Hills, CA: Sage.

Hong, J. Y. (2012). Why do some beginning teachers leave the school, and others stay? Understanding teacher resilience through psychological lenses. *Teachers and Teaching: Theory and Practice, 18*(4), 417–440.

Hoodbhoy, P. (2017, July 01). Pakistan's professor mafia. *Dawn.* http://www.dawn.com/news/1342483

Hoodbhoy, P. (Ed.). (1998). *Education and the state: Fifty years of Pakistan.* Karachi: Oxford University Press.

Hutchings, K., & Michailova, S. (2004). Facilitating knowledge sharing in Russian and Chinese subsidiaries: the role of personal networks and group membership. *Journal of Knowledge Management, 8*(2), 84–94.

Institute for Educational Planning-UNESCO (2007a). Alternative models in reforming school supervision, Module 7. http://unesdoc.unesco.org/images/0021/002159/215935E.pdf

Institute for Educational Planning-UNESCO (2007b). Management of supervision staff, Module 4.

Iqbal, H. (2009, October 18). Education in Gilgit-Baltistan. http://www.dawn.com/news/880919/education-in-gilgit-and-baltista/

Irwin, T. (2018). *Extraordinary influence: How do great leaders bring out the best in others?* Hoboken, New Jersey: John Wiley and Sons.

Jaffer, K. (2007). An analysis of the school inspection system in Sindh, Pakistan. Unpublished PhD thesis. Institute of Education, University of London.

Jaffer, K. (2010). School inspection and supervision in Pakistan: Approach and issues. *Prospects, 40*(3), 375–392.

Jakubik, M. (2008) Experiencing collaborative knowledge creation processes. *The learning organization, 15*(1), 5–25.

REFERENCES

James A. Gibson Library. (2018). *How to use Super Search.* https://brocku.ca/library/help/supersearch-faq/#what

Jennings, P. A., DeMauro A.A., & Mischenko, P. P. (Eds.) (2019). *The mindful School: Transforming school culture through mindfulness and compassion.* New York: Guilford Press.

Jinnah, M. A. (1948). Students role in nation-building. Speech at the Dhaka University Convocation on 24th March, 1948 (recorded by Radio Pakistan, Dhaka). http://www.jinnahofpakistan.com/2010/04/students-role-in-nation-building-24th.html

Johnson, G. M. (2010). Internet use and child development: Validation of the ecological techno-subsystem. *Educational Technology & Society, 13*(1), 176–185.

Joong, P., Xiong, Y., Lin, L., & Pan, C. J. (2009). Investigation into the perceptions of students, parents and teachers in China's education reforms in grade 7 and 8. *International electronic journal of elementary education, 1*(3), 141–154.

Josh & Mak International. (1974). The University Grants Commission Act, 1974 (Act No. XXIII of 1974). https://joshandmakinternational.com/resources/laws-of-pakistan/education-and-universities-laws/the-university-grants-commission-act-1974/

Jovanovic, O., Simic, N., & Rajovi, V. (2014). Students at risk: Perceptions of Serbian teachers and implications for teacher education European. *Journal of Teacher Education, 37*(2), 220–236.

Katzenmeyer, M., & Moller, G. (2001). *Awakening the sleeping giant: Helping teachers develop as leaders.* Thousand Oaks, CA: Corwin Press.

Kelchtermans, G., & Ballet, K. (1999). *Micropolitical literacy and teachers' career stories: A narrative-biographical study on professional development.* Paper presented at the European Conference on Educational Research, Lahti (Finland), 22–26 September. http://wwwedu.oulu.fi/homepage/life/Ecer99gk.htm

Kemmis, S. (1993). Action Research and Social Movement: A challenge for policy research. *Education Policy Analysis Archives, 1*(1), 1–8.

Khaki, J. (2005). Exploring the beliefs and behaviors of effective headteachers in government and non-government schools in Pakistan. PhD thesis, Ontario Institute of Studies in Education, University of Toronto.

Khaki, J. (2008). Leading leaders: A school leadership development experience in Pakistan. *The S.U. Journal of Education, 38*, 18–32.

Khaki, J. (2010). Effective school leadership practices: Case studies from Pakistan. In J. Khaki & Q. Safdar (Eds.), *Educational leadership in Pakistan: Ideals and realities* (pp. 104–126). Karachi: Oxford University Press.

Khaki, J. Shafa, M.D. & Baig, S. (2017). Religion and state in Pakistan: Influences on education with special Focus on Gilgit-Baltistan. In D. Ashraf, M. A. Tajik, & S. Niyozov (Eds.), *Education Policies in Pakistan, Afghanistan and Tajikistan: Contested Terrain in the Twenty-First Century* (pp. 81–104). Lanham, MD: Lexington Books.

Khaki, J., & Safdar, Q. (Eds.). (2010). *Educational leadership in Pakistan: Ideals and realities.* Karachi: Oxford University Press.

Khan, G. (2010). Exploring principal-student relationships in a private secondary school in Pakistan. In J. Khaki, & Q. Safdar (eds.). *Educational leadership in Pakistan: Ideals and Realities* (pp. 129–150). Karachi: Oxford University Press.

Khan, G. (2017). A multinational study of the determinants of student achievement in mathematics and science: Policy options for Pakistan. *Pakistan Journal of Education, 34*(02), 119–140.

REFERENCES

Khan, G., Khan, A., Hussain, S., & Shaheen, N. (2017). Teacher evaluation: Global perspectives and lessons for Pakistan. *The Dialogue, 12*(03), 333–346.

Khan, I. M., Khalil, U., & Iftikhar, I. (2015). Educational leadership: Educational development and leadership programmes in selected countries and Pakistan. *Journal of Higher Education and Science, 5*(3), 272–284. https://doi.org/10.5961/jhes.2015.129

Kilbourn, B. & Roberts, G. (1996). May's first year: Conversations with a mentor. In M. Beattie, H. Grunau & D. Thiessen (Eds.), *Interpersonal sources of development for beginning and experienced teachers* (pp. 117–136). Proceedings of the Stoney Lake Invitational Conference, 10–11 May 1990, Toronto.

Kirtman, L. & Fullan, M. (2016). *Leadership: Key competencies for whole-system change*. Bloomington, IN: Solution Free Press.

Korac-Kakabadze, N., & Kouzmin, A. (1999). Designing for cultural diversity in an IT and globalizing milieu. *Journal of Management Development, 18*(3), pp. 291–324.

Koretz, D. (1998). *Measuring up: What educational testing really tells us*. Cambridge, MA: Harvard University Press.

Krajewski, R. J. (1985). How to build the norms of school culture: Understanding the whys of instructional supervision. In R. E. Bruce, & E. E. Grimsley (Eds.), *Readings in educational supervision* (Vol. 2). History, nature, and purposes of educational supervision (pp. 34–35). Association for Supervision and Curriculum Development.

Kunwar, F. A. (2000). Secondary School Headmasters' Leadership Styles and Their Implications for School Improvement. Unpublished PhD thesis, American University of London, UK.

LaRocque, N. (2001). The role of government in education in developing countries. Paper presented for the Comparative International Education Society Meetings, Washington, D. C. 15 March.

Lave, J., & Wenger, E. (1991). *Situated learning—Legitimate peripheral participation*. Cambridge: Cambridge University Press.

Lawson, C., & Lorenzi, E. (1999). Collective learning, tacit knowledge and regional innovative capacity. *Regional Studies, 33*(4), 305–17.

LeCompte, M., & Schensul, J. (1998). *Analyzing and interpreting ethnographic data*. London: Altamira.

Leithwood, K. & Duke, D.L. (1999). A century's quest to understand school leadership. In J. Murphy, & K. S. Louis (Eds.), *Handbook of Research on Educational Administration* (pp. 45–72). San Francisco: Jossey-Bassey.

Leithwood, K. & Jantzi, D. (2011). Transformational leadership. In B. Davies (ed.), *The Essentials of School Leadership* (2nd ed.), (pp. 37–52). London, UK: Sage.

Leithwood, K., & Duke, D. L. (1999). A century's quest to understand school leadership. In J. Murphy, & K. S. Louis (Eds.), *Handbook of research on educational administration* (pp. 45–72). San Francisco, CA: Jossey-Bassey.

Leithwood, K., Begley, P., & Cousins, B. J. (1992). *Developing expert leadership for future schools*. London: Falmer Press.

Leithwood, K., Harris, A., & Hopkins, D. (2008). Seven strong claims about successful school leadership. *School Leadership & Management, 28*(1), 27–42. https://doi.org/10.1080/13632430701800060

Leithwood, K., Jantzi, D., & Steinbach, R. (2000). *Changing leadership for changing times*. Buckingham: Open University Press.

Leithwood, K. L., & Riehl, C. (2003). *What we know about successful school leadership*. Philadelphia: Temple University.

REFERENCES

Levitt, B., & March, J. G. (1988). 'Organizational learning', *Annual Review of Sociology, 14*(1), 319–340. https://doi.org/10.1146/annurev.so.14.080188.001535

Lewis, J. L., & Sheppard, S. R. (2006). Culture and communication: Can landscape visualization improve forest management consultation with indigenous communities?. *Landscape and Urban Planning, 77*(3), 291–313. https://doi.org/10.1016/j.landurbplan.2005.04.004

Lieven, A. (2011). *Pakistan: A hard country*. London: Penguin Books.

Linares, J. J. G., Díaz, A. J. C., Fuentes, M. D. C. P., & Acién, F. L. (2009). Teachers' perception of school violence in a sample from three European countries. *European Journal of Psychology of Education, 24*(1), 49–59. https://doi.org/10.1007/bf03173474

Lingard, B., & Christie, P. (2010). Leading theory: Bourdieu and the field of educational leadership, *International Journal of Leadership in Education: Theory and Practice, 6*(4), 317–333. https://doi.org/10.1080/1360312032000150724

Little, J.W. (1987). Teachers as colleagues. In V. Richardson-Koehler (Ed.), *Educators' Handbook: A Research Perspective* (pp. 491–517). New York: Longman.

Lomos, C., Hofman, R. H., & Bosker, R. J. (2011). The Relationship between departments as professional communities and student achievement in secondary schools: Teaching and Teacher Education. *International Journal of Research and Studies, 27*(4), 722–731. https://doi.org/10.1016/j.tate.2010.12.003

Lovett, S. (2018). *Advocacy for teacher leadership: Opportunity, preparation, support, and pathways*. Cham, Switzerland: Springer International Publishing AG. Doi: https://doi.org/10.1007/978-3-319-74430-8

Luitel, B. C., & Taylor, P. C. (2009). Multi-paradigmatic transformational research as\for teacher education: An integral prospective. *International handbook of science education*. Dordrecht, Netherlands: Springer.

Maham, R. (2013). To recognize cultural diversity that influences knowledge sharing in an organization. *International Review of Management and Business Research, 2*(4), 1092–1100.

Mahroum, S. (2018). AI raises lots of questions. These are the ones we should be asking. World Economic Forum. https://www.weforum.org/agenda/2018/02/this-is-the-ai-debate-that-we-need-to-have

Male, T., & Palaiologou, I. (2012). Learning-centred leadership or pedagogical leadership? An alternative approach to leadership in education contexts. *International Journal of Leadership in Education, 15*(1), 107–118. https://doi.org/10.1080/13603124.2011.617839

Male, T., & Palaiologou, I. (2013). Pedagogical leadership in the 21st century: Evidence from the field, *Educational Management, Administration and Leadership, 43*(2), 214–231. https://doi.org/10.1177/1741143213494889

Mansoor, Z., & Akhtar, N. (2015). The paradigm shift: Leadership challenges in the public sector schools in Pakistan. *Journal of Education and Practice, 6*(19), 203–211.

Masood, T. (2009, November 29). *Student Solidarity March held countrywide to demand restoration of unions, better education facilities*. Dawn. https://www.dawn.com/news/1519531

McEwan, E. K., & McEwan, P. (2003). *Making sense of research: What's good, what's not, and how to tell the difference*. Thousand Oaks, California: Corwin Press Inc.

McNeil, J. D. (1987). Scientific approach to supervision. In R. E. Bruce, and R. E. Grimsley (Eds.). *Readings in educational supervision* (Vol. 2). History, nature, and purposes of educational supervision (pp. 17–33). Association for Supervision and Curriculum Development.

Mead, S. S. & Stowell, S. J. (2016). *The art of strategic leadership: How leaders at all levels prepare themselves, their teams, and organizations for the future.* New Jersey: John Wiley and Sons.

Memon, M. & Wheeler, A. E. (2000). Improving schools through educational leadership programmes in Pakistan. Paper presented in the 13th International Congress for School Effectiveness and Improvement: Global Networking for Quality Education in Hong Kong 4–8 January.

Memon, M. (1999). Reconceptualizing the role of headteachers as pedagogical leaders in Pakistan: Implications for policy reform. Paper read at the Annual British Educational Management and Administration Society (BEMAS) conference held in UMIST Manchester from 17–19 September.

Memon, M. (2000). The future of heads teachers as educational leaders in Pakistan: Implications for pedagogical leadership. *Education 2000, 3*(3), 24–28.

Memon, M. (2010). Reforming school leadership in Pakistan: A way forward. In J. Khaki & Q. Safdar (Eds.), *Educational leadership in Pakistan* (pp. 280–294). Karachi: Oxford University Press.

Memon, M. Nazirali, R. Simkins, & Garrett, V. (2000). Understanding the headteachers' role in Pakistan: Emerging role demands, constraints and choices. *International Studies in Educational Administration, 28*(2), 48–55.

Memon, M., & Bana, Z. (2005). Pedagogical leadership in Pakistan: two headteachers from the Northern Areas. In J. Retallick and I. Farah (Eds.), *Transforming schools in Pakistan: Towards the learning community.* Karachi: Oxford University Press.

Merchant G. & Ali, S. (2003). *Northern Areas education project-longitudinal study: Cumulative report V–2003.* Institute for Educational Development-Aga Khan University and British Council, Karachi.

Merriam, S. (1988). *Case study research in education: A qualitative approach.* San Francisco Jossey-Bass.

Merriam, S. (1998). *Case study research: A qualitative approach.* San Francisco and London: Jossey-Bass.

Merriam, S. (1998). *Qualitative research and case study applications in education.* San Francisco: Jossey Bass.

Mertler, C.A. (2002). Job satisfaction and perception of motivation among middle and high school teachers. *American Secondary Education, 31*(1), 43–53.

Mezirow, J. (1978). Perspective transformation. *Adult Education, 28*, 100–110.

Mezirow, J. (2000). *Learning as transformation: Critical perspectives on a theory in progress.* San Francisco, CA: Jossey-Bass.

Mezirow, J. (2003). Transformative learning as discourse. *Journal of Transformative Education, 1*(1), 58–63. https://doi.org/10.1177/1541344603252172

Mezirow, J. (2012). Learning to think like an adult: Core concepts of transformation theory. In E.W. Taylor & P. Cranton (Eds.), *The handbook of transformative learning: Theory research and practice* (pp. 73–96). San Francisco, CA: Jossey-Bass.

Michelle, L., & Santamaria, J. (2016). Theories of Educational Leadership. *Oxford Bibliographies Online Datasets.* https://doi.org/10.1093/obo/9780199756810-0153

Miller, D. (1997). Celebrating the 'essential': the impact of performance on the functional favoritism of CEOs in two contexts. *Journal of Management, 23*(2), 147–168. https://doi.org/10.1016/s0149-2063(97)90041-6

REFERENCES

Milne, R.S. (1970). Mechanistic and organic models of public administration in developing countries. *Administrative Science Quarterly, 15*(1), 57–67. https://doi.org/10.2307/2391188

Mintzberg, H. (1973). *The nature of managerial work*. London: Harper & Row.

Mullick, J., Sharma, U. & Deppeler, J. (2013). School teachers' perception about distributed leadership practices for inclusive education in primary schools in Bangladesh School. *Leadership & Management, 33*(2), 151–168. https://doi.org/10.1080/13632434.2012.723615

Nahapiet, J., & Ghoshal, S. (1998). Social capital, intellectual capital, and the organizational advantage. *Academy of Management Review, 23*(2), 242–266. https://doi.org/10.5465/amr.1998.533225

National Assembly Secretariat. (1974). *The Gazette of Pakistan*. http://www.na.gov.pk/uploads/documents/1491891934_240.pdf

National Commission for Government Reforms: Government of Pakistan. (2008). *Report of the national commission for government reforms on reforming the government in Pakistan*. http://www.ncgr.gov.pk/forms/final%20report.pdf

Nichols, S. L., & D. C. Berliner. (2007). *Collateral damage: How high-stakes testing corrupts America's schools*. Cambridge: Harvard Education Press.

Niyozov, S. & Khaki, J. (2017). Summary and way forward (Concluding chapter). In D. Ashraf, M. A. Tajik & S. Niyozov (Eds.), *Education Policies in Pakistan, Afghanistan and Tajikistan: Contested Terrain in the Twenty-First Century* (pp. 177–196). Lanham, MD: Lexington Books.

Niyozov, S. (2001). Understanding teaching in post-Soviet, rural, mountainous Tajikistan: case studies of teachers' life and work. Unpublished Ph.D. thesis, Ontario Institute for Studies in Education of the University of Toronto.

Nonaka, I. (1991). The knowledge-creating company. *Harvard Business Review*, November–December 1991, 96–104.

Nonaka, I. (1994) A dynamic theory of organizational knowledge creation. *Organization Science, 5*(1), 14–37. https://doi.org/10.1287/orsc.5.1.14

Nonaka, I. (2007). The knowledge-creating company. *Harvard Business Review*, July–August 2007, 162–170.

Nonaka, I., & Takeuchi, H. (1995). *The knowledge-creating company*. New York: Oxford University Press.

Nonaka, I., Toyama, R. (2007). Why do firms differ? The theory of the knowledge-creating firm. In K. Ichijo & Nonaka, I. (Eds.), *Knowledge creation and management: New challenges for managers* (pp. 13–31). Oxford: Oxford University Press.

Nooruddin, S., & Baig, S. (2014). Student behaviour management: School leader's role in the eyes of the teachers and students. *International Journal of Whole Schooling, 11*(1), 19–39.

Onoyase, D. (1991). *Theory and practice of educational administration*. Warri: Okienriete Publishers.

Oxman-Martinez, J., & Choi, Y. R. (2014). Newcomer children: Experiences of inclusion and exclusion, and their outcomes. *Social Inclusion, 2*(4), 23–37. http://dx.doi.org/10.17645/si.v2i4.133

Oxman-Martinez, J., Rummens, A.J., Moreau, J., Choi, Y. R., Beiser, M., Ogilvie, L., & Armstrong, R. (2012). Perceived ethnic discrimination and social exclusion: Newcomer immigrant children in Canada. *American Journal of Orthopsychiatry, 82*(3), 376–388. doi:10.1111/j.1939-0025.2012.01161.x

Park, H., Ribiere, V., & Schulte, W. D. (2004). Critical attributes of organizational culture that promote knowledge management technology implementation success. *Journal of Knowledge Management, 8*(3), 106–117. https://doi.org/10.1108/13673270410541079

Polanyi, M. (1958). *Personal knowledge*. Chicago: The University of Chicago Press.

Pratt, T. (2013, December 26). We are creating Walmarts of higher education. *The Atlantic*. https://www.theatlantic.com/education/archive/2013/12/we-are-creating-walmarts-of-higher-education/282619/

Price, H. E. (2012). Principal–teacher interactions: How affective relationships shape principal and teacher attitudes. *Educational Administration Quarterly, 48*, 39–85.

Qutoshi, S. B. & Khaki, J. (December 2014). The role of a principal/headteacher in school improvement: A case study of a community-based school in Karachi, Pakistan. *Journal of Research and Reflections in Education, 8*(2), 86–96.

Qutoshi, S.B. (2015). Auto/ethnography: A transformative research paradigm. *Dhaulagiri Journal of Sociology and Anthropology, 9*, 161–190.

Qutoshi, S. B. (2016). Creating my own living-educational-theory: An autoethnographic-soulful inquiry. *Educational Journal of Living Theories 9*(2), 60–86. http://ejolts.net/node/287

Qutoshi, S.B. (2016). Creating my own living-educational-theory: An autoethnographic-soulful inquiry. *Educational Journal of Living Theories, 9*(2), 60–86. http://ejolts.net/node/287.

Qutoshi, S.B. (2019). Cultural-self Knowing: Transforming self and others. In P. C. Taylor, & B. C. Luitel, B. (Eds.), *Research as Transformative Learning for Sustainable Futures: Global Voices and Visions* (pp. 147–159). Rotterdam/Boston/Taipei: Brill Sense Publishers.

Qutoshi, S. B., & Rajbhandari, M. M. S. (2016). A Philosophical View on and a Technical Approach to Leading a Learning Organization. *Journal of Education and Research, 6*(2), 7–20. http://kusoed.edu.np/journal/index.php/je/article/view/136/81.

Rafi, Y. (2015, June 17). *Pakistan hosts second largest refugee population globally*. Dawn. https://www.dawn.com/news/1188585

Rashid, A. (1993). Blonde Muslims find shelter in Pakistan: Refugees from Bosnia were given a warm welcome in Ahmed Rashid writes from Islamabad. *Independent*. 26 June 1993. https://www.independent.co.uk/news/world/europe/blonde-muslims-find-shelter-in-pakistan-refugees-from-bosnia-were-given-a-warm-welcome-in-a-distant–1493968.html

Ratković, S., Kovačević, D., Brewer, C. A., Ellis, C., Ahmed, N., & Baptiste- Brady, J. (2017). *Supporting refugee students in Canada: Building on what we have learned in the last 20 years*. Report to Social Sciences and Humanities Research Council of Canada, Brock University, St. Catharine's, ON.

Rizvi, M. (2008). The role of school principals in enhancing teacher professionalism: Lessons from Pakistan. *Educational Management Administration & Leadership, 36*(1), 85–100. https://doi.org/10.1177/1741143207084062

Roehrig, A., Pressley, M., & Talotta, D. (2002). *Stories of beginning teachers: First-year challenges and beyond*. Notre Damme: University of Notre Dame Press.

Rogers, R., Schaenen, I., Schott, C., O'Brien, K., Trigos-Carrillo, L., Starkey, K., & Chasteen, C. C. (2016). Critical discourse analysis in education: A review of the literature, 2004 to 2012. *Review of Educational Research, 86*(4), 1192–1226.

Rozovsky, J. (2015). The five keys to a successful Google team. At: https://rework.withgoogle.com/blog/five-keys-to-a-successful-google-team/

REFERENCES

Safdar, Q. (2006). Exploring the Leadership of Early Years: Two case studies from Pakistan. Unpublished MA dissertation, Institute of Education, University of London, UK.

Saqib, M. A. (2008). Introduction. In Ali, S. M., and Saqib, M. A. (Eds.). *Devolution and governance: reforms in Pakistan* (pp. x–xvi). LUMS-McGill Social Enterprise. Karachi: Oxford University Press.

Sarason, S. (2002). *Educational reform: A self-scrutinizing memoir.* New York: Teachers College Press.

Schein, E. (1985). *Organizational culture and leadership.* San Francisco, CA: Jossey-Bass

Schein, E. H. (2010). *Organizational culture and leadership.* San Francisco, CA: Jossey-Bass.

Schön, D. (1991). *The Reflective Practitioner.* Aldershot: Ashgate Publishing Ltd.

Schon, D. A. (1983). *The Reflective Practitioner: How Professionals Think in Action.* New York: Basic Books.

Schunk, D. H. (2000). *Learning theories: an educational perspective.* New Jersey: Prentice-Hall.

Senge, P. (2006). *The fifth discipline—the art and practice of the learning organization.* New York: Currency/Doubleday.

Senge, P. M. (1990). *The Fifth Discipline: The art and practice of learning organizations.* New York: Bantam Doubleday.

Sergiovanni, T. J. (1992). *Moral leadership: Getting to the heart of school improvement.* San Francisco, CA: Jossey-Bassy.

Sergiovanni, T. J. (1998). Leadership as pedagogy, capital development and school effectiveness. *International Journal of Leadership in Education, 1*(1), 37–46. https://doi.org/10.1080/1360312980010104

Shachar, H., Gavin, S. & Shalomo, S. (2010). Changing organizational culture and instructional methods in elementary schools: Perceptions of teachers and professional educational consultants. *Journal of Educational Change, 11*(3), 273–289. https://doi.org/10.1007/s10833-009-9128-8

Shafa, M. D. (2003). Understanding How a Government Secondary School Headmaster Addresses School Improvement Challenges in the Northern Areas of Pakistan. Unpublished PhD thesis, Ontario Institute for Studies in Education, University of Toronto, Canada.

Shafa, M. D. (2010). Challenges of School Improvement: A Study of a Headteacher from the Northern Areas of Pakistan. In J. Khaki & Q. Safdar (Eds.), *Educational Leadership in Pakistan: Ideals and Realities* (pp. 80–103). Karachi: Oxford University Press.

Shah, D. (2003). *Country report on decentralization in the education system of Pakistan: Policies and strategies.* Academy of Educational Planning and Management, Ministry of Education, Government of Pakistan, Islamabad.

Shamatov, D. (2013). Everyday realities of a young teacher in post-Soviet Kyrgyzstan: A case of history teacher from a rural school. In P. Akcali & C.E. Demir (Eds.), *Post-Soviet Kyrgyzstan: Political and Social Challenges.* Routledge.

Shamatov, D. (2014). Education Quality in Kyrgyzstan. In D. B. Napier, C. Aced & A. Pitman, *Qualities of education in a globalized world* (Ed.). Rotterdam: Sense Publishers.

Shamatov, D. (2015). Country study report on pedagogical approaches: Case of Kyrgyzstan. In Hau-Fai Law, E. & Miura, U. (Eds.). *Transforming Teaching and Learning in Asia and the Pacific: Case studies of seven countries* (pp. 90–123). Bangkok: UNESCO.

Shamatov, S. (2005). Beginning Teachers' Professional Socialization in Post-Soviet Kyrgyzstan: Challenges and Coping Strategies. Unpublished Ph.D. thesis. Ontario Institute for Studies in Education of the University of Toronto.

Shane, S. (1995). Uncertainty avoidance and the preference for innovation championing roles. *Journal of International Business Studies, 26*(1), 47–68. https://doi.org/10.1057/palgrave.jibs.8490165

Shareef, R. O. (2010). Journey of a Female Pedagogical Leader in a Traditional Community Context in Pakistan. In J. Khaki & Q. Safdar (Eds.), *Educational Leadership in Pakistan: Ideals and Realities* (pp. 39–56). Karachi: Oxford University Press.

Siddiqui, N., & Gorard, S. (2017). Comparing government and private schools in Pakistan: The way forward for universal education. *International Journal of Educational Research, 82*, 159–169. https://doi.org/10.1016/j.ijer.2017.01.007

Siddiqui, S. (2016). *Education policies in Pakistan: Politics, projections, and practice*. Karachi: Oxford University Press.

Sider, S. (2014). School leadership across borders: Examining a Canadian-Haitian partnership to support educational capacity-building in Haiti. *International Studies in Educational Administration, 42*(1), 75–87.

Sidorkin, A. M. (2015). Campbell's Law and the Ethics of Immensurability. *Studies in Philosophy and Education, 35*(04), 321–332. https://doi.org/10.1007/s11217-015-9482-3

Simkins, T., Charles, S., Memon, M., and Khaki, J. (2001). Headmaster Approaches to Managing Improvements in Pakistan Schools: Lessons Learned from case Studies. Paper presented at the 14th International Congress for School Effectiveness and Improvement, Toronto, Canada, 5–9 January 2001.

Simkins, T., Garrett, V., Memon, M., and Ali, R. N. (1998). The Role of Perceptions of Government and Non-Government Headmasters in Pakistan. *Educational Management and Administration, 26*(2), 131–146. https://doi.org/10.1177/0263211x98262003

Simkins, T., Sisum, C., & Memon, M. (2003). 'School Leadership in Pakistan: Exploring the Headteacher's role'. *School Effectiveness and School Improvement, 14*(3), 275–291. https://doi.org/10.1076/sesi.14.3.275.15841

Sitkin, S. B. (1996). Learning through failure. In Cohen, M. D., & Sproull, L. S. (Eds.), *Organizational Learning* (pp. 541–577). Thousand Oaks, CA: Sage Publications.

Skinner, T. H. (2003). The role of the school principal in contemporary society: A rural Manitoba perspective. PhD thesis, Ontario Institute of Studies in Education, University of Toronto.

Skrla, L., Erlandson, D.A., Reed, E. M., & Wilson, A. P. (2001). *The emerging principal*. Larchmont, NY: Eye on Education.

Smith, K. G., Collins, C. J., & Clark, K. D. (2005). Existing knowledge, knowledge creation capability and the rate of new product introduction in high-technology firms. *Academy of Management Journal, 48*(2), 346–357. https://doi.org/10.5465/amj.2005.16928421

Smyth, W. J. (1984). *Clinical Supervision-Collaborative learning about teaching*. Victoria: Deakin University Press.

Solangi, G. M. (2016). Role of headteachers in government secondary school teachers' job satisfaction: A case study. *Research Journal of Physical Education and Sports Science, 11*, 210–228.

Southworth, G. (2004). *Primary school leadership in context: Leading small, medium and large sized schools*. New York, NY: Routledge Falmer.

Spender, J. C. (1996). Making knowledge the basis of a dynamic theory of the firm. *Strategic Management Journal*, 17(S2), 45–62. https://doi.org/10.1002/smj.4250171106

REFERENCES

Starratt, R. (2011). Ethical leadership. In B. Davies (Ed.), *The Essentials of School Leadership* (2nd ed.) (pp. 74–90). London, UK: Sage.

Stewart, J. (2012). Transforming schools and strengthening leadership to support the educational and psychosocial needs of war-affected children living in Canada. *Diaspora, Indigenous, and Minority Education, 6*(3), 172–189. https://doi.org/10.1080/15595692.2012.691136

Stoll, L. (2009). Capacity building for school improvement or creating capacity for learning? A changing landscape. *Journal of Educational Change, 10*(2–3), 115–127. https://doi.org/10.1007/s10833-009-9104-3

Suen, H. K., & Yu, L. (2006). Chronic consequences of high-stakes testing? Lessons from the Chinese civil service exam. *Comparative Education Review, 50*(1), 46–65. https://doi.org/10.1086/498328

Sun, P.Y., & Scott, J.L. (2005). An investigation of barriers to knowledge transfer. *Journal of Knowledge Management, 9*(2), 75–90. https://doi.org/10.1108/13673270510590236

Swieringa, J., & Wierdsma, A. (1992). *Becoming a Learning Organization: Beyond the Learning Curve*. Wokingham: Addison-Wesley.

Tajik, M. A. (2004). From educational reformers to community developers: the changing roles of Field Education Officers of Aga Khan Education Service, Pakistan. Unpublished doctoral dissertation, Ontario Institute for Studies in Education, University of Toronto.

Tajik, M. A. (2008). External change agents in developed and developing countries. *International Journal of Improving Schools, 2*(3), 251–271.

Tajik, M. A. (2010). Leaders as Agents of Change and Their Change Strategies. In J.A. Khaki & Q. Safdar (eds.), *Educational Leadership in Pakistan: Ideals and Realities* (pp. 169–192). Karachi: Oxford University Press.

Tajik, M. A. (2011). Change agents' orientations to change: Experience from Pakistan. *International Journal of Humanities and Social Sciences, 1*(2), 1–13.

Tajik, M. A. (2012). Improving Quality of Education through Enhancement of Teachers' Capacity: Policy Implications for Higher Education in Pakistan. In A. Bashiruddin & Z. Bana (Eds.), *Education in Pakistan: Learning from Research Partnerships*. Karachi: Oxford University Press.

Tajik, M. A. (2017). Building Communities by Building Schools in the Rural, Mountainous Regions of Pakistan. In D. Ashraf, M. A. Tajik, & S. Niyozov (Eds.), *Educational Policies in Pakistan, Afghanistan and Tajikistan: Contested Terrain in Twenty-First Century*. Lexington Books, USA.

Tajik, M. F. (2010). Leaders as agents of change and their change strategies. In J. Khaki and Q. Safdar (Eds.), *Educational leadership in Pakistan: Ideals and realities* (pp. 169–129). Karachi: Oxford University Press.

Taylor, P. C. (2008). Multi-paradigmatic research design spaces for cultural studies researchers embodying postcolonial theorizing. *Culture Studies of Science Education, 3*(4), 881–890. https://doi.org/10.1007/s11422-008-9140-y

Taylor, P. C., & Luitel, B. C. (Eds.) (2019). *Research as transformative learning for sustainable futures: Glocal voices and visions*. (pp. 1–16). Leiden, The Netherlands: Brill-Sense.

Taylor, P. C., Taylor, E., & Luitel, B. C. (2012). Multi-paradigmatic transformative research as/for teacher education: An integral perspective. In B.J. Fraser, K.G. Tobin, & C.J. McRobbie (Eds.), *Second International Handbook of Science Education*, 373–387. Dordrecht, the Netherlands: Springer. https://doi.org/10.1007/978-1-4020-9041-7_26

REFERENCES

Terpstra, V., & David, K. (1991). *The cultural environment of international business* (3rd ed.). Cincinnati, OH: South-Western Publishing.

Thiessen, D. & Kilcher, A. (1993). *Innovations in teacher education: A review of recent literature.* Ontario: Ministry of Education and Training.

Thiessen, D., & Anderson, S. (1999). *Getting into the habit of change in Ohio schools: The cross-case study of 12 transforming learning communities.* Columbus: Ohio Department of Education.

Ting-Toomey, S., & Oetzel, J. G. (2002). Cross-Cultural face concerns and conflict styles: Current status and future directions. In William B. Gudykunst & B.M. Mody (Eds.), *Handbook of International and Intercultural Communication* (2nd ed.). London: Sage Publications.

Tomal, D. R., Wilhit, R. K., Phillips, B. J., Sims, P. A., & Gibson, N. P. (2015). *Supervision and evaluation for learning and growth: Strategies for teachers and school leader improvement.* NY: Rowman & Littlefield Publishing Group, Inc.

Toth, P. W. & Farmer, T. S. (2001) Brain hemispheric characteristics and leadership style of school superintendents. http://www.nationalforum.com/TOTHaer10e3.html.

UNESCO Report. (1983). *Strengthening Educational Institutions.* http://unesdoc.unesco.org/images/0005/000559/055915eo.pdf

UNESCO. (2000). *The Dakar Framework for Action.* http://unesdoc.unesco.org/images/0012/001211/121147e.pdf

UNESCO. (2006). *Decentralization of Education in Pakistan: Country Report at the UNESCO Seminar on 'EFA Implementation: Teacher and Resource Management in the Context of Decentralization.'* http://unesdoc.unesco.org/images/0014/001471/147130e.pdf

UNESCO. (2009). *Policy Guidelines on Inclusion in Education.* http://unesdoc.unesco.org/images/0012/001211/121147e.pdf

UNESCO. (2015a). *EFA global monitoring report: Education for All 2000–2015: Achievements and challenges.* Paris, France: UNESCO.

UNESCO. (2015b). *Education 2030 Framework for Action to be formally adopted and launched.* https://en.unesco.org/news/education–2030-framework-action-be-formally-adopted-and-launched

UNESCO. (2017). Paper commissioned for the 2017/8 Global Education Monitoring Report, Accountability in education: Meeting our commitments'. https://unesdoc.unesco.org/ark:/48223/pf0000259549

UNESCO. (2018). *Migration, displacement & education: Building bridges, not walls | Global Education Monitoring Report.* https://en.unesco.org/gem-report/report/2019/migration

UNHCR. (2016). *With 1 human in every 113 affected, forced displacement hits record high.* 20 June 2016. http://www.unhcr.org/en-us/news/press/2016/6/5763ace54/1-human–113-affected-forced-displacement-hits-record-high.html

UNHCR. (2018). *Future of Syria.* http://www.unhcr.org/FutureOfSyria/executive-summary.html

UNHCR. (2019). *Figures at a glance: Statistical yearbooks.* http://www.unhcr.org/figures-at-a-glance.html

UNHCR. (2019). *Refugee Education Strategy 2016–2018 Pakistan.* https://www.unhcrpk.org/wp-content/uploads/2018/06/Pakistan-Education-Strategy–2016–18.pdf

UNHCR. (2019). *Syria Emergency.* https://www.unhcr.org/syria-emergency.html

REFERENCES

UNHCR. (2019). *Syria Regional Refugee Response.* https://data2.unhcr.org/en/situations/syria#_ga=2.32486139.417003257.1576105172-615582881.1568642514

UNICEF. (2016). *Beyond 2015: The Education We Want. UNICEF, 2015.* http://www.unesco.org/new/fileadmin/MULTIMEDIA/HQ/ED/ED_new/Beyond2015_UNESCO-UNICEF-Flyer.pdf

United Nations. (2016). United Nations children's rights violations during armed conflicts on rise despite national action plans to end abuse, security council told in day-long debate. *Meetings coverage and press releases.* https://www.un.org/press/en/2016/sc12470.doc.htm

United Nations. (2017). *New UN DESA report finds numbers of migrants continues to rise.* https://www.un.org/development/desa/en/news/population/international-migration-report-2017.html

United Nations. (n.d.). *Universal Declaration of Human Rights.* http://www.un.org/en/universal-declaration-human-rights/

Usman, R. M. (2016, May 12). *Will Pakistan see more school attacks? Dawn.* https://www.dawn.com/news/1222915

Van Manen, M. (1977). Linking ways of knowing to ways of being practical. *Curriculum Inquiry, 6*(3), 205–228. https://doi.org/10.2307/1179579

Van Manen, M. (1991). *The Tact of Teaching: The Meaning of Pedagogical Thoughtfulness.* Albany, NY: SUNY Press; London, Ont.: Althouse Press.

Van Manen, M. (1992). Reflectivity and the Pedagogical Moment: The Normativity of Pedagogical Thinking and Acting. *The Journal of Curriculum Studies, 23*(6), 507–536. https://doi.org/10.1080/0022027910230602

Van Manen, M. (1995). On the Epistemology of Reflective Practice. *Teachers and Teaching, 1*(1), 33–50. https://doi.org/10.1080/1354060950010104

Varner, I., & Beamer, L. (2005). *Intercultural Communication in the Global Workplace* (3rd ed.). Boston, MA: McGraw-Hill.

Veenman, S. (1984). Perceived problems of beginning teachers. *Review of Educational Research, 54*(2), 143–178. https://doi.org/10.3102/00346543054002143

Virtanen, T. (2007). Leadership Metaphors in Superior-Subordinate Relations: Illustrating Latent Leadership Culture in Public Organizations. Unpublished Paper Presented at the Annual Conference of European Group of Public Administration (19–22 September 2007), Madrid, Spain.

Vygotsky, L. S. (1978). *Mind in society: the development of higher psychological processes.* Cambridge, MA: Harvard University Press.

Waheed, A., & Ahmad, M. M. (2012). Socioeconomic impacts of terrorism on affected families in Lahore, Pakistan. *Journal of Aggression, Maltreatment and Trauma, 21*(2), 202–222. doi:10.1080/10926771.2012.639052

Wahlstrom, K. L., & Louis, K. S. (2008). How teachers experience principal leadership: The roles of professional community, trust, ffficacy, and shared responsibility. *Educational Administration Quarterly, 44*(4), 458–495. https://doi.org/10.1177/0013161x08321502

Waldron, N. L., & McLeskey, J. (2010). Establishing a collaborative school culture through comprehensive school reform. *Journal of Educational & Psychological Consultation, 20*(1), 58–74. https://doi.org/10.1080/10474410903535364

Wang, D., Su, Z., & Yang, D. (2011). Organizational culture and knowledge creation capability. *Journal of Knowledge Management, 15*(3), 363–373. https://doi.org/10.1108/13673271111137385

Watkins, C. (2000). Feedback between teachers. In S. Askew (Ed.). *Feedback for learning* (pp. 65–80). London: Routledge Falmer.

Watkins. P. (2005). The principal's role in attracting, retaining, and developing new teachers: Three strategies for collaboration and support. *The Clearing House: A Journal of Educational Strategies, Issues and Ideas, 79*(2), 83–87. https://doi.org/10.3200/tchs.79.2.83-87

Whitehead, J. (1989). Creating a living educational theory from questions of the kind, 'how do i improve my practice?' *Cambridge Journal of Education, 19*(1), 41–52. https://doi.org/10.1080/0305764890190106

Whitehead, J., & Huxtable, M. (2015). Creating a profession of educators with the living-theories of master and doctor educators. *Gifted Education International, 32*(1), 6–25. https://doi.org/10.1177/0261429415575836

Woolfolk, A. & Hoy, W.K. (2009). *Instructional leadership: A research-based guide to learning in schools* (3rd ed.). Boston: Pearson.

Yin, R. (1989). *Case study research: Design and methods.* Beverly Hills, London: Sage Publications.

Zeichner, K. M., & Tabachnick, B. R. (1985). The development of teacher perspectives: Social strategies and institutional control in the socialization of beginning teachers. *Journal of Education for Teaching, 11*, 1–25. https://doi.org/10.1080/0260747850110101

About Editors and Contributors

Asif Khan is currently affiliated with the Department of Educational Development, Karakoram International University (KIU), Gilgit-Baltistan, Pakistan. Recipient of a Fulbright scholarship, he earned his PhD in Social and Comparative Analysis in Education/School Leadership from the University of Pittsburgh, Pennsylvania, USA. Dr Khan's PhD dissertation on the professional development needs of Pakistani school administrators has been honoured as the best dissertation of the year 2010 by the Institute for International Studies in Education (IISE), University of Pittsburgh. He has contributed research papers in various international and national forums on areas such as international educational assistance, school leadership, and management. For the last two years, Dr Khan is working as coordinator faculty development programme at KIU.

Bal Chandra Luitel is Associate Professor of Mathematics Education at the Kathmandu University, Nepal. Educated in Nepal and Australia, and having worked in Nepal, Australia, and Portugal, Dr Luitel's expertise as a transformative education researcher lies in employing multi-paradigmatic research design for portraying the problem of culturally de-contextualised mathematics and science education. He has a PhD in Mathematics Education from the Curtin University of Technology, Australia. Luitel has been working with several Nepali teachers and teacher educators who examine their lived experiences as students, teachers, and teacher educators, thereby developing visions for fostering experiences of meaningful mathematical learning among their students. In this process, Luitel's research programme enables education researchers to engage with a host of research paradigms together with new analytics arising from dialectical, metaphorical, poetic, and narrative logics and genres as a means for conceiving, expressing, and implementing visions of an inclusive and life-affirming mathematics and science education in Nepal.

Duishon Alievich Shamatov works as an Associate Professor at Nazarbayev University Graduate School of Education where he teaches graduate programmes focusing on Educational Leadership. Dr Shamatov has an English teacher diploma from Osh State University, Kyrgyzstan, an MEd from AKU-IED, and a PhD from the Ontario Institute for Studies in Education at the University of Toronto in Canada. He has worked at Osh State University, AKU-IED, University of Central Asia, and Kyrgyz Academy of Education. Dr Shamatov has written several book chapters and published articles in peer refereed journals. He also has experience of conducting research and education consultancies in Kyrgyzstan, Pakistan, Tajikistan, and Yemen. Duishon's areas of interest include teacher education, curriculum development, education quality, and student assessment.

Dhani Bux Shah is currently pursuing his PhD at Melbourne Graduate School of Education, University of Melbourne, Australia. Before joining it, he was working as Assistant Professor at IBA University, Sukkur, Sindh, Pakistan. Previously, he worked as the project coordinator of a provincial level assessment project—Standardised Achievement Test (SAT). He has also been engaged as a consultant in developing, teaching, and supervising leadership programmes for public and private educational organisations. Shah has done M.S. in Educational Research and Evaluation from Northern Illinois University, USA (2017), and MEd from the AKU-IED, Pakistan (2008). He has contributed to various educational institutions, such as the Sindh Education Department, AKU-IED, and Indus Resource Center in different educational areas in enhancing the teaching and leadership skills of the faculty. He has presented his research work at many forums within and outside the country including Malaysia and USA.

Gulab Khan is an Assistant Professor at the Syed Ahsan Ali and Syed Maratib Ali School of Education (SoE), Lahore University of Management Sciences (LUMS), Lahore. Before joining SoE in 2018, at different times over a period of eighteen years, he assumed teaching, research, and leadership positions at the Aga Khan Education Service, Pakistan, the National University of Sciences and Technology, Islamabad, and the University of Swat, Khyber Pakhtunkhwa. Dr Khan has a PhD in Educational Theory and Policy from the Department of Education Policy Studies, College of Education, Pennsylvania State University. Also, he holds MEd (Educational Leadership and Management) from the Aga Khan University's Institute for Educational Development, Karachi, and MSc in Chemistry from the Department of Chemistry, Quaid-i-Azam University, Islamabad. He has rich experience of teaching, leading, and research from school to university.

Jan-e-Alam Khaki has been Associate Professor at AKU-IED, Pakistan for over fifteen years, securing twice the 'Outstanding Teacher Award'. He has taught at graduate level, including PhD and Masters, leading to his assuming the Chair, PhD programme. He has been conducting special courses and seminars for senior leadership of schools, colleges, and NGO organisations on various subjects, including, leadership skills and leadership in a globalised world. Moreover, Dr Khaki has been a national resource faculty at the Higher Education Commission (HEC) Pakistan, the premier national level instuition, to enhance the teaching skills of the faculty members of the public sector universities. He is the chief editor of a pioneering book, *Educational Leadership in Pakistan: Ideals and Realities* (Oxford University Press, 2010). In addition, he has contributed to national and international journals, conferences, and newspapers.

Mir Afzal Tajik is Associate Professor and Coordinator PhD Programme at the Nazarbayev University Graduate School of Education (NUGSE) in Astana, Kazakhstan. He obtained his PhD from the OISE/UT, Canada, and MEd from the AKU-IED, Pakistan. Before joining NUGSE in September 2016, Dr Tajik worked as an Associate Professor and held leadership positions including Interim Director, Associate Director, Head of Graduate Programmes, and Head of Outreach Programmes at AKU-IED. He has also led AKU-IED's capacity building programmes in Afghanistan and Tajikistan. Dr Tajik brings over twenty-five years of experience in school and higher education with teaching and research interests in teacher education, educational leadership and management, school improvement and community-based education. He is the recipient of AKU's Award for Sustained Excellence in Scholarship of Application, 2009.

Mola Dad Shafa, Associate Professor at the AKU-IED, Pakistan also has the portfolio of Head of AKU's two Professional Development Centres in Gilgit-Baltistan and Chitral, both underprivileged regions. Dr Shafa has introduced numerous context-friendly teacher development programmes by reaching out to the inaccessible and resistant-to-change communities to improve children's access to quality education in Pakistan. Dr Shafa's research interests include educational leadership, girl education, and whole school improvement. Dr Shafa has led many international donor funded projects aiming at enhancing the access and quality of education in Gilgit-Baltistan. He secured his PhD in Education from the Ontario Institute of Studies, University of Toronto, Canada in 2003 after doing his MED from AKU-IED. Before joining AKU, he served the Aga Khan Education Services Pakistan (AKESP), a premier private network, for seventeen years, holding various leadership positions, including headteacher, teacher educator, senior education officer, and head of AKESP's first field education office in Gilgit-Baltistan.

Neelofar Ahamed is a doctoral student at the University of Toronto, Canada. She holds MEd from Brock University, Canada, besides having MA, MBA, and MS from Pakistani universities. Her career spans over twenty years of national and international transdisciplinary work experience. Having last served as the regional head for the Virtual University of Pakistan in 2018, she is a team member of SSHRC and Brock University (Canada) funded projects. Ahmed has presented at various international conferences, participated in three videos, a webinar, and serves as a reviewer in international journals. Ahmed was interviewed at the Voice of America, Washington D.C., to discuss refugee students' education in North America and Pakistan. Her scholarly contributions include a major research paper, journal articles, and research reports.

Peter Charles Taylor is Director of the International Transformative Education and Research Network (iTERN) and Adjunct Professor at Murdoch University's School of Education. During three decades at Curtin University's Graduate Centre of Science and Mathematics Education, Peter developed a model of research as transformative learning designed to engage teachers and teacher educators in exploring their cultural histories, reconceptualizing their professional practices, and developing their agency as inspiring leaders. Engaging stories of these educators' transformative learning experiences are recounted in a recent book co-edited with Professor Bal Chandra Luitel, *Research as Transformative Learning for Sustainable Futures: Glocal Voices and Visions* (Brill-Sense, 2019). Peter supports the visionary leadership of his graduates as they transform teacher education programs in universities across Asia, Africa, the Middle East, and the Pacific.

Sajjad Hussain is currently working as a lecturer at the Center for Education and Staff Training (CEST) with the additional responsibility of deputy director Quality Enhancement Cell (QEC) at the University of Swat in Pakistan. Previously, he served at the Elementary and Secondary Education Department of Khyber Pakhtunkhwa. Hussain has a PhD in Education from the department of Education, International Islamic University, Islamabad, Pakistan with specialisation in assessment and evaluation. His teaching and research interests include student learning assessment, curriculum and instruction, teacher education, educational research, educational leadership, ICTy in education, multiple literacies, and educational psychology. He brings an inter-disciplinary outlook to his work. Hussain has contributed to national and international research journals. He also holds keen interest in developing training modules for teachers at different levels.

Sadruddin Bahadur Qutoshi is Assistant Professor at Karakoram International University, Pakistan. Educated in Pakistan, UK, UAE, and Nepal and having worked in these countries,

Qutoshi developed his expertise as a transformative living-educational-theorist and researcher. He is interested in multi-paradigmatic research design for portraying the problems of conventional teacher education and narrowly conceived view of reforms in education. He has been working with prospective teachers, teacher educators, and researchers to challenge taken for granted views of being and becoming an educational leader/researcher with critical reflections on self and others so as to foster deeper level of learning to experience. He has written book chapters and articles on teacher education and research with specific interest to leadership, curriculum, pedagogies, assessment, educational-technology, and teacher education research.

Sharifullah Baig is a Senior Instructor at the AKU-IED's Professional Development Center North (PDCN) Gilgit-Baltistan, Pakistan. With over fifteen years' experience in the profession of teaching and learning, the author is currently engaged in educational research, focusing on the field of human values and student behavioural management, contributing to and disseminating his research work through many journals. His scholarship has been acknowledged by his current University by granting him the 'Outstanding Teacher Award, 2015'. As for qualifications, he has got a master's in Public Administration from Gomal University Khyber Pakhtunkhwa and MEd in Education from AKU-IED. Additionally, the author is privileged to be a global scholar with the 2013 International Editorial Advisory Board of the National Council of Educational Administration (NCPEA) in educational leadership and administration, Greensboro, NC 27402.

Omidullah Khawary is engaged in the reconstruction of Afghanistan through education and social development working with prestigious organisations such as the AKDN and UNO. Currently, he works with the UNICEF Afghanistan country office as a national officer for learning and development. Prior to joining UNICEF, he served as head, human resources management and development at the Aga Khan Education Services, an AKDN organ in Afghanistan. He has two prestigious master's degrees to his credit, the first being in Educational Leadership and Management from the AKU-IED, Karachi, Pakistan (2012) while the second one in the Global Human Resources Management from the University of Liverpool, UK (2016). Khawary is conversant with many languages including English, Farsi, and Urdu.

Qamar Safdar has done her master's in Education and International Development from the Institute of Education, University of London (IOE-UoL) as well as master's in English Literature from Mysore University, India. She also has an Advanced Diploma qualification in the Educational Leadership and Management (ADISM) from the AKU-IED. She served as an Assistant Professor at AKU-IED focusing on educational leadership and Management. She has been the Chair of the Ethical Review Committee and of School Headteachers' Association for Development of Education (SHADE), a unique body in this part of the world. She has contributed significantly to both local and international journals. She is the second co-editor of *Educational Leadership and Management: Ideals and Realities* (Oxford University Press, 2010).

Taj-Ud-Din Sharar is Assistant Professor of Education at University of Chitral, Khyber Pakhtunkhwa, Pakistan. Prior to joining the current university, he worked with Lahore Leads University, Karakoram International University, Gilgit-Baltistan, and AKU-IED's Professional Development Centre, Chitral. He did his Master's in political science from the

University of Peshawar and B.Ed. from Allama Iqbal Open University, Islamabad. He did his MEd and PhD from the AKU-IED, Pakistan. His interest ranges from teacher education and research to educational leadership and management, educational change and development, global education, and post-colonial studies. He has published different research papers in HEC recognised national journals and presented papers in many international conferences.

Takbir Ali is Assistant Professor and Head, Outreach, at the AKU-IED. Dr Ali has earned his MEd from the same university, while he has done his PhD from the Ontario Institute for Studies in Education of the University of Toronto, Canada. He is interested in teaching and research in the areas of teacher professional development, teacher leadership, educational leadership, governance and organisational efficacy, educational change and development, school improvement, and science education. He has published his research in reputable national and internationally peer reviewed journals. He has worked extensively in rural Pakistan through many organisations, including the AKU-IED, implementing many donor funded projects to improve the quality of education.

Zubeda Bana (Late) had been Assistant Professor at the AKU-IED since 1997 with some break in between. She did her MA from the (then) University of London, Institute of Education. She has been the head of a pioneering programme for headteachers called the 'Advanced Diploma in School Management' (ADISM), the first of its kind in Pakistan. She led the Professional Development Centre, Northern Areas (PDCN), an arm of the AKU-IED, leading many innovative programmes in the rural areas of one of the most deserving regions of Pakistan. Prior to joining AKU-IED, Bana served as a teacher educator with the Government of Sindh holding the position of Assistant Professor. She has contributed to many international journals and books. Sadly, she passed away in 2017 leaving behind her husband and two lovely daughters.

Index

18th Constitutional Amendment, 18, 75

A

Achieving Universal Quality Primary Education in Pakistan (MOE, 2013), 136
Action research, 53, 80, 84–5
ADOs, 56, 71–2, 219
Afghanistan, 2, 4, 8, 127–8, 130, 192–3, 199, 201, 208–9, 217, 220
Aga Khan Planning and Building Services (AKPBS), 149
Aga Khan University's Institute for Educational Development (AKU-IED), 3–4, 31, 33–6, 40–2, 49, 74–6, 80–3, 87, 96, 156, 213
Ainura, 117–25
Army Public School (APS), 128, 140
Artificial Intelligence (AI), 29–30
Assistance to Conflict-Affected Persons in Pakistan (2011, 2012), 146
Assistance to Internally Displaced People in Pakistan (2009, 2010), 146
Assistant District Officers of Education (ADOEs), 58–9, 62, 64–6
Assistant Education Officers (AEOs), 161–2, 218

B

Balochistan, 6, 18, 31, 34–5, 42–5, 49, 56–9, 60, 65, 69, 92–6, 100, 107–8, 216
Bangladesh, 2, 130, 153
Behaviourist Theory, 77
Bio-Ecological Model, 131–4, 137, 144–5
Bio-ecological Theory of Child Development, 147
Brock University, 126, 135, 137
Bronfenbrenner's Bio-ecological Theory of Child Development (1999), 127, 131–5, 137, 144–5, 147

Bureau of Curriculum of Sindh, 68
Bush, George W., 128

C

Campbell's Law, 27–8
Certificate of Education: Educational Leadership and Management (CE:ELM), 92, 94, 96–7, 103, 106, 108–9
China-Pakistan Economic Corridor (CPEC), 25
Civil Society Resource Center (CSRC), 149
Combination, 77, 88–9, 94, 195, 198, 212, 215
Convention on the Rights of the Child (CRC), 138
Course Participants (CPs), 83, 86–7, 96–9, 100–6
Critical Reflexivity, 187–8, 213
Culture, 2–3, 15, 26, 28, 32, 36, 43, 47, 61–3, 83, 87–9, 99, 101–2, 116, 133, 139, 148, 152, 175, 192–4, 196, 198–207, 211, 220–5

D

Department of Education and Literacy, 68
Department of Education of Gilgit-Baltistan (DoE GB), 150
Digital Mentoring Project (DMP), 145
Distributed leadership, 78, 90, 154, 222
District Education Officers (DEOs), 5, 31–6, 38, 40–6, 48, 50, 52, 63, 65, 97, 100, 107, 211, 214–19
District Inspectors of Schools (DISs), 161–2
Divisional Directorate, 68
Drawing and Disbursing Officer (DDO), 103

E

Early Childhood Education Development (ECED), 170
ED-LINKS, 33–35, 40–2, 48, 92, 94, 97–8, 107–8
Education for All (EFA), 75, 138
Education Policy 1972–80, 19–20
Educational Development and Improvement Programme (EDIP), 7, 148–50, 152, 154–9, 160–9, 170–2, 214–5
Educational leadership, 1, 3–5, 8–9, 11–12, 32, 34–5, 41, 76, 78, 80, 83, 92, 173, 175–6, 182, 190, 211, 222, 224–5
ERIC, 135–6
Ethical leadership, 78
Externalisation, 195

G

Gilgit-Baltistan (GB), 7, 49, 148, 150, 156

H

Higher Education Commission (HEC), 19, 25–6, 29, 75
Higher Education Institutions (HEIs), 5, 25

I

Individualism-Collectivism, 182, 193, 196
Information and Communications Technology (ICTy), 72, 96, 102–3, 133, 144
Instructional leadership, 78, 85, 88, 102
Islamabad Capital Territory (ICT), 31, 34–5, 42–5
Internalisation, 105, 195, 200

J

JSTOR, 135–6

K

Kalys, 121–4
Kanyshay, 118, 121
Kathmandu University (KU), 174, 181
Kathmandu University School of Education (KUSOED), 174, 182
Kazan Federal University, Russia, 126
Khyber Pakhtunkhwa, 18, 129, 140
Kyrgyzstan, 2, 4, 6, 8, 110–11, 116, 124, 209–10, 213

L

Lahore University of Management Sciences (LUMS), 4, 211
Leadership from the Middle (LftM), 218
Learning and Development (L&D) departments, 197–8
Learning-centred leadership, 78
Less developed countries (LDCs), 1–4, 8, 209–12, 215, 218–19, 222–5
Local level institutions (LLIs), 149

M

Machine Learning (ML), 29–30
Managerial leadership, 75, 78, 88
Millennium Development Goals (MDGs), 75, 138
Monitoring and Evaluation (M&E), 97, 106–7, 218
Monitoring and Evaluation of Debt Conversion for Education (2004–2018), 146
Monitoring, Evaluation, Research and Learning Unit (MERLU) employees, 197–8
MOOCs (Massive Open Online Courses), 29
Moral Leadership, 216–17
More developed countries (MDCs), 1–2, 8, 95, 211–12, 224
Mother support groups (MSGs), 149–50, 158–9, 170
Multi-paradigmatic Research Design (MRD), 173, 176

N

National Action Plan (2009), 136
National Business Education Accreditation Council, 26

INDEX

National Cadet Corps (NCC), 138
National Computing Education Accreditation Council, 26
National Council for Accreditation of Teacher Education, 26
National Education Policy (NEP) 2009, 19, 24–7, 29, 130, 139
National Education Policy (NEP, 1992), 23, 26
National Education Policy 1998–2010, 16, 19, 23–4
National Education Policy 2017 (NEP), 18–9, 21, 25, 51, 75, 130, 138–9, 141–2
National Education Policy and Implementation Programme 1979, 22
Nepal, 2, 4, 174–5, 179–80, 182, 189
Network of Organisations Working with People with Disability in Pakistan (NOWPDP), 149

O

Offices of Research, Innovation and Commercialisation (ORICs), 25, 28
Organisational Citizenship Behavior (OCB), 187
Organisational Knowledge, 192–6, 198, 204, 208
Organisational Leadership, 193, 203, 207, 221
Organisational Learning, 4, 192, 220–21
Organisational Silence, 205, 221
Oxford University, UK, 80

P

Pakistan Engineering Council (PEC), 26
Participatory Leadership Theory, 77
Pedagogical leaders, 74, 79–80, 81, 84–5, 87
Pedagogical leadership, 8, 74–5, 78–9, 81–2, 84–7, 213
Post-Traumatic Stress Disorder (PTSD), 126, 140
Power Distance, 20, 36, 47, 192–3, 196, 199, 203–4, 206–7, 221
Praxis, 79, 139–40, 173, 176, 181, 187, 190
Professional development centres (PDCs), 1

Professional Development Teacher (PDT), 6, 92, 95, 98–99, 103, 105–6, 149, 213
Prophetic Professional Leadership, 216–17
Provincial Civil Service Commission (PCSCs), 71
Provincial Institute for Teacher Education, 68
Punjab, 18, 142

R

Reform Support Unit, 68
Resource-Based View (RBV), 194

S

School development plans (SDPs), 97, 105–8, 149
School Management Committees (SMCs), 65–8, 149–50, 155, 158–9, 170
Servant Leadership, 216–7
Sheffield Hallam University, UK, 75–6, 80
Sindh Public Service Commission, 94
Sindh Teacher Development Authority, 68
Sindh Textbook Board, 68
Sindh, 5–6, 18, 35, 42–3, 45, 49, 51, 56–9, 60, 65, 68–9, 92–6, 98, 100–1, 103, 107–8, 216
Situational Leadership, 78, 86, 90
Situational Leadership Theory, 77
Socialisation, 195
Strengthening Teacher Education in Pakistan (STEP), 49, 56, 68
Sustainable Development Goals (SDG), 137–8

T

Taliban, 127–8
Taluka Education Officers (TEOs), 58, 60, 70–2
Teacher Leadership, 148–9, 151–4, 168–9, 171, 214
Terms of Reference (ToRs), 52, 65, 219
Trait Theory, 77
Transformational leadership, 7, 78, 85, 88, 184, 212

Transformative Educational Leadership, 173, 180, 182
Transformative Leadership, 8, 173–4, 176–9, 180–6, 190, 212
Transformative Teacher Education and Research (TER), 180

U

Uncertainty Avoidance, 192, 196, 202, 204, 207, 220–21
Union Council (UC), 73
United Nations Educational, Scientific and Cultural Organisation (UNESCO), 32–3, 36, 135, 137–8, 142
United Nations High Commissioner for Refugees (UNHCR), 126–8, 135, 137
United Nations International Children's Emergency Fund (UNICEF), 135, 137
University Act 1969, 16–7
University Grants Commission Act (UGC) 1974, 13–17
University of Toronto, Canada, 80

W

War on Terror, 127–8